HELL
AT THE FRONT

About the Author

Tom Donovan is a specialist military publisher and bookseller with over twenty-five years' experience in handling, reading and researching First World War books, diaries and other documents. His other books include *Voices from the Trenches: Life & Death on the Western Front* (with Andy Simpson), also published by Tempus. He lives in Brighton.

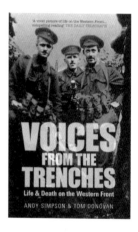

Praise for Tom Donovan

'A vivid picture of life on the Western front... compelling reading' *THE DAILY TELEGRAPH.*

'Offers the reader a wealth of fine writing by soldiers of the Great War whose slim volumes were published so long ago or under such obscure imprints that they have all but disappeared from sight like paintings lost under the grime of ages... no one can read this book without being moved' MALCOLM BROWN

'There is a great deal of fascination with the everyday life of the British soldier of the First World War. One of the best books on this subject is *Voices from the Trenches*' *MILITARY ILLUSTRATED*

'Copious, well-chosen extracts from soldiers' own writings... very highly recommended' GARY SHEFFIELD

AT THE FRONT

Combat Voices from the First World War

TOM DONOVAN

TEMPUS

First published 2006

First published in 1999 as
The Hazy Red Hell by Spellmount Publishers

Tempus Publishing Limited
The Mill, Brimscombe Port,
Stroud, Gloucestershire, GL5 2QG
www.tempus-publishing.com

British Library Cataloguing in Publication Data.
A catalogue record for this book is available from the British Library.

ISBN 0 7524 3940 5

Typesetting and origination by Tempus Publishing Limited
Printed and bound in Great Britain

Contents

Introduction

The 1914-18 war was horrific from beginning to end. The insane daily torture of the human mind and body is unforgivable. It was very rarely glorious. Don't blame the army commanders, coping with a wholly novel set of rules and materiel; condemn, if you will, the human race; the frailty of the Western World; the way in which, even now, it conducts its international arguments.

This collection of Great War experiences demonstrates the *daily* futility of that war: each piece is a microcosm of a broad canvas. It would be possible – but contrived – to find an example of shocking futility or suffering for every single day of the conflict after the BEF first clashed with the German Army. I have restricted my choice to a representative selection from the first to the last month of the war. All the main battles are represented in my selection, as well as numerous minor incidents in every part of the British front line. In making my selection I have attempted to choose pieces that add to an understanding of the Western Front not just in terms of its horror. There were marked characteristics to each battle and some of these are noted in the short introductions provided for each quotation. I have also drawn attention to other points which would seem to benefit from explanation.

THE WAR OF THE GUNS

All but one soldier who contributed to this anthology was an infantryman serving with a British infantry regiment on the Western Front, but if one strand of experience links them all it is, oddly enough, artillery. For while the infantryman went 'over the top' to the sound of the whistles and crashes, to d hand-to-hand combat with the German infantry – if he was lucky (?) enough to get that far – it was inalienably a gunner's war, and everywhere in the front line area that the infantryman went he was at the mercy of long- or short-range guns. The morning and evening 'hates' were a regular feature of trench warfare, as each side 'softened up' known junctions, strong-points and so on in case of an attack. The precursor to every Western Front battle was an intense bombardment (on one day, 8 August 1918, 700 field guns fired some 350,000 shells – as well as those fired by heavy howitzers and the enemy's retaliation; and by early 1918 the Russell Motor Car Co. of Toronto had manufactured over eight million fuses – and they were just one of hundreds of contractors). Once a battle had started the barrage moved on, from objective to objective, while specially designated batteries were employed in counter-battery fire to knock out the German guns, which were of course firing back at all *their* known targets as fast as they could. On a smaller scale, every trench raid required artillery back-up; every relief attracted the attention of the enemy's gunners, and every night the streams of transport running up food and war materials to the front line were shelled as they went. So every front-line soldier lived continuously with the fear and tension of shelling.

   This is not to say that every participant endured terrible experiences every day that he spent on active service – that is very far from the truth – but will reaffirm that the war was appalling on a daily basis.

The Eye-witnesses

The experiences which go to make up this book are selected from a variety of sources ranging from extracts from diaries and unpublished letters held in private collections to published volumes of war experience, these with a cut-off point of 1939. Many of these works were printed in small numbers and through the passage of time they have become difficult to lay one's hands upon, some exceedingly so, so that their contents will be unavailable and unfamiliar to the vast majority of readers. Details of published works consulted will be found in the list of Sources.

There is a difficulty in balancing the experiences of other ranks of the Great War with those of officers: the latter were so much better educated and perhaps had more time in which to write their diaries, and censorship of them was pretty much voluntary, being based on trust, so they could send home much more informative letters. While there are strikingly outstanding published other-rank memoirs, they are few, and as such they tend to be oft quoted. While one or two are quoted here, there are notable exceptions, such as Frank Richards' classic memoirs with the 2nd Bn. Royal Welch Fusiliers, *Old Soldiers Never Die*, first published in 1933 and recently reprinted. Every effort has been made to locate and utilise obscure accounts from the ranks. All the accounts presented here are reproduced exactly as they were written; none has been edited or changed in any way with the exception that very occasionally irrelevant or repetitive text has been excised.

British Army Medical Arrangements on the Western Front

As this compilation is concerned with the front-line experience of soldiers on the Western Front, the daily 'wastage' of life

– both wounded and killed – inevitably dominates its pages. It has been thought as well to outline British Army medical arrangements so that the reader will have some idea of the experiences of the many soldiers wounded herein after they left the fighting line, and to understand the frequent references to Aid Posts, Casualty Clearing Stations and so on.

The wounded soldier's first treatment was most likely to be that which his immediate comrades or he himself could provide using their Field Dressings. Every soldier carried this very basic medical kit comprising two bandages and safety pins, with which they would stem the wound until further aid was available. Frequently rags, jerseys, puttees and so on would be adapted to fill larger wounds and to help make the patient comfortable. There were no pain killers available, although some officers carried their own private supplies of morphia and there would sometimes be a certain amount of rum around – neither could be guaranteed.

Each infantry battalion had a Medical Officer, a doctor who was attached to the unit on a permanent basis to look after its health both in and out of the line. He had a staff of regimental stretcher-bearers who would accompany, or follow immediately behind, an infantry attack to pick up the casualties. While in trenches or during an attack a Regimental Aid Post was established in the front line. The RAP was usually a dugout: cramped, dirty and smelly, the doctor working by the light of flickering candles, discarded bloody dressings and soiled uniforms and kit thrown aside, the treatment taking place on a stretcher or cot. Cases in need of immediate treatment at the hands of the doctor and his trained staff would be brought here, while less severe cases would be carried or directed to make their way back to a Collecting Post behind the lines, from which ambulances and cars would transport patients to the Advanced Dressing Station. Walking wounded, those capable of moving under their own steam, including men who had to be helped along by colleagues, would relieve the pressure on ambulances by making their own way down the line to the ADS. The Collecting Post might be a farm building or the cellars of buildings in a now destroyed village just behind the trenches, always within range of artillery, and here some further hasty treatment would be possible.

Field Ambulances, units of some 241 officers and men including medical officers, stretcher-bearers, nursing orderlies, clerks and so on, fully equipped with horse and mechanical transport, set up the Collecting Posts and looked after the passage of the wounded from the front line as far back as the Main Dressing Station.

The next stage back from the Collecting Post was the Advanced Dressing Station, also the responsibility of the Divisional Field Ambulance and perhaps a mile or so behind the Collecting Post(s) and so in relative safety, but still subject to the attentions of German gunners. Here there would be more shelter, from both weather and shelling, for stretcher cases awaiting dressing or operations, or simply waiting their turn for the ambulance.

Behind the ADS came the Main Dressing Station where treatment could be carried out in relative comfort before a patient was moved to the Casualty Clearing Station.

The CCS was the last link in the chain, large tented or hutted camps where several surgical teams carried out a wide range of operations (many being amputations), and care was provided in the wards before onward transmission of the patient by Ambulance Train to a Base Hospital for longer term treatment and convalescence. It should be remembered that during periods of heavy fighting all the medical facilities described above would be working to over-capacity: everyone working almost twenty-four hours a day as the back-log of cases awaiting treatment built up. Stretchers would be laid in rows on the ground outside waiting their turn in the theatre. Many died before their turn came.

The base hospitals were established on the coast, some in hotel premises such as the former Hotel Splendide at Wimereux, and here the lightly wounded or sick would convalesce until fit to return to their unit, while those whose wounds were severe or would take a considerable time to heal fully would pass through before being transported by Hospital Ship to England for completion of their treatment.

1

1914: The Contemptible Little Army

THE BATTLE OF MONS: 23RD–24TH AUGUST 1914

'Each one of our men was equal to three of the enemy as regards shooting'

As the German army and the rather smaller British Expeditionary Force (BEF) moved inexorably closer in the region of Mons, in southern Belgium, it would not be unreasonable to say that the expectations of the protagonists at every level were unclear. The British Commander-in-Chief, Sir John French, was not sure how large the force was that opposed him. Whether he expected to win the forthcoming fight, hold the line or retreat immediately is not clear. The Germans, on the other hand, were so confident in their numerical superiority that they believed they were unstoppable. Perhaps they were, for the time being, but they received a rude shock when they met the BEF and their advance cost them immense casualties. Both sides advanced under cover of 'screens' of cavalry, probing and scouting ahead. The talk was of 'vedettes' and 'picquets' – terms that would sink in the mud as fast as cavalry itself would in the ensuing four years. The 4th Bn. Royal Fusiliers was one of the first units to meet the Germans at Mons, as related here by one of their soldiers. They manned a line of trenches and other defences around the north and east sides of Mons, met the German attack and retreated, with the rest of the BEF, at the end of the day. They fought through civilian buildings, still surrounded by the populace; a far cry from the later devastated battlefields. Perhaps the enduring experience was that of casualties on a scale unheard of in the British Army for many decades as the mechanised battlefield, although in its infancy, made its presence felt.

On the morning of the 22nd [August], the 1st and 2nd Army Corps were ordered to the theatre of war in Belgium. We were told that we would not meet the enemy that day, but probably the next, which was Sunday. During our march to Mons we passed many former British battlefields – Malplaquet being one of them, where Marlborough had a great victory over the French, also Namur.

We passed through the town of Mons between one and two o'clock, where we were greatly welcomed by the population, who gave us an enormous amount of refreshment, etc. We took up position on the banks of a canal beyond Mons. The 2nd Army Corps was composed of the 3rd and 5th Divisions, which each has three Brigades, four Regiments to a Brigade. The Royal Fusiliers was in the 9th Brigade, composed of the Northumberland Fusiliers, Royal Fusiliers, Royal Scots Fusiliers and Lincolnshire Regiment, so it was almost a Fusilier Brigade. Lt.-Colonel N.R. McMahon, D.S.O., commanded 4th Royal Fusiliers. The Brigade was commanded by Brigadier-General Shaw.

After being told our position, we entrenched ourselves in along a canal close to a railway bridge, which was being held by our machine gunners; there were also obstacles of wire entanglements along the line on the bridge. The evening passed very quietly, there being no signs of the enemy. We stood to arms an hour before dawn, which is a usual order on active service, as an attack is always expected at dawn. There were still no signs of the enemy until about nine o'clock, when we saw somebody try to fix a white flag on to a tree. The officer looked through his field glasses and found that it was two of the enemy's patrol. Myself and three others were ordered to fire at them, which we did, bringing the one down off the top of the tree and also killing the other.

About four hours later, a patrol of Uhlans, one officer and ten men, were sighted on the other side of the canal and our machine gunners were ordered to open fire, which they did, when the enemy's horses turned and galloped away less their riders; nine men were killed and one wounded, who managed to escape. The officer was also severely wounded, so gave himself up to be taken prisoner. He told our captain that he was a baron; he seemed to be rather old – about sixty years of age – and had a long beard. He looked very ill for the want of food; he told our captain (Captain Ashburner, M.V.O., D.S.O.) he had only had chocolate for three days. Our officer was very kind to him, bandaging his leg and arm for him. He then asked if he could go back and pick up his helmet, which he was allowed to do, our captain assisting him over the barbed wire entanglements. He was too severely injured to be able to escape. After he had come back he was handed over to an escort, which took him to the General's Headquarters, where he was quartered.

During the afternoon an hostile aeroplane was seen, which we were told afterwards was a German aeroplane having the shape of a bird named an eaglet. A few shots were fired at it, but without success, and then it proceeded back to where the enemy was in hiding.

Then shortly after, the battle began, our fellows giving a good field of fire, far superior to the enemy's.

But again an aeroplane came over our lines, dropping what we thought were live bombs, but which turned out to be

smoke bombs, to show their artillery our position, which was
then very heavily bombarded.

Then came the sound of trumpets from the enemy's lines,
which was the order to advance, and they came on in vast
numbers, ten to our one, and ten machine guns to a battalion
to our two to a battalion. Each one of our men was equal to
three of the enemy as regards shooting, the Germans firing
from the hip, therefore causing the shot to go high.

They were met by a very deadly fire from our two machine
guns which were on the railway bridge, the officer holding on
until every one of his gunners was killed or wounded, then he
himself fired the gun, while one of the gunners, though severely
wounded, supplied the ammunition. They were both awarded
the V.C., the officer not surviving to receive it. Their names were
Lieut. Maurice Dease and Pte. F. Godley (4th Royal Fusiliers).

We had some very close fighting, one of our men going up
to a German and striking him full in the face with his fist.

About five o'clock the order came to retire, which we did,
being supported by our reserve companies. We retired in an
orderly manner, every man keeping cool, calm and collected
– also fighting our way at the same time.

We retired from a village called St. Ghislain into the town
of Mons, where we were given refreshments by the civilian
population who were still there despite the battle. We looked
a very dirty lot, our faces being black from the rifle fire. The
Roll was called of our Company, which numbered about 85
out of 250, losing one Captain killed, one Lieutenant also.

After forming the remainder of the Battalion together,
which numbered now about 478 out of a total of 1200, we
marched to the grounds of a big estate which was being used
as a hospital – after we left it was blown to pieces by shell fire,
many wounded being in there.

We rested there for about seven hours, which we were very
glad of. The night had turned very cold, I myself having no

overcoat because I had to leave it in the trench to obey orders to retire and having no time to get it.

We were woke up about 2 o'clock, when we resumed our retirement, and took up another position in some houses which had been left by the inhabitants. We made some loopholes in the wall to fire out of. I could not fire myself, because the top of my rifle had been smashed the previous day by a bullet which passed into my chum's thumb next to me. So I was told off to be ammunition carrier, which is no pleasant job to keep running out in the open for two or three hundred yards to fetch ammunition, also being a nice target for the enemy.

Whilst fetching ammunition I passed through a yard of a big stable, which afterwards I found contained a large number of farm horses. This I immediately reported to my Company Commander, as I told him they would be suitable for transport. He reported the matter to the Colonel, who ordered that only six were to be taken to make up for the horses we were deficient of.

The houses our men were firing from were full of furniture and wardrobes, but not a thing was taken by our men, as we had strict orders not to loot, which, however, the enemy did when we retired. I learned that our (2nd) Army Corps was being attacked by three German Army Corps, two of whom were coming straight ahead and the other attacking on the flank, one of them being commanded by Von Kluck, the Crown Prince and Von Bulow.

Later in the afternoon we had the order again to retire. We had not so many casualties as the day previous, though they were rather heavy. We retired to a place called Le Cateau, where we again took up our position.

At daybreak the enemy was throwing the bulk of his strength against the left of our position. The French Cavalry should have come to our help, but owing to the fatigue of their horses were unable to do so.

Our Artillery showed grand fight against our opponents, also inflicting great loss, though our guns were outnumbered. There was fine work done by our cavalry, who covered our retreat by fighting rearguard actions with great activity, thereby inflicting great losses on the enemy.

Our retreat was carried far into the night of the 26th, and throughout the 27th and the 28th, on which date we halted, throwing off the weight of the enemy's pursuit.

From *The Immortal First: A Private Soldier's Diary with the original B.E.F.* by F.Gaunt. Erskine Macdonald. 1917.

SOMERSETS AT LE CATEAU: 26TH AUGUST 1914

'there was no disgrace in retiring'

The 4th Division disembarked at Le Havre on 23 August, entrained for the front and were billeted near Le Cateau by the 24th evening. Sundry movements and skirmishes took place on the 25th and on the early morning of the 26th – the day of the Le Cateau battle – the troops were warned for a rearguard action. They were to fight all day, without much idea of who was where or why, but by the end of it they had disengaged with honour having had considerable casualties and held the German advance. Unlike the other divisions engaged at Le Cateau they had not already spent days fighting or retreating, but they had only been in France three days! The writer of this letter, George Roworth Parr, commanded a platoon of the 1st Bn. Somerset Light Infantry; on the day in question he held his position for five hours under fire, losing three-quarters of his platoon.

At about 3 [a.m.], we were halted in the road and fell down where we were and slept for about half an hour, and then moved on again. Then my company turned about, and we turned some

Germans out of a village, where we also got a scrap of bread and a drop of wine. Then we were withdrawn – shrapnel bursting over us harmlessly as we went. Then we were hurried on, and I was ordered to take up a position with my platoon in a field of cabbages with a road in front. We lay down in the cabbage-field behind the road on the right of the cottage with supports behind in the quarry and the machine gun there too.

At 7.45 a.m. 3 shells burst over us, in quick succession, and hit 3 men and alarmed the rest horribly. We all got our heads down behind our head cover, scraped up with our entrenching tools, just enough to stop a bullet, if you throw the earth well out to the front. I had just borrowed a tool from a man, and scraped up a bit before the firing began. This cover is no good against shrapnel, which bursts over head. Luckily, after those three shells, the Germans fired on the supports, otherwise we should have been wiped out in a quarter of an hour. The Germans had the range plum (or plumb). Then the Rifle Brigade retired across our front to the village on the right and got fired at by some of us, not knowing who they were. Then there was a lull. At about 8.45 a skirmishing line came across the road, in front of the German guns, and I gave my first fire order about 5 minutes later. 'Enemy advancing 1500 – distribute fire.' I don't think we hit anyone as the range was very long and I couldn't see the bullets strike anywhere to correct the range. I shouted back to the machine gun, who had a range-finder to give the ranges, but I couldn't make them hear. Two German guns then walked quietly along the distant road and came into action with the others behind them. I tried to fire on them, but it was 1800 or 2000 yards, and again I could make no one hear behind me. I saw the guns come into action and the observer in his sort of scaffold arrangement. I could see him through my field-glasses turn and shout, when a shell pitched short, and we could do nothing at all! A few more men were hit by shrapnel and the nerve of the others shaken badly (which is what shrapnel is for). Then a machine gun started on our right and hit a few more, and I looked at my watch wondering how long we could stay there for. So far very few infantry came at us, mostly going to the left of us where the rifle and machine-gun fire was very heavy.

I managed to get the men's heads up to fire on the Germans as they crossed our front, and they passed my orders down very well... later a corporal passed down 'Ask Mr. Parr when we are to retire.'

I shouted back that we were going to stay where we were and that our side would counter-attack soon. At about 10.30 I heard the well-known whizz and thud, and felt a violent blow on the back which fetched a grunt out of me, and a corporal said 'You hit, Sir?' I couldn't think what had happened for a minute, and put my hand to the place and found nothing damaged. It was a spent bullet which had ricocheted. Another went through my rolled Burberry just over my shoulder. Later on I looked down, and found a bullet under my nose which just managed to penetrate my head cover before its force was expended. I have got the bullet now.

The machine gun then enfiladed us on both flanks or nearly so, and more messages came to ask about retiring. I told them we were going to stay where we were.

They shouted up to me that there was nobody left on our left flank and that our supports had gone. At about 12.30 I shouted out that we would retire, and we started to crawl back the 50 yards to the old quarry. After some distance a man said to me, 'They're getting hit in, let's run for it'; so we ran the last fifteen yards and dropped down over the bank. Out of 49 that I took into action I had only 12 left. 37 were killed or wounded, so that there was no disgrace in retiring.

To my astonishment I found Frank Bradshaw in the quarry with some more of the regiment and a Major and a Captain in the Rifle Brigade, about 100 men in all. Bradshaw came towards me under the bank with his revolver drawn, saying,

'Are they coming, George?' I said, 'No, we have been enfiladed from both flanks and had to retire.'

Then we waited for the Germans to come on, not being able to put our heads up for the maxim fire; none of us ever expected to get out alive. However, the Germans didn't come on, so we decided to retire and run for it, which we did, and luckily at that moment they had diverted their fire and we all got clear away towards the railway embankment.

Looking around, when I had got over the edge of the hill, I found myself some 50 yards ahead. Thinking this hardly the place for an officer retiring, I turned round and walked up the hill again to where a private in my old company was trying to get a wounded man away. The fire was pretty hot, but we got him down the hill and then had to carry him over the railway embankment. I then gave my Burberry and woolly waistcoat to somebody to hold and never saw them again. (I have got a new waterproof sheet instead.) The bullets were flying over our heads on the line, but neither of us was touched. We had to leave the man the other side of the line, as we were both too exhausted to carry him further. He was very badly hit.

The hill behind the line was covered with our own men retiring on the village, with shells bursting continuously over them. I stood for a moment and nearly took a photograph, with my pocket Kodak, but somehow, as I had to cross over the bit of ground myself, I didn't do it. We rallied what men we could in the village and held it for some time, when we had to fall back. The French subsequently came up and drove the Germans out again. We fell back to another village, arriving about 11 p.m. and managed to get some bread and coffee for ourselves and the men – the first food since about 5 a.m. the morning before!

From *George Roworth Parr, Prince Albert's Somerset Light Infantry, A Short Memoir* by Cuthbert Headlam. Edinburgh: Privately printed. 1915.

BROTHERS IN ARMS ON THE AISNE: 15TH SEPTEMBER 1914

'bullets ricocheted, shrieking like some infernal cat-fight all about us'

Cpl. John Lucy's 2nd Bn. Royal Irish Rifles crossed the River Aisne on a wet 14 September morning under German shelling and small arms fire. Once across, the Irishmen advanced uphill under heavy fire towards the German position and dug-in under the cover of a chalk bank. Lucy's 'A' Company was relieved and spent the night in some caves nearby. Next day they returned to their chalky front-line position.

Just as we came to the little cliff the officer commanding a company on our right came striding towards us; a tall gaunt captain with the light of battle in his eye. A very religious man he was too, always talking about duty, and a great Bible reader. Tall, sinewy, with pale face and pale blue eyes, colourless hair, and a large, untidy, colourless moustache, he came at us looking for blood. He reminded me of a grisly Don Quixote. 'They have gone,' he cried jubilantly and with certainty, in a cracked voice, 'all the Germans have gone away, except about one platoon, which I have located in that wood to our left front. I intend to capture that enemy platoon with my company, but I want volunteers from 'A' Company to move across the open to support me, while I work forward through the wood, which enters the left of my company line. Now, who will volunteer?'

I suppose he knew very well that the native pride of Irish troops could be depended on. Anyway the whole of 'A' Company immediately volunteered to assist. The officer selected the two nearest platoons, which happened to be mine and my brother's. He then sent Muldoon, one of my platoon, up a tree to look across the plateau at the wood, in order to confirm the presence of the enemy for our edification. Mul, as we called him, shinned up, and presently shouted down: 'Yes, there they are, I can see them in the woods.'

'Good,' said the officer. '"A" Company's two platoons will move forward in line from here, keeping parallel to the right edge of the wood, as soon as my company gets going,' and Don Quixote went off rapidly to launch his attack. A rifle shot, aimed at Mul, cut short that lad's curiosity, and he slid grinning and safe to the ground. We fixed our bayonets, as the enemy were close, and sorted ourselves by sections along the plateau edge, searching for easy places to surmount so as to get on to the level of the plateau.

It cannot be said that the operation was very well organized. It was all too rapid, and we got no definite objective, our task being to engage any enemy on our front by advancing to find him and attack him. My brother's platoon suddenly got the order, unheard by me, and up went the men onto the open grassland, led by their officer. Denis went ahead, abreast with this officer, too far in front of his section, I thought. He carried his rifle with the bayonet fixed threateningly at the high port, and presented a good picture of the young leader going into battle. I wished he had not gone so far forward.

Not quite necessary for a lance-corporal. He was exposing himself unnecessarily and would be one of the first to be shot at. I raised myself high over the parapet of our cliff, and shouted to him: 'Take care of yourself,' and I blushed at such a display of anxiety in the presence of my comrades. My brother steadied a moment in a stride which was beginning to break into a steady run forward, and looking back over his shoulder, winked reassuringly at me. The beggar would wink.

Forward he went, and out of my sight for ever.

I had to forget him then, because Lieutenant Waters drew his sword and signalled us. We rose from cover and doubled forward over the grass to the right of my brother's platoon. There was an uncanny silence. We could see fairly level wooded country and some cottages to our immediate front, backed by more broken landscape. With a sinking heart I realised that our extended line made an excellent target, as we topped a slight rise, and went on fully exposed across flat country without the slightest cover. The Germans were waiting for us, holding fire. As we cleared the crest, a murderous hail of missiles raked us from an invisible enemy. The line staggered under this ferocious smash of machine-gun, rifle- and shell-fire, and I would say that fully half our men fell over forward onto their faces, either killed or wounded. Some turned over onto their backs, and others churned about convulsively. With hot throats the remainder of us went on, as there is no halt in the attack without an order.

The wood on our left, through which the other company was advancing, seemed on fire, as it sparkled with bursting enemy shells, and then became almost hidden under a pall of rolling smoke. The wood was a shell-trap, and the company had 'bought it', as the troops curtly say. More men fell, but my section still went strongly. Two men of the nearest section to our left fell, and both immediately sat up and began to tear open their First Field Dressings. They had been hit low, in the legs. A bullet ripped through the sole of my right boot, as I ran on, and jerked my own leg aside. For the next few paces I kept stamping my right foot on the ground, testing it, and half expecting to see blood spurt from the lace holes. This low fire was a bloody business, and most efficient – the kind of stuff we were taught ourselves. I believe I was now beginning to get really afraid of these Germans.

The high rate of concentrated fire continued, and the men were now advancing in a very thin line, with most of their numbers scattered on the grass behind. No officer remained. A sergeant on the left shouted and the men nearest him got down into the prone position. We followed suit, and hastily threw ourselves flat on the grass. Hardly had we done so when a machine-gun raked the whole line, a weak and feeble line now, and shot accurately home into it. Some of the lying men flapped about, others, shot through the head, jerked their faces forward rapidly and lay still. I trembled with fear and horror.

This was a holocaust. The relentless spray of the deadly machine-gun traversed back along the line from the left towards us. The Catholic soldiers blessed themselves in a final act of resignation. But the curve of the traverse came luckily short as it swept across my section, and it traced the ground in front. Little spurts of earth showed the strike of each group of bullets, a few yards before our faces.

This was more perilous than shots going over our heads, because the bullets ricocheted, shrieking like some infernal cat-fight all about us, but it was better than being hit direct. By lucky chance or instinct I saw the enemy machine-gun. There it was, mounted daringly on the roof of a cottage, close to the left side of a chimney, about six hundred yards away, and directly to my front. With all my strength I shrieked the range, described the target, and ordered five rounds rapid fire. There was a heartening response as we opened fire at the first and only target we had seen in this terrible attack.

In about four seconds some thirty bullets were whistling about that dark spot near the chimney as we slammed in our rapid fire, glad to have work to do, and gloriously, insanely, and incredibly the German machine-gun stopped firing, and then it disappeared as it was quickly withdrawn behind the roof.

'Fire at the roof below the ridge of the house, about three feet down,' I ordered exultantly, and I could have whooped for joy. I was now commanding effectively. Damn the rest of the enemy fire. Their rifle-fire was always poor anyway, and blow the shells. They might hit you and they might not. There was none of the deadly accuracy of the machine-gun in these other weapons of the enemy. I breathed a long breath of relief and looked about me.

I looked right and left at my section to see that all were firing.
Bugler Tymble had been wounded in the right arm, and having
discarded his equipment was moving away back. The others on
the left were firing well and steadily. On my right, the nearest
figure lay still with his face in the grass. I roared: 'Are you hit?'
and he raised his head to show a grinning face. I got angry,
and shouted at the scrimshanker: 'Why the hell don't you fire?'
and the man began to laugh. I did not know him well. He had
arrived with the first reinforcement only about ten days before.
He laughed and laughed and dug his face back in the grass. It
was no grim joke, as I then suspected. The man was hysterical
with fear. I did not know hysteria, and could not understand
him. Some of our wounded had bandaged themselves and had
continued to fight. The sight of them made me madder, and I
edged towards the laugher, swearing at him, and I struck him
twice in the ribs with my rifle butt. That steadied him, though
his grin turned to a look of terror. I threatened him with a
court-martial, and told him to pull his socks up. This sounded
damn silly in the circumstances, even to myself, so I crept back
to my central position to supervise the actions of more useful
men. I looked about for more enemy targets, but could see
none. Our cover was better than we had first thought, and most
of my section were lying accidentally against a tiny ridge, so
small as to be almost invisible when standing, yet it provided
us with definitely good cover, and probably saved all our lives.
Shells and bullets continued to kick up earth and grass in our
vicinity. On the left my brother's platoon was suffering badly.
Nearly all the men had been hit, and only a few were returning
fire. The shell-fire too was much heavier over them.

Muldoon rose some yards to my left with his face covered in
blood, which poured down on to his jacket and equipment. He
had been shot through the top of the head. He came to me, and
asked for the platoon sergeant. I said: 'What for? Go back,' and
he said: 'No, got to report first.' And report he did, going down

that awful line, under heavy fire, spurred by a most soldierly but ridiculous conscience to ask permission to fall out. He got back safe, with a peculiar wound, not at all fatal, for the bullet had hit him near the top of the head, and had passed under his scalp, and out at the back, without injuring his skull.

The curious behaviour of some bullets, as in this case, puzzled us then and afterwards.

We were still in great jeopardy, losing men every moment. Nine officers of the two companies – all we had – were knocked out. They fell forward in the advance waving their naked swords.

The Germans, aided by the flashes of these out-of-date weapons, had concentrated their fire with success on our leaders. Two officers had been killed and seven wounded. From this date swords went out of fashion. Our attack had been a fiasco.

Without officers, and sorely stricken, we still held on, until a sergeant waved us back, so we rose and returned to where we had started, exhausted and disappointed. Some of the men walked back disgustedly, not deigning to run for it. I found Tymble under cover, and saw he was quite happy with his wounded arm. He was waiting to go back to Vailly. The Germans followed up our short retreat with shells, and worried us with more casualties among the few survivors. This was very harassing, almost the last straw. Our casualties had already amounted to one hundred and fifty, more than half the strength of the two unfortunate companies. A sliver of shell hit the hysterical laugher of the front line and sent him all diddery. It struck him in the foot, and completely out of control he rushed limping for sympathy to me, shouting: 'Oh, oh, Corporal, what shall I do?' Some one seized him, disarmed him, took off his boots, and led him away, still groaning: 'Oh, Corporal. Corporal, Corporal.' My vials of sympathy were emptied, and I was glad to see the last of him.

A young Cork man named Lane came smiling towards me, with his arm in a sling. He was of my brother's platoon. I asked him about Denis, and he gave me the glad news that he too was slightly wounded in the arm, and had gone down to the village of Vailly with some other wounded. I was pleased and relieved.

The next few minutes reminded me of Butler's picture of the Crimean roll-call, when the senior N.C.O.s listed our casualties from information given by the survivors: '08, Corrigan?' 'Dead, Sergeant.' 'I saw him too.' 'Right, killed in action. Any one seen 23, Murphy?' No answer. 'Right. Missing.' 'What about MacRory. Any one see MacRory coming back after he was hit?' No answer. 'Right, wounded and missing,' and the sergeant's stubby pencil scribbled on. The depleted company moved back the short distance to reserve, and grouped in little parties to discuss their experiences. I left them to seek the orderly-room clerk, who verified that my brother's name had been submitted in the list of wounded of his platoon.

The clerk would not tell me the total casualties. He had been forbidden to speak about them.

Actually my brother was lying dead out in front, about three hundred yards away, all this time, and I did not get to know this for days. Only one man of his section had come back alive.

From *There's a Devil in the Drum* by John F. Lucy. Faber & Faber. 1938.

IRISH RIFLES AT LA BASSÉE: 25TH OCTOBER 1914

'a product of the slums of Dublin, and a stout asset to the British Army'

While the First Battle of Ypres (19 October–22 November 1914) was a mere week-old infant, in France just a few miles to the south the Battle of La Bassée (8 October-2 November) was reaching its conclusion. The Official History *(1914, Part II) explains that: 'The fighting on the La Bassée front, so far as the valour and determination of the troops on both sides are concerned, was as desperate as that at Ypres, but it never had the same strategic or sentimental importance. The capture of the Béthune district, with its coalfields and resources, would undoubtedly have been a very serious loss to France, but not an irreparable one like that of the Channel ports.' Cpl. John Lucy and his section of the 2nd Bn. Royal Irish Rifles were among the troops engaged; at the height of the fighting they were 'encouraged' by the presence of one Sgt. Kelly − 'a Dublin fellow, whom we all disliked because he was too fond of work. An unattractive fellow... a man-driver with a sarcastic tongue.'*

I had a grand dream. Loving friends were about me, a smiling valley held my home, and I stood regarding it, full of my happiness.

I opened my eyes and saw earth, empty cartridge cases, a pair of worn heavy boots, and two mud-caked puttees. I lifted my head from my knees to look at the man who was guilty of waking me.

Sergeant Kelly stood over me.

The night attack had come and gone: we had lined our crumbling trench and fired, and fended it off on our company front, at what hour I do not know, because we were only half alive. Fatigue had us.

The Germans had again broken the line in the night, and had exploited the gap on our left, between us and the next regiment, and some Germans had stolen in behind us, occupying the ground between us and the village.

Sergeant Kelly stood above me, blue-jawed like a pirate, with blasphemy on his lips. 'Get up and fight,' he said. 'The bloody Germans are all around us, and remove that man. Is he dead? He indicated O'Brien, who was collapsed forward on the low parapet, at his sentry-post, his dead face in the wet earth, and a hole in the back of his head. He had been shot from behind by the German infantry in rear.

Young Shea and I lifted O'Brien and propped him in the corner of the trench. The body canted, gave way and fell down sideways, the lifeless limbs slowly adjusting themselves to the accidents of the bottom of the trench. I gazed at it stupidly with heavy eyes, wondering if I should sit him up again. It seemed important that he should sit.

'Will you fight?' said Sergeant Kelly bitterly.

'Fight what, Sergeant?' I asked hazily, more and more bemused at my forgetting that one of my own men had been killed.

'Fight them, look!' he said with a string of oaths, and he clutched me by the shoulder, and pushing me to the parapet showed me the massed corpses of the Germans in front. The field was now simply covered with German bodies, the nearest only a few yards from the parapet and inside our single strand of wire. I thought the sergeant was batty, so humoured him, and looked hard at the motionless slain.

'No,' said the sergeant, 'not there. I'll indicate. Left haystack, two fingers. Three o'clock. Row of eight men. A fresh lot, they're stirring about. On to them quick. Get a move on.'

The miserable German section was lying fully exposed to us on level ground, where they had remained from the moment daylight had caught them, and they were trying to keep still, shamming dead like the masses around them, but small movements and their regular formation had given them away to the keen eyes of Sergeant Kelly.

'Get up,' I shouted to my section, and, firing with them, we put our bullets into the heads of the lying enemy. Two or three of them rose stiffly to their knees to escape, but the bullets caught them and they flopped down again. One man actually managed to rise to his feet and I shot him through the chest. He pivoted sideways, poised a moment, and swung back to his front, then slowly sank down, his head bending towards us, the sun glinting on his helmet badge.

I felt disgusted. We had slaughtered too many already. I was miserable until the German line was still and I prayed for them as I killed them.

There was another bellow from the unwelcome sergeant behind me, and we all saw the reason simultaneously. A single German, a derelict of last night's attack, rose slowly from under our eyes, where he had been lying against our very parapet, and without looking at us he began to limp away, just as the daily bombardment of our line began again. Then an enemy machine-gun whipped the parapet and we ducked. The sergeant, nonplussed by the sudden opening of fire, and enraged at the sight of the German, shouted: 'I'll get that bugger anyway,' and he raked the already wounded German with a bullet through the hips. We could not look at Sergeant Kelly, nor at each other for the shame of it.

Sergeant Benson came into our trench at a run, saying that he had spotted the machine-gun in the right haystack, and had sent a message through to our guns. This was interesting, and in a short time our shells arrived and exploded, but they hit the wrong haystack and set it blazing. The machine-gun stuttered again, and we popped down as the bullets traversed along the trench top.

'Up,' shouted Benson. 'Rapid fire at the haystack.' We fired hard at the stack, and at its top and sides, but with no effect. That gun was well hidden. We learned afterwards, too late, that the enemy had the habit of cutting a tunnel from the back right through the centre of haystacks, and mounted their guns in the tunnel; a clever ruse, as no one would fire at the blank centre of a stack. Anyway, we failed to put the gun out of action and it killed a good many before we left those trenches.

Sergeant Benson's attention was called to the wounded German, who, persistent in his efforts to escape, had now raised himself on his elbows, and was dragging his maimed body after him like a crocodile.

The kind-hearted Benson rose up, exposed himself to the enemy, and shouted: 'Come on in, Allemand, come on in. Don't be afraid.' The machine-gun gallantly ceased fire. I added my voice in French, knowing no German: 'Venez vous ici. Vite. Venez ici.' The German turned at that and came crawling towards us with a smile on his pale face.

Seeing this, Benson exposed himself still more and amused us by promising the German tea and bread and jam. The German came on, and in spite of our warnings the sergeant stooped out over the trench to help him. Then there was a loud crack, some one said: 'My God,' and Benson slipped back into the trench onto his feet, staggered a pace or two, and sagged down dead, with a bullet through his pitying mouth.

We forgot the German in our rush to succour our good chum and his, but it was no use. Benson spouted blood and made no sound. The bullet had come out at the back of his head and blown his poll away.

The German was half over the parapet by now, where he stuck and waved his hand despairingly and deprecatingly towards his own treacherous people. We took him in and laid him gently down under cover near Benson, took off his hairy pack, and placed it under his head, and some one dressed his wounds and gave him water. He was very weak and kept his eyes closed. Sergeant Kelly sneered. He stayed near us for some time, and during the lulls in the shelling he kept us up to the mark by making us stand up, time and again, without reason, under the enemy machine-gun bullets, to resist any invasion of our trenches.

During these alarms and excursions he raged at our small numbers.

Then he devoted his terrible energy to organising us. He made us clear away the dead and place them on the parados

like the company on the left. Under his direction we cleared
the trench of smashed rifles and other debris, and he made us
man our posts more evenly, spreading us out along the trench,
so that our small numbers only allowed one or two men to
each fire-bay.

He glared at the useless dead as if resenting their inactiv-
ity. He wanted more men for his next task of repairing the
smashed-in trenches. He was a great man in a way, and a good
war leader; a product of the slums of Dublin, and a stout asset
to the British Army, though a nasty piece of work from our
point of view, just then.

At last he left us, and disappeared round a traverse, whence
his rasping voice cut through the explosions, cursing some
unfortunate soldier for not cleaning out his rifle breach. The
mud of the trenches had entered the chambers of our rifles
and been baked hard inside by the heat of our firing, making
many rifles useless.

We had to resort to using bacon fat instead of rifle oil to
grease the action of our bolts, and we pulled pieces of old
socks over the metal work of the moveable parts to protect
them from the rain of earth blown over us by the bursting
shells. This earth got in everywhere; into our food, our hair
and eyes and noses, and inside our clothing.

Our supply system had broken down, and no rations had
come up last night, as the Germans had extended their heavy
shelling to the back areas.

My section, now reduced to Kelly, Shea, and the wounded
Grimes, fought on. I think we stopped two further attacks, one
by day and one by night, but my memory fails me, because
dreams and realities become mixed. The two forward companies were taken out of the line on the morning of 26th
October for a belated rest, right back through ruined Neuve
Chapelle to the village of Richebourg Saint Vaast, about two
and a half miles behind. We were silly from lack of sleep and

stumbled about like drunken men. We washed, devoured the food produced for us, and dropped down to sleep anywhere in the house allotted to us as billets.

From *There's a Devil in the Drum* by John F. Lucy. Faber & Faber. 1938.

WIPERS: 5TH–7TH NOVEMBER 1914

'more trenches and fallen trees and wire entanglements than there was level ground to walk on'

This account of the first few days of a lengthy tour in the line east of Ypres during the desperate First Battle indicate that even at that early stage the Salient was becoming a focus for defensive – and offensive – effort. The fighting was often confused, and the defences were being constructed under fire. It is also of interest to follow the trials and tribulations of a brigade commander in exercising his command, coupled with the basic requirement of comfort and food that even generals could not always take for granted.

We marched at 7.30 a.m. *via* Locres and Dickebusch, on the main Bailleul-Ypres road, passing through many French troops on the way. Not far on the other side of Dickebusch we heard that the road was being shelled by the enemy; so M'Cracken ordered the whole force to park in the fields some distance down a road to the west, while he went on to Ypres for instructions.

We had our midday meal whilst we waited there, but it was not pleasant for the men, for the fields were dripping wet and very muddy; they had, therefore, to sit on their kits, whilst the transport had to remain on the road, the fields being so deep.

M'Cracken came back at 3.30 p.m. with instructions, and we moved on, myself being in charge of the movement. We managed to get to Ypres all right along the main road, as the shells were rather diminishing and not reaching so far, and we pushed through the town, entering it by a bridge over the nearly dry canal. Why the Germans had not shot this bridge to pieces before I cannot imagine, as it was well within their range. There were numerous big shell-holes in the open space near the railway station; one or two houses were smouldering; there were heaps of bricks and stones from damaged houses in the streets, and the extreme roof corner of the Cloth Hall had been knocked off, but otherwise the town was fairly normal-looking, except, of course, that hardly any civilians were visible.

At the other end of the town I came across General Haig, and rode ahead with him down the Menin road as far as the village of Hooge, where the Headquarters of the 1st Division were, under General Landon. (He had succeeded General Lomax, who had been badly wounded by a shell exploding at his headquarters, and subsequently died, 15th April.) Here we had a cup of tea in a dirty little estaminet crowded with Staff officers whilst awaiting the arrival of the Brigade.

No part of this Menin road was, in fact, 'healthy', and at night it was generally subject to a searching fire by German shells. The wonder, indeed, was that more casualties did not occur here, for after dark the road was packed with transport and ration and ambulance parties moving slowly and silently back and forth. But the hostile shelling was not accurate, and for one 'crumper' that burst in or over the road twenty exploded in the fields alongside.

Only a day or two before, a couple of heavy shells had burst just outside General Haig's Headquarters at the entrance to Ypres. Luckily the General himself had just left, but poor 'Conky' Marker of the Coldstream had been fatally wounded, and several other officers, signallers, and clerks had been killed.

My Brigade arrived in the dark by the time that I had received further instructions in detail, and was parked off the road (south side) half a mile further on, whilst Weatherby went on to make arrangements for their taking up the line, taking representatives of the battalions with him. I met General Capper (commanding 7th Division) at his dugout in the wood close by, and he told me that his Division had been reduced to barely 3,000 men and a very few officers, after an appalling amount of severe fighting.

Weatherby came back after a time and the battalions and ourselves moved off along the road and branched off into the grounds of Herenthage Château – deep mud, broken trees, and hardly rideable. Here we bade adieu to our horses, who were, with the transport, to stay in the same place where we had had our dinners, right the other side of Ypres and out of shell-range, whilst we kept a few ammunition-carts and horses hidden near Hooge village. All the rest of our supplies and stuff had to be brought up every night under cover of darkness to near Herenthage, and there be unloaded and carried by hand into the trenches.

In the château itself who should we come across but Drysdale (My late Brigade-Major at Belfast, now, alas! killed [on the Somme, 1916]), Brigade-Major now of the 22nd Brigade, the one which, by the law of chances, we were now relieving; and, still more oddly, the other battalion (2nd) of the Bedfords was in his Brigade. It was a cheerless place, this château – every single pane of glass in it shivered, and lying, crunched at our every step, on the floor.

We pushed on over the grass of the park, through the scattered trees, and into the wood, and so into the trenches. Even then, as far as one could judge in the darkness, the ground was a regular rabbit-warren. By the time we had finished with the district the ground was even more so; there seemed to be more trenches and fallen trees and wire entanglements than there was level ground to walk on.

Our own Headquarters were in a poky little dugout, really only a half roofed-in little trench, in a wood, not 200 yards from our firing trenches. There was just room for two – Weatherby and St André (Moulton-Barrett having gone to settle about transport and supplies, Cadell being away sick, and Beilby being left with the transport the other side of Ypres) – to lie down in it, and there was a little tunnel out of it, 6 feet long and 2 broad and 2 high, into which I crept and where I slept; but I was not very happy in it, as the roof-logs had sagged with the weight of the earth on them, and threatened every moment to fall in whilst I was inside.

The Bedfords were put into the trenches on the eastern edge of the wood, the Cheshires continued the line to the south and for a couple of hundred yards outside the wood, and the West Ridings were in reserve at the back of the wood, in rear of our dugout.

I did not like our place at all, for it seemed to me that, being so close to the firing line, I should not be able to get out or control the little force if there were heavy operations on; and this was exactly what did happen.

We had been told that the 6th Cavalry Brigade was in trenches on our left, and the 7th Infantry Brigade in ditto on our right, and that was about all we knew of the situation.

Nov. 6th. Next morning there was a thick mist till 10 a.m., and I took advantage of it to visit the trenches in detail. The left of the Cheshires was within 40 yards of the enemy, who were hidden in the wood in front of them, so, there being no communication trenches, we had to be fairly careful hereabouts. But it was desperately difficult to make one's way about, what with the fallen trees and telephone wires, and little patches of open ground on the slopes, and long, wet, yellow grass and tangled heather in parts, not to mention the criss-cross of trenches, occupied and unoccupied, in all directions. Difficult enough to find one's way in daylight, it was infinitely worse in pitch darkness. No wonder that our reliefs had not been accomplished till nearly 3 o'clock that morning!

We were shelled pretty heavily all the morning, and two of the shells burst so close that they covered us with dirt. Two officers – Langdale and O'Kelly, of the West Ridings – had their legs broken by their dugout being blown in upon them, and three Cheshires were buried by an exploding shell and dug out dead. Another dozen were killed or wounded in their trenches, which were nothing like deep enough, and could not be further deepened because of the water which lay there only just below the ground. About twenty Cheshires were moved back to escape the shell fire, and taken to a rather less-exposed place. At 4.30 the Bedfords reported a heavy attack on their front; but it was confined to rifle fire, and nothing serious happened there.

The remainder of the Bedfords, under Griffith, consisting of two strong companies, turned up at 6 p.m., and the West Ridings were taken away from me, so that my command was now reduced to two battalions, one rather strong (1100 – just reinforced by a big fresh draft), and the other, Cheshires, only about half that number.

On further consideration of the situation, I settled to make Brigade Headquarters at the Beukenhorst Château (later known as Stirling Castle), half a mile farther back, and started the R.E. and a strange fatigue party to dig a funk-hole for us in front of it in case it were badly shelled; but I remember as a particular grievance that when the foreign fatigue party heard they were to go somewhere else, they went off, leaving their work half undone, and with our Brigade tools, though I had given them distinct orders to do neither of these things. But they were now out of my jurisdiction, so nothing could be done except to send them a message to return our tools – which they never did.

Moulton-Barrett turned up in the afternoon with a basket of cold food for us, and took St André away; it was not the least necessary for him to stay, as the dugout was really only big enough for two, so Weatherby and I settled down for the night. We had wanted to move into the château at 7 p.m., but we could not. For it was not advisable as long as an attack was imminent; also, M.B. had not got our message of that morning saying we wanted him to clean up the château for us; and thirdly, the Bedford relief was taking place. So we settled to move next day instead.

But it was not very attractive living in the tiny dugout. We had no servants, we had to prepare our own food and wash up afterwards; it was frightfully cramped, and we were always getting half-empty sardine-tins oozing over official documents, and knives and forks lost in the mud and straw at the bottom, and bread-crumbs and fragments of bully beef and jam mixed up with our orders and papers; and it was not at all healthy going for a stroll as long as the sun was up because of the bullets and shells fizzing about. Altogether, although it was no worse, except as regards size, than other dugouts, it was not luxurious; and as for washing, a little water in the bottom of a biscuit-tin was all we could manage, whilst a shave was a matter of pain and difficulty.

Nov. 7th. We had now come under the 3rd Division (under General Wing temporarily – a very good and charming fellow, a gunner, who had taken over General Hubert Hamilton's command, the latter having been killed, I forgot to mention, some time previously), whilst the 9th Brigade had relieved the 6th Cavalry on the previous day. The Division, therefore, now consisted of the 7th, 15th and 9th Brigades (the latter comprising the Northumberland Fusiliers, Royal Fusiliers, Lincolns, and Scots Fusiliers) – in that order from right to left. It looked, therefore, as if we ought to be soon relieved by the 8th Brigade and return to our own Division. Vain hope! We were not destined to be relieved for another fortnight.

There was a good deal of shelling of the 9th Brigade during the morning, but we personally had not many shells into us, and were fairly quiet till past 2 o'clock.

Suddenly, about 3, a hellish hostile fire broke out in the wood – not in our front, but close on our left. A hail of bullets whizzed over our heads, responded to by our fire trenches; and then, to our horror, we saw our Bedford supports, to our left front, retiring slowly, but in some confusion, on top of us – many of the men only half-dressed, and buckling on their kits as they moved. We jumped out of our dugout, and with the assistance of their officers stopped and rallied them. They were certainly not running, and were in no sort of panic; but they all said that the word had been passed from the right front that the Bedfords were to retire, so they had done so – half of them being asleep or feeding at the time the fire began.

We made them advance again, which they were more than willing to do, and then there was a cheer from the Bedfords in front. Upon which the supports pricked up their ears, rallied to the sound, and charged forward like hounds rallying to the horn.

Violent firing and confused fighting and yelling in the wood for a space, and some wounded began to come back. Then some Germans, both wounded and prisoners, in small batches, and at last the news that the Bedfords had completely repulsed the attack and taken about 25 prisoners, driving the enemy back with the bayonet at the run.

Who it was that started the order to retire we could never find out. It certainly was not Milling, who was commanding in the front trench, nor was it any officer. Quite conceivably it might have been started by the enemy themselves.

What happened, as far as I could make out, was that the right centre of the Northumberland Fusiliers on our left had been pressed back and the Germans had poured through the opening. The right flank of the Northumberlands had sat tight, so the Bedfords in our front line had known nothing of the German success till they were fired at by the enemy in the wood on their left rear. I do not fancy, however, from what the prisoners told me, that the attack was a very strong one – not more, I expect, than three or four companies.

These belonged to the Frankfurt-am-Main Corps (VII.). I examined one prisoner, a regular 'Schwabe' from Heilbronn, a jolly man with a red beard, who told me that his company was commanded by a cavalry captain, who considered it beneath his dignity to charge with the infantry, and remained snugly ensconced behind a wall while he shouted encouragement to his men.

The Bedfords retook three of the Northumberlands' trenches with them, but failed to retake one of their own – together with two machine guns in it–that they had lost, although they tried hard. A Company (Milling's) making three bayonet charges. They behaved devilish well, in spite of heavy losses both in officers and men. Macready, their Adjutant, was shot through the liver (but recovered eventually); Allason (Major) was hit twice – once through the shoulder, and again, on returning after getting his wound dressed, through the thigh; Davenport was shot through the left elbow (we looked after him in our dugout); and two subalterns were killed, besides twenty-four men killed and fifty-three wounded. Of the Cheshires, Pollok, Hodson, and Anderson (the latter a fine runner and very plucky chap) were killed, besides five men killed, nineteen wounded, and eight missing. Altogether the losses were rather heavy. The men were particularly good to the wounded Germans; I remember especially one man, a black-bearded evil-looking scoundrel, who had been shot through the lungs, and rolled about in the mud at my feet, and him they looked after carefully. The last glimpse I caught of him was being helped to a stretcher by two of our own men, also wounded.

There was again no chance of our getting to the château to-night, so another basket of food arrived, and we fed with what comfort we could.

From *The Doings of the 15th Infantry Brigade August 1914 to March 1915* by its Commander, Brig.-Genl. Count Gleichen. Blackwood. 1917.

2

1915: The Arrival of Attrition

'nothing else but murder'

Lt. Charles Pennefather of 'D' Company, 2nd Bn. The Rifle Brigade, wrote to Lt. Chan Hoskyns, recently departed from the same battalion, describing the battalion's part in the battle of Neuve Chapelle on 10-11 March 1915, and the wasteful destruction of the Rifle Brigade.

My Dear Chan,

So sorry I have not answered your letter before, but since the 10th of March we have been passing through such stirring times that I have only just collected my thoughts.

Now if you behave yourself, I will give you a long and vivid description of the battle of Neuve Chapelle, since we were the first to boost through the village.

We left our trenches at Laventie on the 3rd March and went back into billets in the neighbourhood for a week, during this week we had to practice the attack every day. During this time we collected every gun we could find in the neighbourhood, we got 360 ranging from the 13lb. to the 15 inch.

On the night of the 9th the whole brigade moved up to the trenches and hid behind some parapets which had taken us a fortnight to dig.

The attack was to start at 7.30 in the morning. So at 6.30 we all had a good swig of rum and at 7.30 our guns started off a most unholy bombardment the Lord over saw, this lasted for half an hour, it killed about a 100 of the Berkshires and about 10 of ours. At 8.5 the guns lifted and off boosted the Berks and the Lincolns who captured the German trenches. Then away went the R.B. and R.I.R. to capture the village. We simply boosted through the village capturing about 200 Deutchers. Byatt, Verney, Bulkley-Johnson were shot in this part.

We then arrived the other side of the village and joined up with the Indians on our right, and our job was finished since we had broken a gap in the line and we could have gone to Berlin at least if there had been anyone behind, but as you know our brilliant staff had two men and a boy behind and also 20,000 cavalry which they refused to let go because they said it was too foggy, all balls because there was no fog. Meanwhile the unfortunate 24th Brigade got held up on our left and were unable to push on, so we remained in our position for the night.

The next morning 11th the Deutchers had the audacity to attack us, we polished off about 600, so they did not come anymore.

However we got the order to take the German position at any cost from some bloody shit sitting at Boulogne, so went away A & B Coys, a most bloody fire from all corners of the earth broke out, it killed 130 of A and 90 of B, we then decided not to go on.

Never the less I am damned if another message did not come at 4.30 to take the German position regardless of cost, this time C & D. Meanwhile Brockholes, Pilcher, Gilby, Mason and Harrison had been killed. C were to lead followed closely by D, off went C and they lost 110 men, D were just off headed by Mansel and myself when the Colonel stopped us, Mansel got one in the head here, leaving me in command of D Coy.

The higher authorities then decided that the attack was nothing else but murder, not a bad thought after seeing most of the R.B. stretched on the floor. That finished the day's fighting.

During the night we wired and dug like the devil. The next day the Deutchers started to bombard us at 6. A.M. and continued till 4.30 P.M. the most bloody experience the Lord ever invented, it polished off about 50 of us and hundreds of people at the back.

I took a bullet through the hat, which took the hair off my head, I shot the blighter in the stomach.

That night was a bloody night as there were no stretcher bearers and all the wounded got left. Bridgeman got wounded by a shell in the evening, also Barton was wounded in the head and Carle in the finger.

The next day was quieter and gradually we quieted down. We stopped for 14 days. Now we have been taken away for a week's rest somewhere near Sailly and we are going into the trenches which the 7th. Division had.

The Canadians are in Estaires, awful drunkards. There are 2 Territorial Divisions close by too.

Rawlinson bungled the whole show. Davis was alright. Lowry Cole was very brave and nearly got blown up by a shell.

Stephens is quite well, Constable is acting adjutant. Stopford went away as A.D.C. to Robertson before the show, Grey is M.G. officer. Harding has gone to St. Omer to go through a course (M.G.)

We have 12 new officers and 400 men. Hoste & Stanhope and Cable, Rodney, Trench, Raikes and six others have come here.

The battalion lost 6 killed, 6 wounded and 400 men. The Berks had only 7 officers left, the R.I.R. had only 4 left, the Northamptons 1 officer and 100 men left. The Scottish Rifles had all their officers killed. We lost 520 officers and 1,000 men, hell of a bloody lot.

The new trench we dug we came across rows and rows of dead, those killed in October.

I met Baby out here in Estaires (he is on the 7th. Division staff).

This is all the news. Write me and let me know what you are doing.

Cheer Oh, yours ever,
Charles P.

From an original letter in the compiler's collection.

BLACK WATCH AT NEUVE CHAPELLE: 10TH MARCH 1915

'enormous masses of trench material and bodies sailing high above the smoke cloud'

When William Linton Andrews, News Editor of the Dundee Advertiser, *enlisted in August 1914 he was under the impression that he was either a regular or a Kitchener's Army recruit, and wrote for his paper signing his articles 'By One of Kitchener's Hundred Thousand.' In fact he had joined a territorial battalion, the 4th Black Watch, and landed in France with them on 26 February 1915 – three months before the first New Army units arrived at the front. Eight days later they were in the trenches, and just five days after that they took part in their first battle – Neuve Chapelle. They were attached to the Bareilly Brigade of the 7th Indian Division in the Indian Corps and were in a supporting role on 10 March, taking part in the operations until relieved at midnight.*

It was the night of March the 9th, 1915. Snow swept down upon us in the flooded trenches near Neuve Chapelle. We grew colder and colder. I never thought I could be so chilled and still live. It was a biting torture for the body.

We could hardly drag our feet along when orders came to move from the trench to the Port Arthur dugouts, there to snatch a few hours' sleep before we began battle.

These dugouts were welcome only by contrast with wet trenches. They were poor make-shifts of mud huts, often with ground-sheet for roof. They could not withstand bombardment, but they were some shelter from the weather. We huddled in with numbed wits. There was a young runner (a messenger) of the 2nd Black Watch in a dugout where I was put. He shivered at my side, and stammered.

"It's n-n-not that I'm afraid, Corporal," he exclaimed. "It's the c-c-cold. We've only c-c-come lately from India. I'm all right, chum, but I just c-c-can't help it. D-d-do you m-mind v-very much?" I said no, I quite understood, it was purely physical, like my being sick the first time under fire.

The phrase "purely physical" gave the lad great comfort. He used it several times as we talked. We became good friends in those hours of waiting for the battle. He was a brave little fellow, and anxious not to give a bad impression to a Territorial. His battalion was in billets near ours. Some months later I saw him wearing a D.C.M. ribbon, for continuing to carry messages though buried several times by shell-fire.

At 5 a.m. my platoon comrades and I were rooted out to move to a reserve trench. We shambled over ground hardened with frost. It was colder than ever.

We called it a trench, but it was nothing like the fortified cuttings that became familiar later. It was more of a breast-work, a stockade strengthened with sandbags of earth. Joe Lee, Nicholson, and I were together, sitting close to each other, backs to the stockade. Dawn came, and we peered across at the German lines, wondering if Jerry knew we were coming.

At 7 a.m. a German flew out of a low-lying cloud, swooped over Port Arthur, and after coming down to three or four hundred feet, whence he must have been able to see our lines crowded, he raced back. Now we were for it. German guns began, but directed their fire against the Port Arthur trenches, which we had left. Except for our usual morning hate with registering guns at dawn, the British artillery held its fire until 7.30 a.m. Then began, after a single shot that appeared to be a signal, the hell fury of bombardment from 480 guns and how-itzers. The noise almost split our numbed wits. As the shells went over our heads we grew more and more excited. We could not hear each other. Shots from the eighteen pounders were screaming not far over our heads, and much higher up, higher than the highest mountain of Europe, high explosives from the 15-inch howitzers were rushing like express trains. After a while we could trace the different sounds.

There was no difficulty in making out the German trenches. They had become long clouds of smoke and dust, flashing continuously with shell-bursts, and with enormous masses of trench material and bodies sailing high above the smoke cloud. The purely physical effect on us was one of extreme physical exhilaration. We could have laughed and cried with excitement. We thought that bombardment was winning the War before our eyes. Incredible that the men in the German front line could have escaped. We felt sure we were going to pour through the gap.

Looking towards the village of Neuve Chapelle we saw the houses terribly battered, but not crumbled away as we expected. We thought the German artillery must have been swept out of existence. Vain hope. Counter fire opened upon us.

"They're shelling our fellows," Nicholson exclaimed in extreme surprise. They were. We looked along the breastwork and saw about 300 yards away shrapnel plumping along our Black Watch Terriers. Stretcher-bearers ran along the line. Shell after shell came over, each about ten yards nearer Nicholson and myself. But a few minutes and our turn would come. We had no thought of escape. We had to lie and wait whilst the punctual shells worked along the line. "This looks like the end," said Nick.

On my right lay a young architect, Douglas Bruce, who had crept up to us for warmth. "Och," he said, "if we're for it we're for it."

It was the nearest we had yet been to death, and we were surprised at our calm. (We had then seen little killing at close quarters.)

Death was ruling a straight line along our trench. Crash! Crash! Crash! Our turn was coming. Now the line was veering slightly beyond our trench. The shells were falling five yards behind the breastwork, six yards, seven yards, eight yards.

"The next one's ours," said Nick. "Good luck, Linton." We shook hands. We wormed as low as we could. The shell came screaming. It burst ten yards away with a great gnashing roar. Earth drenched us. There was a cry of astonishment and pain at my side, while yet the up-thrown earth was falling.

"Damn them!" said Douglas Bruce very heartily. His mouth was bleeding. He had had a whack on the jaw, and a tooth had been knocked out. He took it calmly.

"Stretcher-bearers," we cried, and a man crept up and did what he could.

The shrapnel passed along the line, growing more and more harmless as it fell further behind the trench. Then it stopped, all was quiet, and a lark sang. Bruce started to walk with a bloody jaw on the first stage of a journey that was to take him back to Scotland.

An order came shouted along. "4th Black Watch, move to the left in single file."

It was 11 a.m. The village of Neuve Chapelle had been taken with the bayonet, and we were ordered to move forward to the captured German trenches. We passed many Indian dead and stinking shell-pits.

There was a point at which we had to jump a ditch. As we jumped we were in full view of the Germans. They were a longish way off, but now and then hit a man as he jumped. Our company commander, Captain Boase, on the other side of the ditch, called on us to hurry. We were bunching slightly as men hesitated to jump. I remember four in front of me. The first ran as fast as he could, and jumped high. Crack! He was wounded slightly, but carried on. Then a little stumpy fellow, as he jumped, was shot dead, his knees sagging as he fell. The next man, oldish and heavy, just flopped into the ditch itself and scrambled out unhurt. Then Nicholson rushed it safely.

Now for it. I took a good run, aimed to jump high, tucked my legs under me, then thrust them forward for the landing, just as though I were jumping for Peele B House at my old school, Christ's Hospital. Bullets whistled past, but all was well.

Curious that that jump stands out so clearly in my memory. I cannot think what happened next, except that there seemed to be more and more fire, and the situation was more and more confused, and the stench of the shell-pits stung the nostrils.

I remember seeing one of our men flop before a shell-burst. He rose covered with earth, and made towards me white with passion, his eyes rolling. "This is madness!" he cried. "The world's gone mad. Why don't you stop it?"

"Wish I could," I said.

"It's murder," he went on. "Why don't the papers stop it?" I spoke soothingly, but he said the same things over and over again, and went off raging.

I remembered being stationed with my section, probably after some hours, to guard a pump at a brewery. As we moved to it we passed a noticeboard still hanging with the word "Danger". Nicholson laughed as if it were the greatest joke of the War. By this time I was too tired to laugh. I was stupid with fatigue, cold, and strain.

The brewery had been severely battered, but was now quiet. Nick and I stood under a wall trying to follow the battle. We saw an English battalion, I think the Leicesters, going into a charge. We were near enough to see butchers' cleavers and hatchets hanging from some men's belts. They moved slowly, the ground being soft with its churning up by shells, in spite of the frost. Though here and there men fell, they kept a straight line. As a man fell his companions drew nearer to close the gap. I remember Nicholson, greatly excited, saying: "Did you ever see anything like it? It's magnificent." But I did not watch the end. I sank down exhausted. I felt sick. My head was on fire with pain.

We seemed to be forgotten in that smoking brewery where the lyddite still stunk. After a while a shell roared at us, went red with fury, and smashed the pump like a maniac. My occupation was gone. How could I be said to be guarding a pump that no longer existed? I looked at the remains with heavy pathos.

Leaving a man on guard, I hunted about for a Black Watch officer. I saw Captain Boase ducking and stumbling in No Man's Land, and went towards him. He told me he had found two wounded men, and asked if I had seen any R.A.M.C. fellows. I had, at the brewery. I took him to them, but when he asked if they could bring in the wounded they said it was too dangerous, and not their job anyway. One man had been shot in trying to reach them.

"We'll do it," Nick and I said, and Joe Lee and young Paton, coming up, volunteered also. We borrowed a stretcher, and, with Captain Boase leading, ran out to the wounded men. We brought in a German first, a Bavarian, all bloody about the thighs. The poor wretch had been wounded on patrol. He was heavy to carry, but we got him to the brewery. He was intensely relieved to be picked up, and shook hands with us all several times, having no English and we having no German.

Then we brought in the Englishman. He was very quiet, almost unconscious. There was a good deal of rifle fire about us, but no one was hit.

I felt better now. It was best to be doing something. And I began in those moments to respect Captain Boase in a way I had never done before. He had seemed a little too anxious at home, not ready enough to trust a man to do the decent and proper thing, but here he was master of himself, a good Samaritan, a true officer. I was ready to follow him anywhere.

I asked him what we were to do next. You will see that I was still the civilian, in spite of my khaki uniform: the real soldier would have waited for orders.

He said one of our companies had had heavy casualties in capturing a sniper's house, and our bombardment had not done all the damage we expected. Ammunition was running short, and probably we should be wanted either to carry ammunition or to take a German trench by assault. Meanwhile I was to keep my section at the brewery and await orders.

Leaving a man on duty, Nick and I wandered about to see what was to be seen. Men lay dead along the battered German trench. Our shells had done unimaginable harm. A German officer's body had been cut in two, and the upper half had fallen into the British front-line trench.

An Indian's head had been blown off, and was not to be found, but the most harrowing sights of all to us were those of young soldiers of the 2nd Black Watch, looking pathetically young in their blue-black kilts, and with the gay bloom of the red hackle in their bonnets.

An Indian boy came rushing over towards us, whirling a bicycle round and round his head. We thought he meant to assault us, but he was grinning and laughing as hard as he could. We tried to soothe him with the soldier Esperanto: "Teek teek, Johnny. Allyman no bon." We made no impression upon him. He was out of his mind.

From *Haunting Years: The Commentaries of a War Territorial* by William Linton Andrews. Hutchinson. nd (c.1932)

A SOUVENIR HUNT: 14TH–24TH MARCH 1915

'the man I was investigating had his head blown off, and though some of his brains were on the knapsack, I could see no signs of a helmet'

2nd Lieutenant Frank Lynch was commissioned in the 4th (Special Reserve) Bn., The Connaught Rangers, on 15 August 1914. On 11 March 1915 he joined the Rangers in France (the 1st and 2nd Bns. had merged in December 1914 due to their heavy losses). The next day they went into the front line at Neuve Chapelle but their attack was cancelled at the last minute and they came out of the line. After one day out they did a tour in the trenches from 14-24 March, and the day after they came out Lynch wrote this letter to his cousin describing his experiences and particularly a foray into No Man's Land in search of souvenirs.

I need not describe to you the operations that took place when we first came out here [Neuve Chapelle], as they were all in the papers, but let it suffice to say that I did not take part in any bayonet charge although we lined up for one once, but the Brigadier changed his mind. It took us from 5pm to 3am to get to our allotted place in the trenches, through thick mud the whole time, and really they are not worth the trouble when we did get there. This place is really overrated as a health resort, and I do not know what makes people so keen on this God-forsaken country. As an Indian Officer said to me the other day, "I don't see why the Germans should want to fight for this country at all, there is so much mud!"

Well as soon as we settled down in the trenches "The Bosches" started shelling us – a most unpleasant operation. There are several varieties of shells and different methods must be employed for dodging each. The most common kind is "Whistling Rufus" a 5.9 inch Howitzer firing shrapnel. It comes along making a noise like the D.U.D.C. [Dublin Urban District Council] steam roller going up a steep hill. One can hear him coming and can take cover. Then there are "Johnsons" and "Wooly Bears" both fortunately rare in these parts. The worst shell of the lot is the "Pip Squeak," a small high explosive shell that comes along so fast that there is no time to get out of the way. One of them burst beside my dug out on St Patrick's Day [17th March] (I was away having lunch at the time) and killed seven men outright and wounded some more, and demonstrated the fact that my dug out was not shell proof. After that I changed to a safer residence.

A few nights ago an officer and two sergeants were going out to investigate some dead Germans, just in front of the German trenches, and it was suggested that I should go with them "for purposes of instruction." We set out on our long journey (our trenches are about 300 yds from the Huns) and reached the dead bodies in safety. Then the Huns started sending up flare lights and we about thirty yards away from their trenches. We lay absolutely still among the corpses in the hopes of being mistaken for dead Germans. The bodies had been dead some weeks, and the aroma was not exactly that of violets. All the time we could distinctly see horrible German faces peering over the top of the trench. After a while the excitement died down, though we could still hear the gents jabbering and swearing in their trench, and we proceeded with our investigations. We got a full German knapsack each. I would like to have got a helmet, but unfortunately the man I was investigating had his head blown off, and though some of his brains were on the knapsack, I could see no signs of a helmet. Well we got back safely at last and investigated the spoils. The principal constituents of a German's pack seems to be "War bread" and cigars. The war bread ought to be very useful to fire from the 42cm. Howitzers when the Germans run out of ammunition, as its specific gravity (I think that is the word) is considerably higher than lead, and I should think would weigh heavy upon the stomach. I have kept several souvenirs out of the packs. Some of our men actually ate the war bread.

We had heavy rain in the trenches the last couple of days and there were several inches of thick oozy mud. However we are safely out of the trenches in billets now and hope to get a bit of a rest. Had I the imagination of my younger brother I could give graphic descriptions of how I led a bayonet charge and captured the Kaiser etc. but as it is I have not departed from the truth, and though "truth may be stranger than fiction" it is not half so interesting. I must close now, and I trust you will write to me soon. Kindly remember me to all the family.

Your affectionate cousin

F.W.Lynch, attd. the Connaught Rangers

DEVIL'S OWN AT SECOND YPRES: 26TH APRIL 1915

'Come on the Rangers – Come on the Connaught Rangers'

The Second Battle of Ypres – an all-out German effort lasting thir-ty-three days – commenced with their releasing poison gas, at 5 p.m. on 22 April, in the Salient to the north of the town, where the line was held by French Colonial troops. Hardly surprisingly these men broke and ran. No troops previously had encountered gas and its effects assumed exaggerated proportions. The Connaught Rangers, part of the Indian Corps, were rushed up to make a counter-attack where the breakthrough had taken place. Their attack on the afternoon of 26 April is described in this letter from the commander of 'D' Company to the father of one of his dead subalterns, 2nd Lieutenant Francis William (Frank) Lynch. The Connaughts' losses that day were fifteen officers (of the twenty engaged) and 361 other ranks. While the attack as a whole failed, the correspondent, Major Deacon, appears to have acquitted himself with great credit, holding an advanced position with his sixty remaining men together with small detachments of several other regiments for the next twenty-four hours. He was awarded the DSO and the French Légion d'Honneur.

Dear Mr Lynch

You have doubtless received by this time the official intima-tion of your son's death, but I thought you would be glad of some further particulars. I would have written before, but we only got back last night to where any regimental books are kept, and without them I did not know your address.

Owing to the German attack at Ypres, we were hurried away from here on Saturday, 24th April, and spending two days on the march up, arrived there on the morning of the 26th about 1.20pm. We were sent forward to attack the German trenches opposite the left of the British line, where the French joined us. My company, in which your son was, was on the left; and we advanced in columns of platoons, his being the rearmost one.

We had to cross about 1200 yards of rolling ground, and got a bad hammering on the way, losing two officers of the company before we had got very far. Young Hewitt and your son were, however, safe until we left a farm which was about 300 yards from the German line. There the Germans sent this abominable gas down upon us, and we had to edge off to the right, coming under an abominable cross fire from machine guns and rifles as we did so. We crossed a grass field, and gradually got some men up under cover of a hedge on the far side of it. From there Hewitt went on with some men, and your son, who arrived a little later, took on those who were with him. The last I saw of him alive he was laughing and shouting out "Come on the Rangers – Come on the Connaught Rangers." He got within a short distance, some 60 to 80 yards, of the German line, when he was shot dead, through the head.

Practically everyone that passed that hedge was killed or wounded I am sorry to say, but your son was doing his duty and doing it nobly, in urging his men forward. If we had been backed up by another regiment or two perhaps we might have got into the trench, but anyhow we are told that we did what was wanted, in keeping the enemy from using his reserves elsewhere.

Your son's body was brought back at dark, and eventually reached the Battalion Headquarters, where it was buried, along with those of two other officers, Robertson and Irwin, the Company Qr. Mstr. Sergt. of the company and several men. The place is just south of the forked roads in La Brique village, which is about three-quarters of a mile a little to the north and east of Ypres. The spot is marked on a map of the ground which I afterwards made, and which will be preserved amongst the Battalion records.

Your son had not been with us very long, but he had endeared himself to us by his modest unassuming manner and his cheerful acceptance of things as they came. We all regret his loss very much, so can sympathise with you in your sorrow. An inventory of his kit is being made regimentally, and you will be communicated with regarding it. With my sincerest sympathy for you and Mrs. Lynch in your sad loss,

Believe me,

Yours very truly,

H.R.G. Deacon

Self-inflicted? April 1915

'A thumb hung by a shred of skin'

When this incident occurred Cpl. Andrews' 4th Black Watch had only been at the front for six or seven weeks, but they had already been through one battle and consistently in the front line. Apparently it was an existence that was more than one man, at least, could endure.

There was a day when the cold seemed to get into our bones. The night had been frosty, but now it rained, the trench was muddy, and No Man's Land was grey with patches of mist. We had had no mail for a day or two, and our stock of comforts was low. We were not as a rule snappish in the trenches, but that day we were, having been working all night for several nights, and disturbed in the daytime by shelling.

I had to post sentries in two or three fire bays, and now and then go along to neighbouring N.C.O.'s to see that all was well. The mist all about made me a little fidgety. The enemy might be creeping up. One never knew.

I stopped to talk for a while with a private on my sentry rota, a man who had always a hungry, disconsolate look. In billets he had only one joke. He would suddenly call out "Tins outside," or some order like that. This puzzled me for a long time. I found it was what warders called out in a prison, and there was great laughter when some of them, pretending to be old gaol-birds, rushed to put their little food tins in line.

For the most part this soldier was morose. He never had any letters. He was that most pathetic creature, a friendless and unhappy man. Looking up and down the trenches to see that no one was near, he clutched my arm. "Corporal," he said, "I've a present for ye." I thought he probably had some souvenir to sell, but he pointed to a warm cardigan under his tunic. "I'll give ye this, corporal. It'll keep ye warm."

I would not take it. He needed it himself.

"Man," he said, "ye've been very good to me. I'll never forget how ye shared your parcels. I want you to see that I'll no forget."

I was touched by his gratitude, but fancied something shifty in his eye. I told him when he was on duty next, and went off to a neighbouring fire bay. In due course I warned the would-be giver of the cardigan for duty, and left him with a periscope watching the shifting vapour in No Man's Land.

A few shots were coming over from time to time. They were probably fired from fixed rifles, which had been set on suspected sentry posts in our line and did not require a German to show himself when firing. It was easy to fix them on flashes seen at night time, and then fire from time to time during the day.

Within an hour I heard cries of "Stretcher bearer." I hurried along the fire bays to see what the casualty was. My sentry had been shot in the hand. A thumb hung by a shred of skin. He was explaining to a sympathetic officer how he had bobbed his head up to look at the creeping mist, and at the same time was scratching his ear, when a shot burned his thumb like flame.

The officer was nervous. It looked as though the enemy might be crossing No Man's Land in force, hidden in the rolling mist, with snipers active to keep our sentries down. We put two sentries at each post instead of one, and all N.C.O.'s were warned to be alert. Whilst these arrangements were being made the wounded private was taken to a first-aid post, and later got home safely.

I felt sorry for the wretched fellow. Most of us had much to keep up our spirits – proud and affectionate letters from home, parcels every week, our faith in doing our duty, and living up to the ideals we had been taught at school, but he had no affectionate home, or pride of craftsmanship, or school sense of honour to keep him going.

I said nothing of the suspicions that rose in my mind that that shot thumb was a self-inflicted wound.

From *Haunting Years: The Commentaries of a War Territorial* by William Linton Andrews. Hutchinson. nd (c.1932)

FESTUBERT: 9TH MAY 1915

'Jerry knew all about our crammed communication trenches, and was sowing death where it would reap the biggest harvest'

Still attached to the Bareilly Brigade, the second battle in which the 4th Black Watch was called to take part was the ill-prepared Aubers Ridge-Festubert attack. As at Neuve Chapelle, they were to take part in a supporting role, and escaped going 'over the top' by the skin of their teeth. Nevertheless, they had a far from pleasant experience, as this description by Cpl. W.L. Andrews reveals. The regimental history of the Black Watch adds: 'The position of the Battalion during and after the assault was peculiarly trying. It could neither advance nor move to right or left, but had to lie still and endure a trying bombardment from the German guns.'"

At eight o'clock [a.m.] came the time-honoured words, the order for which we had waited so impatiently: "By the right, quick march."

My company carried tools, the others ammunition. Many units were going up, and there was much traffic of ammunition and guns. It was five hours before we reached our appointed position, an entrenched line where we were to await the bombardment.

We were somewhere near Festubert. Though at Neuve Chapelle we had had a good idea of what we were after, here, coming to what to us was a fresh bit of the line, we had only vague ideas of the battle plan.

Once the sweat of carrying our rifles, spades, picks, and ammunition had dried on us, we began to feel bitterly cold, and were glad when we got an order to move into dugouts. Six of us were put in one that was carpeted with straw. Sometimes we looked out and saw the stars shining. We listened for the noises of battle, but all was quiet except for the distant rumble of German carts on paved roads. It seemed that Jerry was bringing up rations as usual.

Chick Wallace, one of our best singers, was in our dugout, and we got him to sing our favourite on such occasions. "There's a wee hoose". It made us think of our homes, and the old folk, and our sweethearts. It was only a music-hall song, but to us it was a hymn before battle. Chick was never to see his wee hoose again. He was blown to pieces an hour or two later.

At five o'clock a battery behind us started to hammer away, and in a moment or two there sprang up what seemed to be miles of British artillery fire. We looked out. It was a good day for the observers, the sky clean of any speck of cloud. The continuous shattering roar of our guns was varied now and then by the swish of German shells over our heads

"Stretcher-bearer!"

The familiar cry went up, never to cease all day.

Wounded men were now walking back in our narrow trenches. English soldiers were pressing forward with ammunition. One had a football tied to his haversack.

At seven o'clock word passed along: "The German trench has been taken." We were very cheerful, everything considered. (This rumour proved to be untrue.)

We waited long past the time when we expected to move. This was ominous, for it meant that we were still a long way from the German second line, whatever had happened to the first. A sergeant put his head in at the dugout. "Get your men out quick, corporal, and move forward as fast as you can. Force your way up. We mustn't be late on any account. Do not stop for the wounded. Get on."

It took us some hours to make our way to a position a little behind the front line. We were under heavy shrapnel fire almost all the way. At one point we had to rush across the open under fire. Whilst I was running my water-bottle broke loose, and I lost it, but I did not stop to pick it up.

The trenches were horribly jammed, and the cries of the wounded Seaforths and Gurkhas wanting to get past was piteous. But our orders were clear. We had to force ourselves forward. There was no stopping to exchange a friendly word with some poor cripple who wanted help.

Our bombers were in front of my section. A small shell – some called it a pip-squeak, a name not very familiar with us then – banged into the middle of them. Two of my friends,

Jimmy Scott and Spark, were badly hurt, and Harley slightly.

We were getting far more fire than we expected. Jerry was surprising us. We never thought we should have anything like this trouble to get to the front line. We were all wedged together in the trenches, men of different units, bombers, riflemen, runners, wounded, and dying. We were so thick at some points that if a shell came we could not crouch down.

We of the Black Watch elbowed our way ruthlessly to the front. It was madness to stay there in that jammed trench, and be shelled to pieces.

When we came to the front line, or near it, there was more room, and we could lie at the bottom of the trench. Nick and I had kept together. A box of bombs had been left in our fire-bay. Nick pointed to it, laughing. I pushed it as far away from us as possible. There was nothing else to do but wait for orders.

I brought out my little notebook and scribbled a few words. This was part of my entry at 3.30 p.m.: "Under bombardment. Nerve-wracking medley of roar and clatter. We are lying as low as possible. From the bottom of the trench I can see white puffs (shrapnel in the sky), also dense yellow-brown clouds where German high-explosive shells strike near our trench. Overhead aeroplanes are like filmy silver-grey moths against the glorious sky. Rushing winds accompany the whooshing and whooping and whistling of the shells, and earth continuously topples over into the trenches. Have just been struck by a piece of shell – only a scratch on my right hand."

The bombardment continued for perhaps an hour. The German fire was vigorous and accurate. We were showered again and again by volcanoes of shell-torn earth. The call for stretcher-bearers never ceased.

About four o'clock we moved forward to a trench close to the firing-line, and were still vigorously shelled. There came a check. Men were bunching in front. Nick and I dropped to our knees for cover. Something struck the earthen wall hardly six inches from our faces and burst. Our faces were blackened, but we were not hurt. Nick said afterwards it was a rifle-grenade, yet a rifle-grenade bursting six inches away from our heads must have killed us. We argued about it later, but never came to a conclusion. It was one of those inexplicable escapes which came to every soldier.

We now saw why our progress had been checked. A narrow trench was crowded with dead, dying, and ammunition. Each of us had to take a box of ammunition and push on to the front trench. Here, too, we were shelled, though not as vigorously as before. Evidently Jerry knew all about our crammed communication trenches, and was sowing death where it would reap the biggest harvest.

We were still not wholly dispirited. We had still seen very little of the battle. Except for a brief dash, we had been in trenches the whole day, and had not seen one German. We did not know what had happened in front of us, except that obviously the German front line had not been taken.

We sat down in the fire-bay to wait. Our platoon-officer came and sat with Nick and myself.

"It looks bad," he said. "I don't believe our shrapnel's the slightest damn use for destroying trenches."

The bombardment had slackened, and we had a peep into No Man's Land. I shall never forget the sight. This is the note I made of it at the time: "Ghastly spectacle of dead and wounded in a long line – 'looking like sandbags', one man said. Our A Company had charged with the 4th Seaforths and lost heavily. They got ten yards from the parapet, and were mown down by machine-guns that burst out simultaneously. The Indians had gone over and had suffered the same fate. There was the frightful smell of charred flesh from a casualty whose clothes had been set on fire by a shell."

A runner came along with messages. Mr. Sturrock went to report to another officer. He came back with a stoical face. "Sorry, boys," he said, "we go over next."

"Shall I tell the men?" I asked.

He replied: "No, not yet. They'll know soon enough. Just see they've got bayonets fixed ready."

Then he had another good look at No Man's Land.

"Not an earthly," he said, meaning there was no chance we could reach the German front line. It did not appear to be battered by our fire. A soldier who had fought in South Africa came to me and said: "My God. They're lying out there on the wire like our fellows at Magersfontein."

We could hear the groans and curses of the wounded, and shouted to them that we would bring them in at dusk. An officer's servant, Private Smith, sprang over the parapet and went out to his master lying wounded, and stayed with him till the dark fell, but the rest of us were forbidden to try to succour our men. It was our job to go over next, and nothing else mattered.

The order came to get ready.

"I shall never see Forthill again," said Mr. Sturrock. That was the county ground where he had played cricket.

Nick said to me with affected self-pity: "Isn't it a shame that we're going to have a wonderful experience that we can't put into print? I could write such a grand article on how it feels to die young."

I was more practical. "Bags I that shell-pit in front where the two Seaforths are," said I.

At that moment a high officer came rushing up. He had only just been able to get through the press.

"My God!" he said. "Do you think you Terriers are going to succeed where regulars have failed?"

"Our orders are to go over," said Mr. Sturrock, quietly.

"Then for God's sake cancel them," said the other officer.

The word passed like a flash. There was no need to issue formal orders. We knew we were saved. Once again that day, by a million-to-one chance, we had been held back from death.

When we put up memorial crosses for those who had fallen in the action of the 9th of May, there was a sergeant-major who put a white cross on the grave of his son, and a private who put a cross on the grave of his father.

From *Haunting Years: The Commentaries of a War Territorial* by William Linton Andrews. Hutchinson. nd (c.1932)

LAST GASP AT SECOND YPRES: 24TH–25TH MAY 1915

'I remember standing somewhere in front of the German trenches, with a wounded pal's revolver, that he slipped into my hand, yelling at my men some of the filthiest language ever heard. They were appalled, and I rallied a dozen or so; as it happened, they were all killed almost at once'

'Second Ypres' officially ended on 25 May 1915 after the failure of the last German attack, The Battle of Bellewaarde Ridge, which commenced on Whit Monday, 24 May. It was the end of thirty-three days of very severe fighting and the Germans had failed. But the last attack was as ferocious as the first and during the 24th, the 1st Bn. Suffolk Regiment were moved up from reserve to take part in a counter-attack. They passed through Ypres, marched up past Zillebeke and at about 5p.m. reached Witte Poort Farm, where they immediately lined up and went into their attack. Already weak in officers and men (they had come out of the line on 9 May and been congratulated by the Commander-in-Chief, Lord French, on the part they had played in the Battle of Ypres!), they sustained around 140 casualties out of a total strength of less than 400. The attack is described by Lieutenant E.G. Venning, one of the company commanders.

I am resting now after some fairly strenuous work. Somebody told the powers that I should probably crock up if left in position much longer, so they sent up and relieved me. Now I am in a nice little wood, the shells pass over, and fall short, but they don't touch us here, and I'm supremely contented. I've had my clothes off and caught all intruders; it only remains to get a bath, but that is a great luxury to hope for. A man is actually coming from a far town to cut my hair this afternoon. I've had rather phenomenal luck out here; twice I've found myself the only officer left. I can tell you no news owing to the Censor's vigilance, or rather to the fact that we are on our honour to impart nothing; but I can tell you the happenings of weeks, nearly months, ago at Ypres (the regiment has long left there and I can tell you nothing of where we are now). I had rather a ghastly time then. I remember a certain two days during which we attacked incessantly in the open, and I had to lead two bayonet charges. You can't really gather what that means, and I can scarcely tell you. There was an open field between ourselves and the Germans, and I got my men to the edge of it (having lost Lord knows how many from shell fire), and we started a fire fight with rifles and machine-guns at about 5 yards. After some time of this I saw the right move, and gave my orders accordingly; it was my first charge, my first real big fight. We tried to spring across that field, but the fire was one solid block of lead. Literally I could see no chance for a fly in it, and a high staff personage told me it was the heaviest he had ever heard in that district (the worst on the line). We struggled along some of us. I remember falling about 10 yards ahead of my Company with a slight shrap hit in the back, that didn't even draw blood, and the shock of the revolver at my waist being broken by a bullet; then I heard my sergeant-major's voice (he's one of the finest men I know) saying, "Where are you, sir?" He said, "That's right, sir, I'm with you when you get up again." Well, we did get up again, and

I had to drop back owing to difficulty getting my remaining men on. I had a shot at one, and missed him, but it settled the rest, a man by me shouting, but he had his head and shoulders taken off; they sagged back from him, you know, riddled in a line, and I fell behind the rest of his body just in time. Then my men broke, and I remember standing somewhere in front of the German trenches, with a wounded pal's revolver, that he slipped into my hand, yelling at my men some of the filthiest language ever heard. They were appalled, and I rallied a dozen or so; as it happened, they were all killed almost at once, and I was left, so far as I could see, alone. Then I ran off the field faster than I have ever run in my life, dodging, taking cover behind dead men, and in shell holes; at the edge of the field I pulled myself together. Why they didn't get me on the skyline I have no idea. I disguise none of my clothes, and am palpably an officer, revolver and all, including a dead cigarette. I had another talk to the men below, and tried to get them back, but in the middle of it I heard my C.O.'s voice. He said, "It's all right, old man, I ordered them to fall back here." I had heard no order at all, and lost a good many lives rallying. Of course, when I heard it was an order, I dropped on my head off the field into a ditch and lay there. Lord, it was good to be under cover. The rest of it was a rotten affair; we were surrounded and retired. I was too sick and tired to move, and just lay among the wounded, smoking innumerable cigarettes; in two or three orders came the order for another attack in a different place, that was worse. We attacked at dawn; the poor old C.O. was killed among many others. At the end of it I came near to blowing my own head off with my revolver, but a wounded Northumberland officer saved me, and I carried him off the field in a coat. It was a beastly business. Since that time I have had some queer goes and weird escapes. A day or two ago I was sniping a sniper; he sent one across that burst the sand-bag in front of my head; the bullet came clean through the bag, but there was just enough sand to turn it a little sideways, and the heat and whirr of it all I felt. That happens so often, though, that one takes no count of it. It's a queer thing, but my impression of all this mighty business is the utter smallness of it all, the infinite smallness; the meaningless orders, obeyed by brainless heads, all willing to do their little best, until some tiny men cart them off to a little grave behind one of the small houses one uses for headquarters...

From *War Letters of Fallen Englishmen* edited by Lawrence Housman. Gollancz. 1930.

MINE AND COUNTER-MINE AT ZILLEBEKE: 23RD JULY 1915

'The men of the listening post were not found... they had been thrown several hundred yards by the explosion'

Under the muddy battlefields of France and Flanders, particularly in the sector from Ypres down to Vimy Ridge, but occasionally farther south, too, a complex system of mine warfare was enacted. From small beginnings early in 1915 there were, by 1917, miles of tunnels and chambers as large as decent sized rooms were filled with tons of explosive, ready to blow under the enemy's trench. If the tunneller's task was to blow the enemy out of his trenches, his prime concern was often his opposite number, mining from the other direction. Small charges, called camouflêts, were laid to bring the enemy's tunnel down on his head; sometimes tunnels met and there was hand-to-hand fighting and firing in the dark and confined space 100 feet below ground level. This piece, from the battalion history of the 1/5th Leicestershire Regiment, describes the infantry experience of the mine warfare existing around them.

There was at this time such a network of mine galleries in front of "A1," [trench] that Lieut. Tulloch, R.E., was afraid that the Boche would hear him loading one of the galleries, so, to take no risks, blew a preliminary camouflêt on the evening of the 21st, destroying the enemy's nearest sap. This was successful, and the work of loading and tamping the mines started at once. 1500lbs. of ammonal were packed at the end of a gallery underneath the German redoubt opposite "A1," while at the end of another short gallery a smaller mine was laid, in order to destroy as much as possible of his mine workings. The date chosen was the 23rd, the time 7 p.m.

At 6.55 p.m., having vacated "A1" for the time, we blew the smaller of the two mines – in order, it was said, to attract as many of the enemy as possible into his redoubt. To judge by the volume of rifle fire which came from his lines, this part of the programme was successful, but we did not have long to think about it, for at 7 p.m. the 1500lbs. went off, and Boche redoubt, sandbags, and occupants went into the air, together with some tons of the salient, much of which fell into our trenches. A minute later our Artillery opened their bombardment, and for the next half hour the enemy must have had a thoroughly bad time in every way. His retaliation was insignificant, and consisted of a very few little shells fired more or less at random – a disquieting feature to those of us who knew the Germans' love of an instant and heavy reply to our slightest offensive action. "Stand To," the usual time for the evening "hate," passed off very quietly, and, as we sat down to our evening meal, we began to wonder whether we were to have any reply at all. Meanwhile, three new officers arrived–2nd Lieut. R. C. Lawton, of "A" Company, who had been prevented by sickness from coming abroad with us, and 2nd Lieuts. E. E. Wynne and N. C. Marriott, both of whom were sent to "B" Company, where they joined Capt. Griffiths at dinner. They were half way through their meal when, without the slightest warning, the ground heaved, pieces of the roof fell on the table, and they heard the ominous whirr of falling clods, which betokens a mine at close quarters.

Before the débris had stopped falling, Capt. Griffiths was out of his dugout and scrambling along his half-filled trench, to find out what had happened. Reaching the right end of "50," [trench] he found his front line had been completely destroyed, and where his listening post had been, was now a large crater, into which the Boche was firing trench mortars, while heavy rifle fire came from his front line. Except for a few wounded men, he could see nothing of Sergt. Bunn and the garrison of the trench, most of whom he soon realized must have been buried, where the tip of the crater had engulfed what had been the front line. For about 80 yards no front line existed, nor had he sufficient men in the left of his trench to bring across to help the right, so, sending down a report of his condition, he started, with any orderlies and batmen he could collect, to rescue those of his Company who had been only partially buried. Meanwhile, help was coming from two quarters. On the right, Col. Martin of the 4th Battalion, also disturbed at dinner, was soon up in "49" trench, where he found that his left flank had also suffered from the explosion, but not so badly. His first thought was to form some continuous line of defence across the gap, if possible linking up with the crater at the same time, and, with this object in view he personally reconnoitred the ground and discovered a small disused trench running in front of "49" towards the crater. Quickly organizing parties of men, he sent them along this cut, first to continue it up to the crater, then with sandbags for the defence of the "lip". He himself superintended the work inside the crater, where he had a miraculous escape from a trench morater, which wounded all standing round him. At the same time, R.S.M. Small, finding a dazed man of "B" Company wandering near Battalion Headquarters, heard what had happened, and without waiting for further orders sent off every available man he could find with shovels and sandbags to assist Capt. Griffiths. Half an hour later, Capt.

Bland also arrved with two platoons of "C" Company, sent across from the left of our line, and by dawn with their help a trench had been cut through from "50" to "49". This, though not organized for defence, yet enabled one to pass through the damaged area. At the same time the miners started to make a small tunnel into the bottom of the crater, so that it would no longer be necessary to climb over the lip to reach the bomb post which was built inside.

During the next day we were fortunately not much harrassed by the enemy, and were consequently able to continue the repair work on "50." "B" Company had had 42 casualties from the mine itself, of whom eight were killed and seven, including Sergt. Bunn, were missing, while in the rest of the Battalion about 30 men were wounded, mostly by trench mortars or rifle fire when digging out "50" trench. At the time of the explosion the enemy had thrown several bombs at "A2", and it was thought for a time that he intended making an attack here, but rapid fire was opened by the garrison, and nothing followed. On the evening of the 24th we were due for relief, but, as "50" was still only partially cleared, and we had not yet traced all our missing, we stayed in for another 24 hours, during which time we thoroughly reorganized the sector, and were able to hand over a properly traversed fire trench to the Lincolnshires when they came in. Before we left we found Sergt. Bunn's body; he had been buried at his post, and was still holding in his hand the flare pistol which he was going to fire when the mine exploded. The men of the listening post were not found until some time later, for they had been thrown several hundred yards by the explosion.

From *The Fifth Leicestershire: A Record of the 1/5th Battalion the Leicestershire Regiment, T.F., during the War, 1914-1919* by Capt. J.D. Hills, M.C. Loughborough, The Echo Press. 1919.

IF YOU WANT THE OLD BATTALION... 30TH JULY 1915

'A machine gun was playing along the top of the trench incessantly. It was too narrow to pass anyone by, and I had to make people kneel down in the water and crawl over their backs. The wounded and dead lay in rows in front of the trench in the open'

Recruiting for Kitchener's Army began with his 'Your Country Needs You' appeal on 7 August 1914, the day after he was appointed War Minister. Of the first rush of men – 'K1' or the 'First Hundred Thousand' – the authorities could take their pick as there were more than enough volunteers. The men recruited to the ranks tended to be of better quality, that is to say in physique, social class, education and worldly experience, than the peace time volunteer. For officers the cream of the nation's universities and public schools came forward into the breach; many had some military training from Officers' Training Corps and they were instilled with the duty of leadership. All ranks were keen to train fast and get to the front. The first division of the New Army was the 14th (Light) Division, composed entirely of Rifle and Light Infantry battalions (except for its pioneer battalion, the 11th King's Liverpools – the very first New Army battalion to be completed). The Division arrived in France in May 1915 and almost immediately took its place in the line in the Ypres Salient, but their troops were still inexperienced when, in a part of the line they had not previously held, they were subjected to a new form of nastiness – liquid fire. This was in fact petrol projected via pipes from canisters carried on German soldiers' backs and ignited. Its moral effect probably outweighed its killing capacity, but when it was unleashed, in concert with machine-gun bullets and bombs, the first line at Hooge, held by the 8th Rifle Brigade crumbled away. The 8th was commanded by Lt.-Colonel R. C. Maclachlan, a regular rifleman who in 1914 headed the Oxford Committee for awarding commissions, so he had the pick of the new young officers. In his battalion were former captains of Eton and Marlborough, tennis and rugby internationals, graduates and undergraduates of Oxford and Cambridge. By the end of the day's fighting his battalion's casualties amounted to nineteen officers (out of twenty-four) and 479 other ranks (of 758). The following harrowing account of the battle was written by Lieutenant Hon. E.J. Kay-Shuttleworth, the second son of Lord Shuttleworth, who was serving with the 7th Rifle Brigade which was rushed up to support the counter-attack of the 8th Battalion. Kay-Shuttleworth was killed later in the war, as was Maclachlan, commanding a brigade in August 1917. In February 1916, whilst recuperating from a wound received near Ypres in December 1915, Maclachlan wrote to an old friend: 'I went out with a grand crowd, and believe to this day we were as good as a good Regular Battalion, but we never got the ghost of a chance, and 8 months of the Ypres Salient has now sapped the life out of those few (and you can count them easily) that remain of the old lot.' Was Hooge, 30 July 1915, glorious? Sydney Woodroffe of the 8th Rifle Brigade won the first Victoria Cross to go to the New Army – posthumously. His brother Leslie, in the same battalion, was wounded (he was killed in 1916; a third Woodroffe brother had already been killed with the Rifle Brigade in May 1915). Hooge was the beginning of the end for the First Hundred Thousand. They would not win the war, that was left for later generations of volunteers, but they played their part nobly.

On July 29th I left the Hospital at Mont des Cats and proceeded to join my battalion which I expected to find in the Ramparts. On reaching the transport however, which was in a field 300 yards N. by W. of the big dressing station on the Poperinghe-Vlamertinghe road, a quarter of a mile West of Vlamertinghe, I discovered that our battalion had remained seven days instead of five in the trenches round the Crater, (exploded mine on 19th July) and the Stables of the Château at Hooge; and were coming out of the trenches that night. I awaited them in company with Hunter, Winter, and Coombs;

I received news of the battalion's severe losses, due mainly to bombing attacks, minenwerfers and aerial torpedoes, resulting in just over a hundred casualties in seven days, during which time Thomas Gent and Ronnie Hardy had been killed, and Shoveller and Merriam wounded. I talked late with Coombs and Major Ashby of the 7th K.R.R. and went to sleep, (the first time I had slept out of a bed and out of doors for fourteen days) in a comfortable bivouac, which Nalley put up for me against a linseed stack, about 11.15 p.m.

We rather anticipated trouble owing to the unusual activity of enemy aircraft during the day; there was a large (5 inch, I believe) new anti-aircraft gun only a few hundred yards from our camp which we watched at work: it was firing incessantly the whole afternoon. About 2 a.m. I became conscious of the arrival of some of the battalion from the trenches: most of them did not come in till 3 a.m. I was awake then and noticed a particularly violent bombardment taking place, as I thought, south of our sector of the Line.

It grew in intensity, and I could not help listening to it, and wondering what was happening.

Suddenly I heard Captain McIlwaine asking for the Colonel's bivouac (which was behind mine) I then heard him say, 'Here is a message from the Brigade. that we are to hold ourselves in readiness to move at any moment.'

I leapt up and dressed at once, it was just after 4.30 a.m. at the time: I went and found the other officers asleep in a barn. I woke them up and broke the unpleasant news to them. They rose and dressed, they had had only an hour's rest after seven of the most arduous days of their life. Not one of them knew any more than I did what was happening: I went out to meet the Colonel talking to the Adjutant. Gradually the shelling diminished in vigour, and we began to think it was all over: we took off our equipment, and many lay down again to sleep a bit longer.

I talked for a little bit with Marriott and Lawson, who told me details of Thomas's death, and also mentioned that though the last two days had been comparatively quiet, yet they had noticed the German batteries registering all day long on various spots. I then returned to lie down in my Bivouac: I had scarcely reached it when I heard the word, 'Prepare to move at once.'

Meanwhile our mess sergeant had been warned to prepare some breakfast for us; it was not yet ready; most of us had a cup of tea, a chunk of bread, and put a piece of chocolate in our pocket, and then went off to see the men get their extra ammunition. The men were splendid and fell in quickly, taking off their packs, and thus (mostly) leaving their iron rations behind: they carried 250 rounds of ammunition each, and we moved off soon after 6.30 a.m. We walked fairly fast to where the railway crosses the Vlamertinghe–Ypres road and there halted for some time. Ammunition wagons for the guns were galloping by incessantly; fortunately the road was a very broad one.

We then moved on to a place just opposite the Asylum at Ypres, where the Colonel and Stewart rejoined us. They had gone on to get orders.

The news was then broken to us that shortly after the 8th R.B. had relieved us the 7th K.R.R. had relieved the 8th K.R.R. (who had been on our right). The Germans had exploded a mine under the Stables at Hooge, and then begun a violent artillery bombardment of the whole section of trenches held by our Brigade. Shortly afterwards, with the aid of a new invention, never before used by them against the British Army, they began to advance against us; we were unable apparently to see what they were doing, but they turned a great number of sprays towards our trenches which emitted a thick smoke and a liquid; the liquid suddenly burst into flames, and liquid fire poured over our parapet, and into our trench.

All sorts of rumours were current, e.g. that the Germans had pierced six lines of our trenches, that we had begun a general advance etc., but the truth seemed to be that in front of liquid fire, and a sudden bomb attack afterwards, we were driven back to the main road, and then out of the two trenches we held just south of it; we took up a new position along the edge of Zouave and Sanctuary Woods.

This occurred about 4 a.m.

They apparently attacked Zouave Wood later unsuccessfully. We were then told the plan of Attack.

The 8th R.B. were to attack on the left, the 7th K.R.R. on the right. We were to be in support of the 8th R.B. and the 8th K.R.R. were to support their 7th battalion; the D.C.L.I. were to come up after us, and act as our supports. We were informed that the 42nd Infantry Brigade would attack at the same moment along the Menin Road to our left. The preliminary artillery bombardment was to commence at 2 p.m., the attack was to be made punctually at 2.45 p.m.

The idea was that the 8th R.B. would spread out from the Strand to Bond Street and that they would be in two lines, and that we should be in three lines behind them. B first line, C second line, D third line. A was carrying up reserve ammunition.

The thick lines on the map are trenches: XXX denote those taken by the Germans: those marked ZZZ denote those taken by us in the counter-attack. After we had received these orders, we were kept waiting for half an hour by the D.C.L.I. (who were to act as our reserves and who had to join on to our Battalion in order to come up to the trenches in daylight by the safest way). At last they arrived and thence we proceeded in single file.

We had had orders to lie down and keep very still in the event of the appearance of enemy air-craft. In consequence of these orders, we were further delayed three or four times before we entered the communication trench running along Zillebecke Lake. However, we were scarcely shelled at all, though we had two casualties on the way up from shrapnel which were probably destined for the men bringing the ammunition up to the neighbouring batteries.

I was in the rear of B Company, Captain S.H. Drummond led C Company immediately behind me, and he became more and more anxious as time went by. It was already 1 p.m. when we reached Zillebecke Lake, and further delays occurred after that. Eventually I reached the end of the leg of Zouave Wood at five minutes to two... The wood was in a most chaotic state: very damp, huge and numberless shell holes, broken-down trees, derelict dugouts, trenches flattened out and contorted by shell fire. No place could have been more awkward for walking through, far less for advancing through in line under heavy machine-gun fire from the trenches, and incessant shell fire.

The roar of bursting shells began just as I reached the turning of the wood. Finch (Capt. Hon. C.D. Finch, commanding B Company) had gone to receive further orders as to our formation from the Colonel, who was stationed at B in my plan. I never saw him again after leaving the Asylum at Kruttstarsett. He was wounded by a piece of shell after receiving the Colonel's orders, but before he could impart them to me. The orders had been changed: our company in front, and the battalion following, were now to attack C8 along the line of Bond Street. I never knew this until later in the day. All I knew was that we were to attack *behind* the 8th battalion between Bond Street and the Strand.

Apparently Captain Drummond reached Gilbert Talbot, who was leading C Company, and told him this, for according to the new orders, C Company were to attack *outside* the wood.

Probably Finch told Marriott of the change, because apparently Marriott attacked on the right line, and thus diverged from Lawson and me who attacked straight out of the wood.

At 2 p.m. our guns began bombarding the enemy's trenches: at a moment's notice several German batteries began dropping huge shells all round us, and plastered Zouave Wood with 'crumps.' However, by degrees, over fallen trees, through tangled brush-wood and broken branches, we pushed on through the wood. The earth rocked from the explosions, while the air was so thick with dust and smoke that it was impossible to see through the wood.

On the whole we had surprisingly few casualties during the bombardment, though the men got badly scattered. The worst misfortunes were that our Company Sergeant-Major (Cole) and Sergeants Fairhead, Hoffman and Bonham were all wounded before we could begin to advance. At 2.10 p.m. a bullet struck my wrist watch, which was in a steel case on my right wrist: it broke them, but left me unhurt. The trouble was that I was without the time, and I crawled over to Lawson and found his watch had stopped. What bad luck! We crawled on to the edge of the wood and decided to charge the moment we saw anyone else doing so. At last after what seemed ages I saw Gilbert Talbot running forward a good way to my left. I also saw Marriott going in the same direction, not quite so far off. Lawson and I got up and rushed out of the wood with all the men round us; that included Sergeant Cuthbertson, Corporal Merrigan, Basketter, Townsend, and Prosser. Sergeants Cuthbertson and Basketter were shortly badly wounded; the other three are missing and we believe dead.

We were immensely surprised to see no 8th battalion men in front of us, or to our right; almost at once we found ourselves up against our own barbed wire, with a machine gun playing backwards and forwards along our line. A shell then knocked us down, and wounded Lawson slightly in the thigh.

We were under such very heavy machine gun fire, and so few of us, that we decided to lie there for a moment until the next line arrived. The next line never arrived: we saw no movement on the right or left of us, and began to dig ourselves in. Townsend, who was lying next me, was shot through the head and I used his entrenching tool. Lawson and I got next each other and discussed the situation. Should we try to get through the wood and attack? We were only ten strong at the most and some of them were slightly hit; it was uncertain whether we had taken any trenches or not. Or, should we withdraw to the trench along the edge of the wood and hold that? As the field of fire was rotten where we were, and we were quite isolated, we decided to withdraw. Only about two besides myself reached the trench unhit. We tumbled headlong into the ditch, which was two feet six in water. There I bound up Sergeant Cuthbertson's arm, and Griffith's arm, saw Lawson's leg, and begged him to have it tied up. Lawson with the utmost gallantry said he would stick on in the trench. We found a few people there; a few crawled into it from behind; some wounded crawled back. I asked Sergeant Cuthbertson to go and be properly dressed, as he wished to do so, and told him to find the Colonel and tell him where we were and what had happened. He got back but never delivered my message.

I then left Lawson to hold that end of the trench and began to explore the right. I kept coming on men in, in front of, and behind the trench. These I put into the trench and told them they had to stick there whatever happened. They all set to work to clean their rifles, and hold on to this very narrow trench, an old communication trench. I soon met Sergeant Bourne with some men, whom I put in touch with Lawson. They had left the wood, missed the direction, and done much the same as I had.

Then I found Philip Collins: he had only just been shot, and then lay at the bottom of the trench. He had come up somewhere from the left rear, and had been trying to find out what had happened and what was going on in front of us. He had got up too high above the parapet, and had been shot instantaneously through the head. A machine gun was playing along the top of the trench incessantly. It was too narrow to pass anyone by, and I had to make people kneel down in the water and crawl over their backs. The wounded and dead lay in rows in front of the trench in the open: under very heavy shell fire, they were nearly all fetched in after dark by our gallant men.

I found a large number of the 8th battalion men there, and one K.R.R. I took them all under my orders and forbade them to leave the trench. I went on, and at last came to Lieut. Pope, a new officer who had only joined our Battalion on Monday, and who was doing his best to consolidate a further portion of the same trench with some men of D Company. I later found Norbury further on with more men of D Company; how they reached that position I do not understand, but after three hours' hard work we got a continuous line of our men holding the trench along the inside of Zouave Wood from Bond St. to the Strand. The end of the wood I found out from Norbury, was held by Captain Sheepshanks of the 8th R.B. His men faced E. and we faced N. We had not the least idea what had happened to the 60th on our right.

Norbury and I met and decided to make our way back to the Colonel and inform him of the situation. I had previously written a brief note and sent it back. On our way down the communication trench I met Colonel Maclachlan and Major Tod and Captain Parker of the 8th R.B. They were in a complete haze as to what had happened; I explained all I knew, and then went on to see our C.O. He seemed pleased to see me, and received my information. He told me that the D.C.L.I. had arrived to relieve us, for which I was profoundly thankful. It was then about 6.30 p.m.

When I got back to our trenches, I received a note to say that Lawson and about twelve men had been released by the D.C.L.I. and had withdrawn, but there were no more men to relieve us. We were severely hampered all the time by the wounded lying in the trench, who could not be moved or attended to; the stretcher-bearers worked marvels for them, but had too many to deal with. Norbury and I later went back to the C.O. and he told me to search for the D.C.L.I. and make them take over our trench. I went up SSS and at that junction found Sergeant Bourne who told me that the D.C.L.I. had arrived at the other end of the trench. I went off to the left to meet them and arrange the relief. It was then dark. My men had walked twenty miles, and had only had one meal in the last twenty-four hours, not to speak of the fighting. As I went along the trench I heard a cry in front, and went out and found Captain Woodroffe of the 8th R.B. shot through the legs. I asked for a volunteer to help me to bring him in, and Woodford offered himself. Together we managed to carry him in from about thirty yards in front of the wood, about forty to fifty yards from the trench. The Germans were keeping up a heavy fire all the time and sent up a quantity of Vérey lights, but thank God none of us were touched.

Subsequently a lot of my men fetched the wounded back, and I hope all wounded on our side of the barbed wire were got in before morning.

I recollected that further to my left Captain S.H. Drummond had been reported wounded in front. So when I got to that place I called out 'Bones' and to my delight the reply came, 'Yes, here I am, who are you?' I said I would come out and fetch him in, and he said 'Thank God, help at last!' When I got there I was awfully disappointed not to find Drummond but another man. I asked him who he was, and he said 'Bone of C Company' – a very curious coincidence. The D.C.L.I.

were eventually found. They had gone to the wrong place and had relieved the wrong people, but at any rate they were insufficient to relieve me, as I had over a hundred men of B and C Companies and of the 8th R.B. under me.

I returned to the Colonel, withdrawing fifty 7th R.B. men from the front line, and putting them in to hold the trench I have marked on the map RRRR. Colonel Maclachlan was there and very pleased to hear my news about Captain Woodroffe. He had been reported to him as killed. While there, two more Companies of the D.C.L.I. arrived and I guided them up to relieve me, to relieve Norbury also and Sheepshanks. On the way back, as I led my men out, a whizz-bang fell just in front of me on a hard path outside the wood and took the skin off my shin. It gave me a terrible fright and for a moment or two I went quite mad: but I have a recollection of Maxwell and Nalley taking me back to the Colonel, where Stewart gave me some neat whisky which restored me to my senses quickly.

I reported that I, Norbury, and Sheepshanks had all been relieved and were on the way out. How thankful we were to leave those trenches.

Then we began to collect the Battalion to return and walked back to bridge 14 across the open. Very heavy shelling proceeded the whole time: it was awful and nerve-shattering, but quite miraculously no one was hit.

On the way out Heavens! though what a lot of shrapnel came over, and 'Heavies,' too, directed for the guns: none too far off us. We walked pretty quick to the Asylum and got there about four o'clock.

Just beyond in a field a most welcome sight greeted us, our cookers with hot tea and biscuits for us. First drink or food I had had since 6.30 a.m. the day before, except for one bar of chocolate, a little water, a little brandy and the Adjutant's whisky, and a tiny sandwich Winter gave me.

We did not wait long but tramped on home, and I am glad to say our horses awaited us there, and so I was able to ride back the last four miles.

So sad, so tired, on the way back we met our cheery friend Quartermaster Coombs, and when he said that he was glad to see me surviving tears came into my eyes...

We had a little breakfast and got to bed about eight o'clock, but I could not sleep. I rocked over and over with horrors to think of the remnants left of our magnificent battalion. They had been so well trained; they were all so fond of each other, and now we were only 450 strong including at least a hundred transport men, etc., who had not been in the fight.

From *Edward James Kay-Shuttleworth, Captain 7th Rifle Brigade, Staff Captain 218th Infantry Brigade 1890-1917* [a memoir] by his wife, Mrs Sibell Kay-Shuttleworth. Printed for private circulation. 1918.

EARLY MORNING HATE: 4TH AUGUST 1915

'and in a moment hell would be loosened all round us'

The 'morning hate' – in some measure – was universal on the Western Front. Each side's daily pre-emptive strike against the possibility of a dawn attack was to shell the opposing front-line trenches for a period. This account of a day in the line near Hooge was written by Henry Arthur Foley, then a Lance-Sergeant in 'C' Coy., 6th (Service) Bn. Somerset Light Infantry.

August 4th was no exception to the rule of early-morning hate. How we dreaded those cold, grey dawns, and waited with eyes almost hypnotically strained to the west to catch the first twinkle of the guns as they spat out in their fearful unison of sound. As the light slowly grew, we would feel just a glimmering of hope that perhaps this morning they would rest and let the day dawn in peace. And then those dreaded flashes, and in a moment hell would be loosened all round us. This morning, in the full blaze of the strafe, as seven of us sat crouched in the little shelter under the parados of our fire-bay, a high-explosive shell pitched just in front of the parapet, blowing it to fragments. The air was filled with smoke and debris, and we had the sensation of experiencing a dozen concentrated earthquakes. Our doorway luckily was not blocked, and we scrambled out, in spite of the entreaties of James, a miner from Wales, to "hold the roof, for God's sake, hold the roof". We squirmed out, over the tumbled ruins of our parapet, round into the neighbouring bay, and there awaited the next instalment. It came, but not so close; and gradually the bombardment slackened.

It rained a good deal during the day, and, deprived of our home, we spent a pretty cheerless time. That night, however, sandbags were procured, we got to work with a will, and before dawn had erected a "brand new Phoenix from the blaze", in the shape of a new and greatly improved parapet. I was so tired next day that I slept through most of it, and at 11 p.m. that night (August 5th) a battalion of the 6th Division relieved us. To them had been given the job of retaking the lost trenches. They came in wearing "fighting order", and seemed in wonderful spirits. On our way out we lost Tinknell, a Bridgwater man, who was hit in the stomach by a stray bullet and died very soon afterwards.

From *Three Years on Active Service & Eight Months a Prisoner of War* by Henry Arthur Foley. Bridgwater, Somerset, Printed for Private Circulation. 1920.

The Battle of Loos: 25th September–11th October 1915

'heavily shelled, as also was Loos, where houses were crashing to the ground every few minutes'

Pte. F.A.Bolwell with the 1st Bn. Loyal North Lancashire Regiment went over the top on the first day of the Battle of Loos. Two main features of the attack were the British use of gas although the wind was not blowing in the right direction, and the fact that the German wire was uncut. All along the line there were severe casualties and in some places quite significant entries were made into the German lines, of which something might perhaps have been made had reserves been near at hand. After the first day, Bolwell's battalion continued to take part in the battle, holding the line mainly, and he was wounded in the closing stages.

The 1st Division took the centre, with the 15th Scottish Division on the right and the 9th Division on the left. The 1st Division faced a part of the line known as "Lone Tree," named after a tree between the two lines and the only one there. The Division had battle Headquarters at Larutwar Farm, and Brigade Headquarters in a part of the trenches known as "Daly's Keep". At 6.40 a.m. on the morning of the twenty-fifth of September the attack was to be launched, first by the Royal Engineers letting off asphyxiating gas; when that reached the German lines or was three parts of the way across, the Infantry were to follow. Of the 2nd Brigade the 1st Loyal North Lancashires and the King's Royal Rifles were the two regiments selected, and to them was given the honour of going over first, the King's Royal Rifles on the right. Punctually at the time given the gas was let off, accompanied by smoke bombs, but unfortunately before it reached half the distance across, the wind changed and it blew back upon us. However, over we went, and, as our distance to the enemy's lines was quite eight hundred yards, we covered them by short rushes. On reaching the enemy's wire entanglements we found that they had not been sufficiently damaged to admit of our access to the enemy's trench; so we held on for reinforcements, which arrived in the form of the 2nd Royal Sussex; but we could not make headway against the enemy's machine-guns, although the Divisions on our left and right had advanced a considerable distance. A Brigade consisting of several Territorial Regiments in the Division was then sent to our aid, and this time we got through, taking several hundred prisoners. The divisions on the left and right of us had advanced, the enemy opposed to them had retired and were to all intents and purposes cut off, so they had perforce to surrender. This gave us practically a clear run of about half a mile, and we saw, as we passed, that our objective at the chalk-pit was the village of Loos on our left. Fighting in Loos village was very furious indeed. This chalk-pit is situated on the Loos-Lens road, and on the left of it is a wood, where, after charging through it for spare Germans, we dug in.

At 4 a.m. on the morning of the twenty-sixth we were relieved by the 21st Division of Kitchener's Army, as we had obtained our objective. We went back to our old original trenches, leaving the 21st Division to carry on. Our ranks were sadly depleted, having lost many men; it was an awful and ghastly sight coming back over the ground we had taken. About two o'clock that afternoon we heard that the 21st Division were not doing well, and that a couple of field-batteries which had taken up position immediately behind the old German front line had been put out of action, as well as two batteries to the right of Larutwar Farm, which was packed from end to end with wounded, waiting to be taken away. The motor-ambulances worked night and day.

Soon after this, the 24th Division, another of Kitchener's Divisions, came into action to relieve the 21st, very few of whom remained. This Division stopped in for nearly twenty-four hours, and retook some of the ground that the 21st had lost. The afternoon before the Guards Division, fresh from − − , where they had been in training, and the New Welsh Guards also went into action, making an attack on the Hohenzollern Redoubt. They did good work, I believe, in taking part of it.

On the night of the twenty-seventh we were ordered out from our old line to the old German support line in reserve; but next morning were taken out again and back to Mazingarbe, a small village behind Vermelles. We had eight hours' rest here, and that same night proceeded to the recently captured village of Loos, where were packed piles of dead Germans and men of the 15th Scottish Division. It was indeed an ugly sight. From one cellar we turned out twenty Germans, and we also took one who had been working an underground telephone. We spent one night in this cellar, and the following night proceeded through the village to Hill 70, where we filled a gap and dug a line of trenches, digging most of the time through solid chalk. While there we were heavily shelled, as also was Loos, where houses were crashing to the ground every few minutes.

Three days afterwards we were relieved by a French Division and went back to Neaux-le-Mines for a well-earned five-days' respite. After that we were put into trenches at Vermelles, and on October the tenth the enemy made a determined attack on the 9th King's Liverpools and Gloucesters, 3rd Brigade, to whom we had then been attached. The enemy were well driven off, but both regiments had to be taken out that night, and we went up in the place of the King's Liverpools, and were situated in our old trenches near the chalk-pit. Here, on the morning of the eleventh of October, we were badly shelled: we lost a machine-gun team and the gun was knocked out. I was then ordered to take a message into Loos village to the 3rd Brigade Office, requesting them to send up another gun-team at once.

Coming back from this message I received my wound, getting a nasty knock through the leg, severing the arteries and smashing the bone. After binding it tightly, I managed to make my way to the first-aid dressing station, a distance of nearly a mile and a half. Thence I proceeded to Mazingarbe, but, owing to hæmorrhage, I did not get my wound dressed until I was sent back to Lozingham, where I was sent to the operating tent of the 23rd Field Ambulance. Whilst awaiting my turn, I watched the surgeons take from another man's knee a bullet. Two days later I was sent to Rouen, where I spent ten days; from there I came home to Salisbury Infirmary, and I was in this hospital for twelve weeks undergoing three operations. I was, on becoming convalescent, sent to the Red Cross Hospital, Salisbury; and here I spent another month, and proceeded at the end of that time to the house of Sir Vincent Caillard at Wingfield. At this house I was given massage twice a day; and after a month was sent on to Sutton Veney. After three weeks I was given my discharge, and proceeded to the depôt in Lancashire, where I finally signed my papers and re-entered back to civilian life after having had one year and 246 days on active service.

From *With a Reservist in France: A Personal Account of all the Engagements in which the 1st Division 1st Corps took part* by F.A.Bolwell. Routledge. nd (c.1919).

Festive Fighting: 25th December 1915

'"the happy morn" was heralded in with the scream and crash of shells and the devils' rattle of machine-guns'

The 1914 Christmas truce came as a surprise to all concerned, and met with official disapproval. Although there were three more Christmases before the war ended there was to be no repetition of the first occasion, although Pte. H. Raymond Smith of the machine-gun section of the 1/8th Worcesters recalled having alarmingly unwarlike thoughts as the second Christmas of the war drew near. In fact, for the soldiers in the line, any hopes of a holiday were short lived, and on this second Christmas the harsh winter conditions made the trench existence more than usually unbearable.

Towards the end of December, 1915, the weather in France became very severe, with frost and snow, succeeded by bitter east winds and icy rain. Trench duty at night became a martyrdom. At one time the frost was so severe that the bolts of our rifles froze so stiff that we could not work them, despite the fact that they were coated with oil. At this time our sentry-go was two hours on and two hours off throughout the night, as through sickness and casualties we were short-handed on the machine-gun teams. Normally we did two hours on and four off. Those two hours standing on the fire-step, gazing into No Man's Land, often seemed more like ten. In the darkness one could usually see a portion of our own barbed wire belt, just in front of the parapet, and staring at those posts for hours on end was apt to make one's imagination play tricks. Surely what one had thought was a post had moved! At these times it was essential to keep a tight grip of oneself. The knowledge that many lives depended on one's vigilance kept one on the alert the whole time. When our period of sentry duty came to an end and we were relieved, we took our frozen rifles down into a dugout where there was a brazier burning to have them thawed. My feet got completely numb with the cold on the fire step, and I remember the agony I went through in the dugout while the blood was beginning to circulate in them again. The miseries of a winter campaign are almost impossible to exaggerate!

It fell to our lot to spend Christmas Day, 1915, in the trenches. I remember that some days before I suggested that several of us should go out into no-man's land, as far as the

Seven Sisters (a line of poplar trees) near the German trenches, and serenade the Boches. My suggestion was that our opening number should be "Hail, Smiling Morn!" It was pointed out that this might be about as far as we should get! Actually when Christmas morning dawned I was on duty with the machine gun, with Sergeant S– , in Botha Trench. Our guns opened a heavy bombardment on the German trenches, and their artillery replied, shelling the trenches and the back areas. When they started shelling we opened with the machine-gun, and for some time "the happy morn" was heralded in with the scream and crash of shells and the devils' rattle of machine-guns.

The second Christmas of the Great War there was no repetition of the extraordinary truce which took place in several parts of the line on Christmas Day, 1914. The High Command took care of that. Orders were issued that there was to be no fraternising with the enemy, and "orders is orders". As a matter of fact, in our part of the line, as it became light, several Germans called out "A Happy Christmas, Tommy," and our men replied with "A Happy Christmas, Fritz." At one point they commenced to climb out of their trenches, but a few rounds fired high over their heads sent them back again. Seasonable greetings, however, were exchanged between friend and foe throughout the day, and as far as possible "a good time was had by all!"

From *A Soldier's Diary: Sidelights on the Great War 1914-1918* by Captain H. Raymond Smith. The 'Journal' Press. Evesham. 1940.

3

1916: When the New Army Bled

Box Barrage at Vimy Ridge: 21st May 1916

'the whole structure rocks again like a toy model with all the screws loose. Some of the wounded, panic-stricken again and almost beyond control, jump up shouting and are only quietened with difficulty. Almost immediately another big shell falls overhead'

In March 1916 the BEF took over some twenty miles of front line previously held by the French in order to relieve the pressure brought to bear on the latter by the German offensive at Verdun. The new line included Vimy Ridge, a sector that had been relatively quiet hitherto although of tactical importance as it was one of the few geographical features of any prominence on the Western Front. At the northern end the western (or Allied) side sloped gently up to a crest some hundred yards wide, with a much steeper drop on the eastern – German-held – side. Each side held an edge of the crest. With little warning two battalions, 7th and 8th Londons of the 47th (London) Division were moved up on to the ridge on 19 May 1916. From the time they came into the line they suffered from continuous minenwerfer fire, and on

*20 May began to be subjected to a new form of artillery bombard-
ment, a "box barrage," i.e., among, behind and along the sides of the
troops and designed to cut off movement to the rear, or the arrival of
reinforcements. It was possibly the most intense barrage of the war thus
far, and the precursor to a localised attack. Cecil Thomas, who wrote
the following harrowing account, was a very young private soldier
who had only recently joined his battalion. This was to be his first,
and last, time in action.*

We crowd into the dugout, Lew and I now being half-way
down the entrance passage, squatting on one of the steps.
Almost immediately we are vouchsafed a possible explanation of the mysterious lights [earlier seen], for, with a crash
and a roar the previous shelling, heavy as it was, is more
than doubled, and a barrage, almost as heavy, goes overhead
to its destination behind us. Although nearly midday, the
brilliant sunshine is turned to semi-darkness by the dust,
the smoke, and the gas, the whole earth shakes and trem-
bles, clods and stones fly through the air, and those at the
entrance to the dugout push their way inwards away from
the inferno.

Surely it can never last at this rate! But it does. On and on
it goes, without pause between the bursts – just one long roar
and upheaval. They will be sitting down in church at home
now, praying for the safety of those over the water. Lord! how
we pray for ourselves. They say many pray in danger who have
never prayed before, yet those of us who have regularly paid
our daily orisons in safety are the first to realize that now we are
really praying for the first time, in the full realization of our own
microscopic smallness and the impossibility of all protection save
from above.

Perhaps they will be walking home now, along that path
through the fields, the long way round, to give themselves
appetites for Sunday dinner.

What senseless fool, what short-sighted imbecile planned these dugouts and these trenches? Four dugouts, dugouts for men, officers and stores, all placed together at the junction of the communication trench with the support trench, like desirable suburban villas round a railway station. With the view afforded from the top of two mine craters and an observation balloon, the Germans must know perfectly well that the front line has been given up, and they are, therefore, able to concentrate on the second line. That means this group of dugouts within a length of about twenty-five yards.

By all the laws of gun-laying there should be immediate annihilation for us, and it is the devilish mathematical certainty of it all, the thoughts of gunners miles away making schoolboy calculations on paper and reducing their margin of error to zero that saps at our foundations of courage and hope. An enemy to face or a chance, however slight, of avoiding, either by our own effort or by miscalculation on the other side, that which now seems inevitable would make all the difference, but to sit still while the shells fall on top and all around us without cessation or diminution tests the stoutest.

Crash! Darkness is upon us; the whole passage and dugout sway from side to side like a ship on a rough sea; the four sides seem to contract, the timbers bellying inwards as if in an endeavour to crush us. Clouds of dust pour downwards from the entrance, and upwards from the dugout itself, coming into the latter from the hole in the roof. A direct hit just over us. Another in the same place will be right through and on us before we know it – which will be just as well.

The wooden strut above my head, and the side supports bearing it up, are all three cracked and bend crazily inwards. At every fresh explosion they 'give' a little, like strung bows, and I find myself with my hands above my head trying to hold up the cross-piece which is most damaged. Little can my strength avail against that weight of earth if it ever falls, but the mere action, the preparedness to make some resistance at least against this form of sudden death, has in it a germ of comfort, and my hands go back above my head. Outside is annihilation, but the fear of being buried alive or of being slowly crushed to death is now almost as great.

Hour after hour the appalling tornado goes on. Surely it cannot continue. Even if all the German gunners have gone mad, members of the Quartermaster's staff must even now be hurrying to tell them that this senseless waste must cease. There cannot surely be many more shells left to fire. I don't know how much it costs to make a shell, but each one of our small band must by now have cost them thousands and thousands of pounds, and still we live – all but three, and one or two missing. Mathematically the thing is absurd. We should all have been dead long ago, and yet, down in our shaking burrows, we still exist.

Half-past two. A nudge at my shoulder. "Say, Tommy, would you like a piece of Cook's birthday cake?" I take a piece, pass the remainder to others farther up, and send back our combined thanks. There is nothing wrong with the cake, but in my parched mouth it tastes like sawdust and I can hardly swallow it.

A shadow looms up at the entrance – an officer. This must be Coles, our other Lieutenant, whom I have not previously seen. He staggers in with a bad cut on the forehead and a large bruise beside it. They have scored a direct hit on the Captain's dugout, breaking in the passage-way and for a moment blocking the entrance. One of the cross-beams fell in on Coles who was directly beneath it, injuring him as I have mentioned. It was some time before he could force a way out, but, having done so, he has come round to see if we are still alive. Twice in those few steps has he been blown over and for the moment at any rate he is only half conscious of his surroundings.

His responsibilities, however, hasten his recovery. One almost envies him his duties of leadership. At such a time as this, the realization that men are looking to him for guidance and that what little can be done may only be instigated by himself gives a man an added strength, a self-forgetfulness, which is no small thing. On the other hand, the feeling of dependence upon another's will, the necessity of relying upon another's judgement make a private prone to self-pity and more than ordinarily fearful. When I had Garstin [a wounded comrade] to look after I was far less afraid than I previously was without him.

With a visible effort, Coles pulls himself together and orders out the first six men in the passage-way to man the trench. Such incessant shelling cannot be purposeless and must portend an attack sooner or later. Ergo, the trench must be manned.

Those of us who have watched the bombardment during the eternal hours doubt the wisdom of this in our inmost hearts. While this shelling last we are at least safe from any infantry advance. If it lifts it will be quite a different matter. However, an order is an order, and out we go.

I am in the first six, but, being the farthest down the passage, am the last out. The first man has taken the place nearest the dugout, the others following, so that I find myself farthest from its haven of refuge.

Again, since the morning, have the contours of the ground changed, and not in shape only, for so universal have been the upheavals that the soil which before had, for the most part, lain white under weeks of drought, has now changed to a reddy moist brown as the subsoil has been subverst.

I take my end place and look for the rifle, but it has been blown up and only a broken portion is sticking out of the ground. Another is passed along and, leaning it against the parapet, I follow the example of all the rest, save the look-out at the periscope, and lie flat on the fire-step squeezing myself as tightly as possible against the protecting sand-bags of the trench side. But only for a moment. A shell exploding quite close sends up a great shower of earth and stones which, falling, inflict no small bruises and I at once realize that it is far better to crouch – that the horizontal is even more dangerous than the semi-vertical.

The shelling is devilishly accurate, particularly that of the batteries firing the 'whizz-bangs,' which with a sudden rush and a bang seem just to graze the top of the trench above us each time.

How the earth shakes! Pressing against the parapet, I can feel it move from side to side, away from me and again into me as it reels in its torture this way and that under the sometimes simultaneous explosions. Every minute brings its fresh quota of guns, all seemingly trained on this little sector, sending in shells from all angles, whilst occasionally, so occasionally as to make us laugh bitterly, our solitary battery fires a salvo.

Another heavy clod falls on me, bruising my shoulder, and, seeing that Lew, who is next to me, has a steel helmet on I shout to him to pass the word for one for me, if there is a spare. After some minutes a helmet is passed along and I hasten to put it on, first of all trying to fix it over my khaki cap (for it is the first time I have handled one) then, realizing that it is an alternative and not an additional headgear, discarding the latter, and strapping the former tightly under my chin.

My fingers are yet on the chin-strap when, with a sickening thud, a great stone falls right on my head, the world is filled with myriad lights and, for a moment or two, I am stupid. On coming round again I find a great sharp-pointed flint at my feet and, feeling my helmet, my fingers run into a big dent just to the right of the dome centre. A minute earlier and I could hardly have escaped, but I have already had so many lucky chances since five this morning that I forget to be thankful. The past and even the present have ceased to exist. It is the immediate future, from moment to moment, which alone concerns.

I now have a sickening headache, the steel helmet bearing down upon my throbbing forehead. Surely our time will soon be up now – half an hour was to be the spell. I look at my watch but find the glass broken and the hands bent. It simply cannot be much longer even if the seconds are measured by single eternities. Dare I take off this helmet to relieve this awful throbbing? A squelch of mud flattening itself on a sand-bag in front of me as I crouch low reminds me of worse things than head aches and the throbbing has to continue.

"'ware gas!" comes a sudden shout from the periscope. "'ware gas!"

Frantically I tear at the wallet holding my gas helmet, drag off my steel protector and pull the mask over my head, holding my breath tighter and tighter as the seconds elapse. At last I get the nozzle in my mouth and with a great gasp relieve my pent-up lungs. Pray God it works – and does not leak. If only I had not been such a fool as to throw the reserve one away.

We are holding our rifles now, for a gas attack is almost sure to mean infantry behind, though there is no diminution in the shelling whatever. I am twisting and turning the gas helmet so as to get the goggles properly in front of my eyes and, having done so, put the steel helmet on again, the chin-strap hanging loosely. The cloth at the bottom of the gas helmet I have tucked tightly into the neck of my tunic and am already only one stage worse off than being actually gassed. Hot as I was before, the heat is now intolerable. The perspiration is rolling off me, down my forehead, on to my eyebrows and thence on the goggles, on to which it sticks hopelessly, distorting the vision.

The man at the periscope is straining every nerve watching the yellow cloud, but gives us no sign. Perhaps it is not gas, or perhaps there is insufficient wind? Certainly we can feel no breeze which would justify hope of a successful gas attack. If only we dare remove our helmets! But this foe is too subtle to take risks with. I have seen too many of his victims trying to recuperate in England to try a throw with him.

A knock on the back makes me crouch down expecting further falls, but another follows and I find it is Lew signalling to me that our spell is up. The others I see have already gone in and a second six are creeping out. These have got their gas helmets on, but raised up on their foreheads in the manner of mid-Victorian ladies with their veils before partaking of afternoon tea. It cannot, therefore, be gas – probably the solid band of fog formed by the smoke of the shells which, to the sentry's tautened imagination, had suddenly appeared as fresh clouds. Better to warn unnecessarily than too late.

I hurry under cover as quickly as possible and squat about three steps down. Opposite me is Coles with the features of a youngster and the lines and expression of an old man. Pale as death, with grime all over his face, and channels of perspiration, his steel helmet perched ludicrously on the side of his head on account of the swathes of bandage with which the stretcher-bearer below has skilfully dressed his gash, one cannot but admire the set mouth and firm chin of this junior lieutenant. His age is about twenty-three and his experience at the Front about two months.

On and on goes the shelling; the earth tremors being empha-sized again in here by the creaking timbers of the passage-way. Surely another five minutes must use up all their stores. It is now about half-past three, Lew tells me. Hour after hour of this ludicrous waste, all to annihilate a few persistent pygmies.

Again the earth is suddenly darkened. That was a big one, and near.

A sound of awful screams and of fierce scuffling outside follows. A man comes tearing past me down into the deep-est depths of the dugout, moaning piteously, holding both his hands over a face which is featureless under a swelter of blood. Blindly he knocks his head against the cross-beams of the roof as he stumbles past, bumping heavily through us in the congested and narrow passage.

Horrified we draw aside as another even worse follows him, like a madman flying from a pursuing demon. A third and fourth force their way past us and we hear them yelling, screaming and stamping as they rush madly backwards and forwards at the bottom of the dugout, while to their clamour is added the noise of those, some of them wounded, who were lying down there and who are now being trampled on in the darkness.

Numbed by the sudden horror of it, we scarce know what to do, and, soldier-like, look to the officer for a lead. He calls for the next six men for sentry duty, which means the first six – including myself again.

Having collected us in the passage, he goes out into the trench to survey the damage. A shell falls right inside the trench and, even as he stands in the door-way – one, two, three more fall just on the edge. With a shake of his head he makes up his mind, and beckoning to the others to come in, shouts to us: "You can't go outside, but stop well up the passage and see that one man is always on the periscope." Then, calling to Stanmore and another N.C.O. to follow him, he goes down to help the stretcher-bearer to quiet the maniacs below.

It occurs to me, if that shell fell actually in the trench, my fourth rifle, which was left on the fire-step as usual, will no longer be in serviceable condition. Nothing seems to matter now, however. Let come what may.

Hardly has Coles gone down than an explosion outside is followed by a clatter and half the periscope falls to the ground outside. The rest has disappeared. To look out now, therefore, is a matter of putting your head over the top, for the steel observation plate has long ago been blown in. Not a healthy occupation, for the snipers are on the watch and within a minute nearly score a hit.

The dugout itself is now crammed with wounded, and endeavours are being made to get them to lie down quietly on the ground. The whole floor is thus occupied, and all able-bodied men are ordered into the passage-way. The doubtful wisdom of leaving rifles on the fire-step during a bombardment is now apparent, for we find we have only two among the lot of us, the rest all having been blown up. At the same time it is equally clear that, if each of us now crouching on the congested steps had a rifle to carry as well, the confusion in the case of sudden exit would be terrible.

Five o'clock. Teatime at home. The thought sharpens the realization of my parched throat. If only I could have brought my water-bottle through. Like most of the others I have had nothing to drink since midnight and only a small square of cake to eat. For hours the wounded have been crying for water, and what few water-bottles were available were long ago handed down to them and consumed. Every minute now this question of thirst becomes more pressing, intense heat and prolonged nerve strain combining to intensify it, so that it begins to occupy our thoughts to the exclusion even of the shelling.

Suddenly our eyes begin to water copiously and very painfully. An old hand shouts "Tear Shells," and we pull down our gas-helmets and tuck them in round our necks. We are in time, but the sweltering heat inside the helmets is awful. A mine goes up somewhere and the whole structure rocks again like a toy model with all the screws loose. Some of the wounded, panic-stricken again and almost beyond control, jump up shouting and are only quietened with difficulty. Almost immediately another big shell falls overhead, sending in clouds of yellow lyddite smoke through the door-way at one end and the hole in the roof at the other. Again there is pandemonium below.

Most of us who have no actual pain are now almost comatose, and it's only the fear of being buried alive while I am unconscious that enables me to keep myself awake. Lew, near me, has been fast asleep for some time. I am still crazily supporting the broken cross-beam over my head and trying to look impassive, but, actually, am praying in an agony of fearfulness. All the others look stolidly indifferent and I would give a good deal to know if inwardly they are as calm as they look, or if, in reality, their nerves are as much a-quiver as mine.

Surely this cannot go on longer. Right through the day noise has been heaped upon noise, and now another mine goes up somewhere. How the dugout rights itself I don't know. Sooner or later it will rock an inch too far, the timbers will finally give and we shall be just crushed underneath the fall.

How thirsty I am and how my head aches! We have raised our gas-helmets now, for the tear shells seem to contain only a weak mixture and, although our eyes are continually watering, this is less discomfort that the boiling breathlessness of the helmets.

Half-past six. Church time at home. I wonder if they have any conception at all of what we are going through. If they only knew – but that would make things ten times worse. It is at least some sort of comfort to know that only we ourselves are involved.

Surely it must stop in a few minutes now – say five. The Germans cannot have supplies left for more than five minutes more. But no! Still it goes on. Another five minutes then. One, two, three, four seconds gone. One minute, two minutes, three minutes. It is not slackening. Must we allow still another five? Eternity – time is surely standing still, motionless like the sun, with its pitiless rays and imperceptible motion, the two laughing together at our extremity.

I keep saying to myself: "How long will this last – how long do bombardments generally last? What is their customary duration?" A fool's thought! Of course there is no fixed time! And yet there might be. Those who have been through other bombardments may be able to interpret certain signs of coming cessation. Supposing I ask Lew. I can't ask him – he'll think me such a raw idiot.

And yet I must know something. I must find some end to it in my mind or I shall go mad.

I nudge Lew.

"This can't go on much longer, can it, old man?"

He stares stonily, vacantly at me.

"Wait – we can only wait – I don't know. Can't tell." Wait. The word rings in my ears – dances before my eyes, each letter on a separate square card. Other cards appear with more letters. They form in a line for a moment into 'WAITING' and then break up into all sorts of moving formations, like a juggler's balls.

They suddenly appear again, quite tiny, on a small bag, a bag, I think, of gunpowder. It begins to swell and swiftly comes towards me, growing terrifically as it comes, the words getting larger and blacker, until it bursts in my eyes, and the whole process starts all over again. Waiting, WAITING, WAITING – something seems to tell me that if any of these imagined bursts coincides with a real one outside, my number will be up.

Coles has just come in again after going along to the Captain's dugout to see how things are there. He has been away some time and tells us that although the distance is only some ten or twelve yards he had to take refuge in the remains of the intermediate stores dugout, and was pinned there, half in and half out as it was shelled into further collapse. The Captain's dugout has again been hit and the Captain himself injured, but not too seriously.

God! How the wounded men are shouting. If only we had some water for them. That also was a reason for Coles' expedition, but he has returned empty-handed. He says Captain Maitland has sent back several messengers at intervals during the day with details concerning our plight and requests for reinforcements, but the possibility of any of them having got through is very slight. The field telephone was knocked out of service before six this morning and on three separate occasions men were sent out to find the break and repair it. The repair has not been effected and no one has come back.

In any case, we ourselves are the first to realize the impossibility of getting reinforcements past the barrage which continually goes over our heads, or, even supposing they arrived, of giving them any shelter in the remnants of our dugouts.

Another hit on top has just caused a panic down below, falling so close that it actually enlarged the hole in the roof. How we still remain alive is beyond comprehension. The range is so exact now that several successive shells have fallen clean into the trench, and the fire-step is blown out of all semblance, while the once vertical parapet looks like a gently sloping breakwater of sandbags rather badly disarranged after a storm.

On it goes, minute by minute, and second by second. It is getting somewhat dark now and in our heart of hearts we knew something must happen soon. Nothing, however, will come until the shelling lifts. That will be our sign; and what we shall do then we are not quite sure. We are too far gone to plan ahead, but I have a hazy idea in my own mind that there may be some bombs or a broken rifle lying about the trench outside which could be used. The only two rifles we possess are just inside the entrance of the dugout. The look-out man there takes a quick look over the top every few minutes, but it is a risky business as the enemy have rifles trained on to the spot, and were it not for reminders from Coles the sentry would probably not look at all.

There must have been an interval longer than usual after the last look for, suddenly, without any warning, without even the slightest diminution in the shelling, there is a sound of rifle shots just overhead, and the man standing nearest the entrance shouts: "Look out, they're here!"

Those of us near the bottom of the steps rush up to get out, but those near the top, finding themselves unarmed, face to face with German rifles, rush down. For a moment we push against each other, then the lower ones, realizing the position, turn round and turn back into the dugout. It is all a matter of seconds, as also is what follows.

Down below, covering the floor of the dugout, are the wounded. It is pitch dark and I suddenly feel myself lurching blindly over their recumbent bodies. Backwards and forwards we go, walking over them, unable to avoid their wounded flesh, not knowing what to do, our yells and curses as we strive to find a way out, mingling with the cries of the poor fellows beneath our feet.

Coles is the man of the moment. Running across the dugout he tries to get out through the hole in the roof, but, finding this impossible, comes back and stands at the bottom of the passage-way, now deserted. At the top end are Germans peering down.

"Now then, men," he shouts, "you can't stop here. We must rush out. Off you get at once, you, and you, and you," touching the three men nearest to him.

For a moment they hesitate. With a rifle in their hands they would be up like a shot, but a soldier suddenly finding himself facing an armed enemy without his rifle, that very portion of himself that he carries all day and sleeps with all night, is like a civilian who all at once realizes himself naked in the midst of clothed onlookers. There is more than fear in their hesitation; there is the number helplessness of a nightmare.

As he stands there, something comes hurtling through the air from a above – a bomb. With amazing coolness, Coles catches it and throws it back whence it came. Another and another follow in quick succession and these he treats similarly, so that all explode above among the original throwers.

Then, realizing the impossibility of getting out that way, he leaps across the dugout again and, with scratching hands and wriggling body, at last manages to force a way through the hole in the roof.

I follow him, but get stuck half-way in and half-way out. There is an explosion behind me and I am blown the rest of the way, though am not actually wounded. Yells and screams below tell of the havoc done and I am afraid Lew, who was preparing to follow me, must have been hit, for he does not appear.

I find myself at the bottom of a big shell-hole, at the top of which is Coles, standing upright, firing his revolver as coolly as if at practice, aiming apparently at the men commanding the entrance to the dugout.

I shout down into both halves of the dugout for a rifle, for, as far as military effectiveness goes, I am a civilian in all but uniform. There is no response from my dugout whence the cries of wounded men are still coming, but after excited fumbling in the other half a muzzle at length is pushed through. The safety catch is shut, the magazine closed and it is all my fumbling fingers can do to open it and get the rising cartridge driven home.

All this time – the matter of fifteen seconds or so – I am crouching down below ground level, with Coles above me. Even as I look at him a small hole suddenly appears above the right top pocket of his tunic. I can almost feel the thud of the bullet myself, but he seems quite unconscious of it. The frenzy of the moment is upon him and he probably does not even know he has been hit.

Just as I drive home a cartridge into the breech of my rifle another similar hole shows in his tunic just near the armpit. He has now emptied his revolver, and as I jump he commences to reload it. Instinctively, I face first towards the German lines whence I have always expected the enemy to appear, then, realizing that Coles is firing the other way, I spring round to see a group of Germans with rifles pointing at us, shooting.

Coles is just closing his loaded revolver when blood suddenly spurts from one of his fingers – a third hit – and he cannot keep on longer. Realizing the hopelessness of it all, he drops his revolver, letting it hang loosely on his lanyard, and puts up his hands, shouting to me: "It's no use, we shall have to give in." Down goes my fifth rifle, and I am captured.

No man could have done more than Coles or shown greater bravery, and if any man can have a clear conscience at being taken prisoner it is he.

As for myself, my first feeling is one of relief at the end of the terrible suspense of the last sixteen hours. Yet we are actually in greater danger than ever, for, now that it is too late, our artillery seem to have found guns somewhere and are plastering the whole Ridge, while behind us the German first line of attack is evidently heavily engaged with our reserve line, way back near the valley. The spent bullets from our fellows' rifles are thick as hail around us.

Still, to know that the worst has happened, to get out into the fresh air after the nightmare in the dugout is a relief. Being a prisoner is a shameful thing, but, having actually been taken, death has lost its terror; and we stand up in all the din of the bombardment no longer fearful and caring not a jot now whatever happens. They will probably question us, and then shoot us. They rarely take prisoners, I know. But that is future, the dugout is past, for the present let me breathe the open air deeply. Nothing else matters.

My second feeling is one of terrible disappointment. After all the waiting to come out, to be captured, and not captured only, but taken without firing a shot. To have gone out from England, through France, and then into the hands of the enemy without drawing the trigger even once as some justification of my training and equipment, that's where the rub lies. Five rifles have been mine in two days, yet not one has been fired. There is acid bitterness in that.

From *They Also Served: The Experiences of a Private Soldier in German Camp & Coal Mine 1916-18* by Cecil Thomas. Hurst & Blackett. 1939.

Diversionary Attack on "The Triangle": 30th June 1916

'we were upon them with bayonet, club and trench-knife, and in a few instants we were pounding on over their dead bodies'

A diversionary attack was intended to mislead the enemy into believing that the main thrust of an offensive was elsewhere than where it really was, and confuse him so that he was unsure as to where to deploy his reinforcements. Just as the start of the Somme Offensive was delayed several times, diversionary efforts had to be postponed until the right time. So, on 23 May 1916 the commander of the 2nd Infantry Brigade told the 2nd Bn. King's Royal Rifle Corps that it was selected for an attack to take place a few days later against 'The Triangle,' a fortified arrangement of trenches near Loos, and well away from the Somme. On 30 May the attack was cancelled, which 'caused the most lively disappointment amongst all ranks, who, after our careful training and preparations, had been looking forward to getting to grips with the Germans' (vide KRRC Chronicle, 1916). These preparations had included practise assaults on a specially dug simulation of 'The Triangle' position behind British lines. In mid-June it was announced that the operation would again take place, and finally it did so on 30 June. Rifleman Giles Eyre was one of a band of forty bombers specially selected and trained to lead the assault. He describes the attack and ultimately the retirement that is the concomitant of a diversion, as it is

never intended to be reinforced, however successful the initial assault.
He also describes the death of Rifleman William Marriner VC which
he witnessed – just one of some 225 casualties in the 2nd KRRC
that day.

Next evening at dusk, rested and replete, we were chaffing
while putting the finishing touches to our gear in readiness for
the night's activities, when Sergeant Wilson's form appeared at
our dugout door and his gruff voice roused us with:

"Tumble up, men! Time to get moving!"

"Right you are, Sergeant!" sang out Oldham, and blowing
the candle stub, turned to us:

"Come along, boys, up we go!"

"Walk up, walk up, my lucky lads, put it all on the jolly
old spade and up she goes!" chortled O'Donnell, rattling a
pebble in his tin mug in mock make-believe of Crown and
Anchor.

We stepped out onto the duck-boards of the support trench,
our accoutrements clinking as we banged against the trench
sides.

It was pleasant to come out into the open after a day spent
dozing and frowsting in the stale, close atmosphere of our
funk-hole. We breathed deeply, filling our lungs gratefully.

The darkening sky, with drifting fleecy clouds rosied at the
edges by the rays of the setting sun, now a molten ball of fire
low in the west, the warm, balmy air, a sparrow's twitter – June
was closing in a blaze of glory and summer splendour.

Only an occasional harsh crack of rifle or at intervals the
deeper toned cr-rump of mortar shell bursting up on the slag
heap, now looming dark on our right front, marred the essential quiet of summer. Far away in the distance the continuous
rumble of guns which had not stayed their booming for the
past week smote on our ears like the thunderous crash of surf
on distant shores. And yet, these sounds and the evidence of

warlike activity notwithstanding, it would have been difficult for the uninitiated to believe that the British front line lay ahead and that a paltry hundred yards or so beyond it a wary and watchful enemy lurked.

The other groups were issuing from their dugouts on their way to Company headquarters. With O'Donnell still humming softly we moved on in the sergeant's wake to be joined farther on by Maddocks and Unwin and the calf-faced Norfolk lad. Such was our group. Clinking and clattering we entered the dimness of the headquarters dugout, where we could distinguish amongst the shadows the members of the three other assault parties huddled against its walls. Candles stuck in bottles stood on the table made up of ammunition boxes, and their curvetting light seemed to accentuate the darkness in the corners. Behind the table and facing us sat Captain Sherlock, flanked by Mr. Walker and the Sergeant-Major, their faces thrown into vivid relief by the light of the spluttering candles.

"Are all the men here, Sergeant-Major?" asked the Skipper, looking up from the maps he had been conning over and turning to him as we took our places.

"Yes, sir, all present now!" rapped back old Mac smartly. We stiffened as our Commander's glance swept over us in a quick, keen inspection.

"Well, men, you know what must be done. The Triangle must be assaulted and thoroughly wrecked. No hesitation, no pause to look after casualties. The wounded must make their way back as best they can. Quick, sharp action is wanted. Penetrate as far down the Boche trenches as possible, then build your blocks and stand fast until three red flares go up from our line, when you will retire onto the Battalion. The Battalion will occupy the Boche front line behind you, while the Royal Sussex will attack the craters and the Boche trenches on the slag heap. Is this all clear? Jolly good luck to you all and give the enemy hell! Mr Walker will be in command of the bombing attack. Carry on!"

His sharp, clipped words had the desired effect. I felt my blood course through my veins strongly, and glancing round in the semi-darkness of the dugout I could see the men's eyes glitter with excitement and their hands grasp their weapons convulsively. It was hard to envisage that in a short space of hours many of these fellows, together with countless others from the attacking battalions, would be groaning and moaning in trench, traverse, shell-hole or stretcher, or staggering blindly through the desolation and horror around them, wounded, shattered and marred for life, while many more would lie stark and still in the finality of death. This last June night would witness anew Man's senseless power of destruction hurled at Mother Nature in a scornful gesture of defiance.

Mr. Walker, in battle order and wearing a private's tunic, stood up, whispered with the Skipper a moment, shook his hand and led the way out, we followed in his wake.

Darkness had deepened. Very lights drifted fitfully on the skyline. Our artillery had begun to register and shells were screeching overhead to fall and burst in the Boche wire and on their parapets.

Oldham in front of me turned and whispered, grinning: "Roll on Blighty!"

Zhee-Bang! Zhee-Bang! Zhee-Bang! Sudden vicious swishes and a flight of Boche light-calibre shells burst on the lip of the trench, causing us to duck quickly and covering us with dirt. Apparently the Germans were beginning to wake up and were commencing to pepper the approaches to the front line. Swearing and spluttering, Marriner behind me muttered: "By Christ Eyre! The asterisks know something is up!"

Our pace got brisker and finally we entered the firing-line. Dim figures crouched alertly on the fire-steps, bayonets fixed and eyes staring into the murk. The Northamptons were standing-to. Traverse by traverse, we wormed our way onwards, up a narrow gulley and finally into the forward sap. On our right the Double Crassier towered above us dark and awesome like some uncouth monster. Flares were going up and down over the whole front, illuminating the waste fitfully. Crouched against the sap-head, we talked in whispers, tense with the strain of waiting.

"By God, Eyre! I wish the show would start. I am shaking like a bloody jelly!" I heard O'Donnell say. Marriner, a little way farther down, was giving harrowing and bloodcurdling descriptions of previous raids to the Norfolk boy, who, with his vacant looks and drawn face, presented a faithful picture of a sheep led to the slaughter. The wind freshened... we shivered... each one of us thinking of the task that lay ahead of us. Suddenly our guns at the back broke out into a mad cacophony of sound. The rush of shells overhead and the crash of their explosions blended into one awful roar, deafened and numbed us – setting our nerves quivering. The German front line became an inferno of spouting earth vomiting red and yellow glares. Flares went up in bunches from their advanced and support trenches and their machine-guns commenced their tac-tac-tac questing over no-man's-land. We shook with excitement, straining like eager dogs at the leash. The acrid smell of cordite, the fumes and smoke, the back rush of air from near explosions, the roar of guns now merged into a mad tocsin intoxicated us. We ceased to be rational thinking men. Our only goal became the hazy red-lit hell of heaving earth, a bare hundred yards ahead, and we were eager to enter it.

"Assault party, get over the top and lie down in front!" came the whispered order. Quickly we scrambled over, Marriner followed me as we stooped and crawled through the gaps which had already been cut in our wire. We stumbled on and lay down in a straggling line, Mr. Walker and a runner on our left rear.

All at once hell broke loose. The Boche counter-batteries had come into action and were splashing masses of shells that fell behind us onto our front line like hail. From the slag-heap sudden glares, smoke, spouts of earth, the dull sound of explosions and the staccato rattle of machine-guns came in waves of awful sound. The world seemed suddenly to have changed into a very maelstrom of noise.

Then the artillery paused abruptly. A few seconds' strange hush clapped down, smothered all the battle noises as if a giant stopper had been suddenly clapped on a pot of hissing boiling water, and then with redoubled fury it resumed its crazy roaring as it lifted to blast the German back areas flat. At the same instant a great glare lighted up the landscape for a fleeting instant with a lurid flame, to be followed with an awful crash which blinded and deafened us. An avalanche of stones, earth, bags, wire and heaven knows what else, fell and bounced all around us crazily. The mines had been sprung along our front! Zero!

Whistles shrilled out. With inhuman cries and tautened nerves we sprang up and, cursing, roaring, singing, scrambled forward towards the Boche like a band of fiends.

Holes, twisted wire, debris of every kind, seemed to grip and drag at me as I scrambled over the twisted heaps that had been neutral ground. Stumbling and recovering, helmet bobbing up and down, slugs pinging all around me, bewildered and deafened, but determined, I ran forward, tearing through the wreckage of the enemy position like a madman. All caution dropped from me as if it were a discarded mantle. I became intoxicated with battle lust, my one thought was to destroy everything that stood in my way. Ahead, abreast and behind me the rest of the party were running and scrambling with hoarse cries.

Marriner, rifle slung behind him, hands grasping grenades, overtook me, jumped on the German trench-top and, scattering his grenades before him, jumped in yelling like a fiend:

"Do them in! Kill the bloody swine!" I followed him. We came to a wrecked dugout adit. From some hole in the trench a few Germans emerged, bewildered. I could just distinguish their flat caps in the half darkness. But before they had properly set foot in the trench and recovered from their surprise we were upon them with bayonet, club and trench-knife, and in a few instants we were pounding on over their dead bodies. Crash! Roar! Crash! Tac-tac-tac-tac! A Noise like a million hammers in my ears. Rodwell, O'Donnell and other shadowy figures, hard to identify in the gusts of drifting smoke, were running about, stabbing, bombing and destroying. A communication-trench appears before us, we plunge down it. Bodies scrunch under my feet, unheeded. We halt, panting, before a dugout entrance. I take a pin out of a Mills, chuck it in the canvas bag full of grenades I am carrying and sling the whole lot down. I can hear it rattle and bump down the steps, then a muffled roar, a swirl of dust and smoke, a few smothered cries quickly extinguished and the whole adit disappears in an avalanche of earth and splintered wood. Machine-gun and rifle-fire breaks out on our front. Grenade burst further down. The Boche, having recovered from his initial surprise and the stunning effect of our bombardment, is attempting to counter-bomb his way up.

"This way, boys!" yells Marriner suddenly and, running like a madman, he vaults on the trench-top, runs down a few yards, heedless of everything about him, and starts dropping his grenades on the heads of the Boche further down in the trench.

"Here are the bastards!" he shouts. "Give 'em hell!" Like hounds in full cry we crash through the bays, destroying everything in our path, and burst on a crowd of saucepan-helmeted Germans, bewildered by the bombs and herded together. A short fierce struggle, groans, cries. Hands go up. We herd our prisoners over the top and shoo them towards the British lines in charge of Unwin. I wonder what that simple Norfolk yokel must have felt like as he prodded over a dozen hefty Germans onwards with his bayonet. Anyhow, he is comparatively safe for the rest of the night and out of harm's way!

Sharp thuds further down on our left warn us that the other bombing parties are hard at it. From the slag-heap a sudden murderous burst of machine-gun-fire sweeps over us and I see one or two men fall. A terrible scrap is going on up there in the craters, judging by the sounds. The German artillery has now shortened its range and is now plastering the whole triangle with its shells, regardless as to whether it is held by friend or foe. Suffocating fumes sweep over us. Bags and earth crash round, the trenches rock like express trains to the shock of bursts. The Very lights going up in multicoloured profusion illuminate the scene like a gigantic Brock's display. We advance further down carefully. A turn in the trench. We have reached our appointed limits.

"Up with a trench-block, boys!" yells Oldham. Feverishly we fall to work with trench-tool, bayonet and bare hands, scooping earth, piling sandbags and debris to form a barricade. Rodwell and I crawl up on the trench-lip on either side and with rifles ready we strain our eyes towards the Boche support line just further on. The battle has now spread northwards, the Royal Sussex and our Battalion have crossed the bags and are now throwing out the Boche from his front line along the whole Brigade front. As far as the eye reaches the horizon is a red sullen glare splattered with gusts of dark smoke. Machine-guns are cackling and spluttering everywhere. Nothing but thuds, noise and crashing roar all around. The ear-drums seem to burst with the constant thud, thud, thud of explosions. The Germans are trying to launch a counter-attack from their support trenches. We descry a line of straggling figures clambering over the parapets while the thud of grenades further down the trench warns us that the enemy is working his way up the trench as well. They make a sudden determined rush.

A yell bursts out from the line held by the British: "Stand to! here they come!" and a roar of rapid fire breaks out. The bullets whizz by me like a storm of angry bees rattling and plomping like hailstones. I fire and fire until my rifle becomes too hot to hold and the bolt sticks and won't act. Some Boches make a rush for the block below. The world becomes a red haze to me. Cries, yells, groans, and then comparative quiet. All over! The counter-attack crumples up and the Boche scuttles away to what cover he can get in shell-holes and trenches. And then Marriner loses his remaining senses. As Rodwell and I slide back into the trench he lets out a roar, scrambles over the trench-block and runs down in pursuit of the retreating enemy. Neither Rodwell nor I can resist the urge. We clamber over the block and follow him. I slither and stumble over a still-twitching form. Moans and wailing cries come from dim shapes crouching and lolling against the trench sides. And then as I round a corner and glimpse Marriner in the very act of bayoneting a prone German – a whistling swish seems to fill the world. A soul-splitting roar, a terrible glare blinds me for the nonce. I feel myself lifted up as if by a giant hand and flung like an empty sack against the further end of the bay. I hit the wall and slither down, while a cascade of earth and bits of all kinds whizzes by and around me. I feel as if my body is being torn asunder by red-hot pincers, breathing is a superhuman effort. I stagger up dazedly with whirling senses. Part of the trench in front of me has disappeared, leaving a huge shell-hole behind, the sides have fallen in. For a moment I seem to feel as if I have no bones left in my body.

Gingerly I begin to paw at my legs, chest, and over my body, to see if I am hit. I seem all right. But what is all this sticky liquid and gobs of flesh spattered all over me? The explanation flashes across my numbed and dazed brain. Marriner caught full tilt by a shell has been blown to fragments. I shudder and sicken at the thought, then scramble frantically over the debris blocking the trench, to find Rodwell pale and wan, crouching on its further side. "By God, Eyre! Are you all right? I thought we were all gone," he says shakily.

"Yes, I think I'm all right, but old Marriner is blown to bits!" I gasp. We run back and get over the barricade.

The Boche shelling gets worse as we get back to the block where the rest of our party are standing alert and watchful. Fighting was getting heavier all along as the Boche gradually began to push our fellows back. His machine-guns were sweeping the trench-top, their slugs pinging and whizzing unpleasantly. The triangle by now was a mere wreck of broken trenches, heaps of burst sacks and earth, gaping holes and splintered wood. Anxiously we peered back for the three red signal lights. A shower of grenades over the barricades! Blam! Blam! Blam! we retaliate. We hear movement, tinkle of accoutrements and croaking whispers. The Boche is near us. At the same moment the three red lights rise up in the dark sky! With a last shower of bombs to halt the Boche we leg it as fast as we can over all obstacles up towards the trench-line. Just about time too! Hoarse shouts behind and the sullen bursts of grenades warn us that the Germans have got over the barricade and are hot on our heels. "Come on, move in front for Christ's sake" yells Rodwell. The Boche bombardment is becoming heavier and heavier. The very sky seems to be vomiting shells which burst and bounce everywhere. Roars of bitter battle from the slag heap. It must be pretty hot up there amongst the craters and mazes of trenches. Panting and gasping we debouch into the ex-Boche front line, to be greeted by a spatter of Lewis gun-fire and a yell to halt.

"Stop your bloody firing you f–s! It's No. 3 party!" yells out Oldham savagely. We scramble over a heap of sandbags placed at the entrance to the communication-trench just as the first grenades from the pursuing Germans lob over.

"Here they are, boys!" cries a voice. "Fire into the bastards!" Trrrr-trrrr! goes the Lewis gun, pouring a dose of slugs down the communication-trench and knocking the foe over like ninepins.

I look around me and see a huddle of figures crowding this trench. It is filled with a medley of men from all our four Companies, and Mr. Walker is urging the men to dig fire-positions in the parados. On both flanks of the front line the Germans have re-entered the trench and are systematically bombing their way down, crowding us in towards the centre. Unless some move is made soon we shall all go to blazes or to Germany! Men are falling here and there, twisting and twitching in the agony of death. Cries for stretcher-bearers rise on every hand, but in most cases remain unanswered. It is as much as we can do to hold on now, and there is no time or opportunity to minister to our stricken comrades. It is a case of all sound men to fight it out, and to hell with the consequences.

"Stick it out, men!" encourages Mr. Walker. "A covering barrage will be put down shortly and we shall get back then."

I look round at him. His left arm is bandaged and the tunic-sleeve ripped off. His face is streaked with blood, dirt and sweat. He must have had a pretty hectic time by the looks of him!

The sound of grenade-bursts gets closer and enfilade fire from the machine-guns on the slag heap falls on us in waves and takes a heavy toll.

A tattered scarecrow gripping a pistol in one hand and a nasty-looking trench-club in the other sidles up to me and whispers: "Well, Eyre! I think it's all up with us unless that bloody barrage comes down quick. The blasted Huns are getting too damned near!"

I look. It's O'Donnell, and in queer shape. Spattered with chalk dust, uniform in rags where the barbed wire has caught at him, face and hands a mass of nasty scratches, all caked with dried blood and dirt.

Just then an excited R.E. officer, flourishing a revolver, appears from nowhere and yells out hoarsely:

"Retire, men, retire! You are being murdered for nothing here!"

Some of the men hesitate, others without further ado begin to scramble out of the trench.

"Stand fast!" roars out Walker, and turning to the newcomer: "No man quits this position unless I get a direct order from my Commanding Officer or the barrage is put down. Dig, men, dig!"

The R.E. officer mutters something and subsides. We resume our toil feverishly. The Boche artillery continues to slam at us and his bombers get closer and closer. From his support line a hail of machine-guns and rifle-fire compels us to keep low. Things are getting serious when a hurricane of shells from the British guns falls like an awful blanket of fire, steel and dancing flame between the foe and us. The word to retire is passed down and as best as we can, hale, halt, and lame, we scramble out of the Boche trench, rush through the remains of his wire and pick our way gingerly across no-man's-land, now littered with fresh human sacrifice. Gasping and panting we jump down into our own front line. The Boche fire has increased. His artillery are spraying our whole system with all kinds of crumps. Our front line has become mere heaps of tumbled earth, dead men and broken wire.

"All men of the Rifles will make their way back to the 'Garden City' cellars." I am greeted with. I obey, I push my way through the men crouching against the trench walls of the front line, get to the communication-trench and away down towards Maroc. It is now between 3 and 4 a.m., dawn is in the offing. Objects are becoming clearer every moment. The communication-trench has been badly smashed up and parties are toiling to make the damage good before daylight puts a stop to their work. Straggling groups are still coming up it laden with burdens. Stretchers filled with groaning wounded slowly moving down. Progress is difficult and very slow. A constant: "Mind my leg, chum!" "Look out, there's a hole ahead!" "Get out of the way, you big asterisk!" "Halt in front, the rear has lost connection!" keep impinging on my ears as I amble on.

Gradually I get moving quicker and I descry Oldham and Rodwell in front of me.

"By gosh, Eyre," says the latter, "it's been pretty hot, eh? I wonder how many poor blighters are done in?"

"Coom on, boys, let's get a move on," cries Oldham, looking back. "Daylight will soon be here."

Crash! bang! Another shell burst near us.

"The bloody Huns are after us with bells. Get moving Oldham," cries Rodwell anxiously.

The last turn. We enter Maroc High Street. Groups of men here and there, talking low, smoking nervously and marching off into the half light. Across the road, in a half-ruined house, a glare of candle-light. The dressing station! Doctors and orderlies working like mad. A filthy reek of blood, disinfectant and iodine makes my nostrils quiver. Stretchers littering the doorway, with moaning occupants twisting and turning. Walking wounded, their bandages showing in the growing light, with drawn faces, stagger and stumble down the street towards the ambulances waiting on the main road leading to Bully Grenay and Mazingarbe.

We, jaded, tired, weary, move on with shuffling feet towards the "Garden City" at the bottom of the street, careless to the sights and sounds round us. We are all in! We only look up when a body of German prisoners, seventy or so, swing by, guarded by soldiers with fixed bayonets. As I turn towards the broken railings leading into the "Garden City" a last incident impresses itself on my consciousness. Down the road, from the direction of Loos, comes a huge German, stumbling now and then, with bandaged eyes and hands tied behind him, and goading him on with a bayonet an excited, diminutive rifleman from "A" Company, scarce eighteen by the looks of him, with tattered uniform, helmet awry, a huge grin and shining eyes. "Caught him all on me own!" he cries to us. "Come on, gee up, you big louse!" It takes a lot to damp the spirits of the men of the Old Corps.

Morning is well on its way as we reach the cellars. Dixies of hot tea await us. Hastily we hold out our canteens, swallow the hot liquid, then wordlessly we get below, fling off our equipment and, dirty, weary and tired, we flop onto our packs and overcoats and are asleep in the matter of moments, seeking in oblivion that rest and forgetfulness that war denies us.

From *Somme Harvest: Memories of a P.B.I. in the Summer of 1916* by Giles E.M.Eyre. Jarrolds. 1938.

GOMMECOURT: 1ST JULY 1916

'they afterwards buried nearly 1,400 of our Brigade'

This extract from the history of the Fifth Bn. Sherwood Foresters, written by one of their officers, recounts the grim experiences of that battalion on the first day of the battle of the Somme. The same story could have been told of many battalions. But the attack on the Gommecourt salient, a fortified village and park of deceptively placid appearance, was never intended to succeed. Two divisions, 46th (North Midland) and 56th (London) were to converge on the village and 'bite it off,' according to the elaborate plan, but in fact they were merely making a diversionary attack to draw German resources out so that they could not reinforce their line farther south. They were sacrificed as part of the overall plan, for however successful their attack, there was no intention to reinforce them; rather fewer than half of them came back – the rest had been doomed from the start.

The attack, part of the Somme offensive, was designed to reduce the salient west of Gommecourt, and so ease the pressure on the flank. The scheme provided for a week's bombardment previous to the attack, and this naturally involved a certain amount of retaliation, which added very considerably to the discomfort in the trenches.

The 56th Division were attacking from the south, meeting the 46th Division east of Gommecourt. Thus the 46th was on the left of the whole Somme offensive, with the 35th Division (who were demonstrating only) on its left.

The assault was on a two-brigade front, the 139th on the left and the 137th on the right, with the 138th in reserve. The Fifth were on the right and the 7th on the left, with the 6th Battalion in support and the 8th in reserve.

The Brigade line was roughly from the La Brayelle Road on the north to the northern end of Gommecourt Wood on the south, where the 139th Brigade joined up with the 6th North Staffords (137th Brigade). The front allotted to the Fifth was from Little Z southwards to Gommecourt Wood. This frontage was opposite a section we had not previously held, nor had we been in the front line from which the assault was to be made.

The communication trenches allotted to us were from north to south: Regent Street, Roberts Avenue, Rotten Row, and Stafford Avenue.

Regent Street commenced at Fonquevillers Brewery, ran due east, then crossed La Brayelle Road in a south-easterly direction, and met our front Line 150 yards south of the road. This was the northern boundary of Retrench (support trench). Roberts Avenue ran practically parallel with La Brayelle Road, crossed Green Support Trench and Retrench, and then met the front line at Russian Sap, which was the centre of our Battalion front.

A Russian Sap is a tunnel driven close to the surface towards the enemy line as the commencement of a communication trench in that direction. When the time for the advance arrived the top crust of earth was forced in, this being left to the last moment, so that enemy aeroplanes should not be able to identify it as new work.

Rotten Row, at the western end of which Battalion Battle Hd. Qrs. were established, joined the front Line about 100 yards south of Roberts Avenue.

Stafford Avenue, the right of our position, joined the front line about 100 yards south of Rotten Row, close to the point where the communication trench to the jumping-off position joined up.

This jumping-off trench for the first wave had been hastily dug the night before, but was only three feet deep, full of water, and completely dominated from the enemy position. It was about 120 yards in advance of our front Line and 250 yards from the enemy front at the nearest point, which was south-east; but this distance increased to the north until opposite Little Z it was 300 yards.

Companies were organised in four waves, each of two platoons, with two platoons in immediate support. D company, Capt. Naylor, was on the right; A company, Capt. H. Claye, in the centre; C company, Major Wragg, on the left; and B company, Capt. Kerr, as a carrying party.

Battle equipment consisted of "fighting order" – 200 rounds of S.A.A., four sand bags, two Mills bombs, two gas helmets, haversack, waterbottle, waterproof sheet and wire cutters.

We left Pommier on the evening of the 30th for Fonquevillers, Battalion Hd. Qrs. going into a cellar on the Gommecourt-Fonquevillers Road, at the junction of Colonel's Walk.

Companies moved up to the front about midnight, disposing themselves in Retrench. Shortly afterwards Col. Wilson, with head-quarters, including police, runners, signallers, pioneers and scouts, moved over the open to Battle Hd. Qrs. The trenches were impassable – mud, water and traffic. The party was continually tripping over wire and dropping on machine guns and trench mortar positions, moving in single file, and not making much more than half-a-mile an hour. This head-quarter party was fully loaded with consolidating gear, latrine pails, notice boards, direction arrows, charcoal, picks and shovels, in fact everything that is included in an ordnance catalogue. Mention must also be made of a basket of pigeons, which in the end did serve a useful purpose, but not their legitimate one.

At 3.30 a.m. it was found that all the Companies were in position. Hot coffee, with a tot of rum added, was brought up at 4.45 in petrol tins, eight per company, and was very acceptable, everyone without exception being wet through and perished with cold.

The coffee-carrying party was supposed to be clear of the trenches by 6 a.m., but a number was seen when all was over in Retrench, killed by shells and still holding the tins.

Our barrage commenced at 6.25. This was the signal to move up to the advanced trench from Retrench. Smoke bombs were thrown at 7.25, and the first three waves moved to the assault five minutes later.

Enemy machine guns were clipping the top of the parapet, or rather where it had been an hour previously. A party of 20, waiting foot on firestep, ready to spring over on the word, had just made their spring when a burst of machine gun fire caught them, and all fell back dead or wounded.

The smoke screen was very dense and seemed to cling to the earth and our sodden clothing. No sooner was the parapet crossed than everyone was lost to view, and it was only by bumping into anyone that companionship was recognised.

The enemy set up a triple barrage of artillery, trench mortar and machine gun fire as soon as our attack was launched.

The first three waves attacked with great dash, but casualties during the advance were very heavy, and the enemy position was strong and well-organised.

The fourth wave was delayed by their heavy loads and the muddy state of the trenches, which caused them to be 15 minutes late in moving over the top. The carrying company was still more delayed, but made a splendid effort to get through; although carrying loads almost too much to attempt on a good track, they advanced at 8.10 a.m., when the smoke screen had to a great extent dissolved. They were consequently met with a withering machine gun fire from several directions. This completely checked any advance, with the result that the 6th and 7th Battalions were unable to move.

The two machine gun sections of the Fifth, attached to the 139th Brigade Machine Gun Company, went over with the Battalion under command of Capt. Robinson (Brigade Machine Gun Officer), but were wiped out before covering more than 150 yards. Capt. Robinson went on and reached the enemy wire, where he was wounded and entangled. Capt. Green, R.A.M.C., found him in this difficulty, extricated him, and reached a shell hole; later, having nearly reached our Line, Capt. Green was killed. Lt. Godfrey, No. 9 platoon of C company, with the remains of the platoon reached the wire, where he and Major Wragg were killed.

Sergt. Bowler, Bombing Sergt., was one of many killed immediately before advancing from the jumping-off trench, and if it were possible to ascertain the casualties before the advance, it would probably be found that companies were reduced to practically platoon strength before they started.

It is now known that many men of our first three waves reached the enemy second Line, 110 yards beyond the first. Doubtless, owing to the anticipated early arrival of supports, the precaution of mopping up the first Line was not taken, nor was it possible to leave a garrison. Consequently, the enemy emerging from their dugouts opened fire on them from the rear, themselves relying on their barrage for protection from our supports.

Efforts were made later in the day to extricate this party, which could be heard firing occasionally, but without success.

At 3.30 p.m. a fresh bombardment was begun by the right Brigade, and continued on our front preparatory to an attack by the 6th Battalion, but it was cancelled.

Daylight patrols were sent out at 5.5 p.m. to ascertain the situation, and at 6.10 p.m. the 8th Battalion took over the original front line from the remnants of the Fifth and 7th, and were later relieved by the 5th Lincolns, with a view to an attempted rescue of any of the Fifth and 7th who might have been left in the enemy trenches. The attack was not pressed home, and eventually one company of the 8th Battalion was detailed for the gruesome task of bringing in the dead and wounded, but they did not meet with much success.

The R.S.M. went over with Col. Wilson and the Adjutant (Capt. Lewes), but immediately lost touch with them in the smoke. He ran into Sergt. Taylor on his way back wounded, eventually got up to and into the German front line, and after a bit of a rough house got out again and "lay doggo" in a shell hole until night, when in making his way back he came across Lt. F. Oliver of the 6th Battalion (who went out with us as Ord. Room Sergt.), out with a party looking for wounded; he eventually reached Bienvillers just before the remnants of the Fifth.

The attack by the 137th Brigade was held up and a retirement made, which left the right of the 139th Brigade and the left of the 56th Division in the air. This caused the 56th, which had reached Gommecourt, to retire, with the result that the end of the day found the remnants back in the original line.

At 7 p.m., the Fifth were relieved, and marched under command of Major Checkland, M.C., to Bienvillers.

Thus ended a disastrous day. Looking back with the knowledge we gained of this ground the following year, it is a marvel that the enemy first Line even was reached, and if it were necessary, one could extol at length the qualities of manly courage, strength and endurance that enabled some, under the conditions existing, to reach the second enemy line and there hold out until exhaustion of ammunition caused them to be overwhelmed.

That the attack was not altogether futile is shown by the statement made to the Fifth on parade shortly afterwards by General T.D. Snow, the Corps Commander, who, after complimenting us very highly on our heroic attack, said: –

"The losses have not been in vain. I can assure you that by your determined attack you managed to keep large forces of the enemy at your front, thereby materially assisting in the operations that were proceeding further south with such marked success."

Our casualties had been enormous. Fifteen officers were killed or died of wounds, seven were wounded, and three taken prisoners; other ranks, 469 killed, wounded and missing.

Our strength in the morning had been 28 officers and 706 others. On the roll being called at the end of the engagement we were three officers and 237 others.

The total casualties of the Division were 164 officers and 2,820 others. The enemy admit their casualties to be three officers killed, ten wounded, and 182 others killed and 372 wounded, with 24 missing. They claim that in the sector of our attack they afterwards buried nearly 1,400 of our Brigade.

From *The War History of the Fifth Battalion Sherwood Foresters Notts & Derby Regiment 1914-1918* by Captain L.W. de Grave. Bemrose & Sons. Derby. 1930.

CAPTURE OF BAZENTIN WOOD: 14TH JULY 1916

'a Dulac picture of some goblin forest'

Those units of Kitchener's New Armies that had not already experienced action were unequivocally 'blooded' on the Somme, but not necessarily on the famous First Day. Captain D.V. Kelly was Intelligence Officer of 110th Infantry Brigade, comprising four battalions – 6th, 7th, 8th and 9th – of the Leicestershire Regiment, which had arrived in France at the beginning of August 1915 but had had a relatively peaceful existence until the battle described in the following piece. They were in reserve and not used on 1 July, and committed to battle for the first time in the dawn attack of 14 July to assault the German second position on a ridge from Longueval to Bazentin le Petit. The piece is superbly descriptive of the shattered woods (two weeks into the four-and-a-half month battle) that became household names during that sickly summer. Also of interest are Kelly's comments on the then new creeping barrage, communications during battle, the rôles of senior officers in action and his own job as a junior staff officer.

Orders came for the Brigade to move on the night of 13th/14th July to a position in front of Mametz Wood, and from there to attack Bazentin Wood. On the 13th I walked over to Mametz Wood to see General Rawlins, who commanded the 62nd Brigade, and was in a German dugout on the western edge of the wood, which was to be our headquarters also. The wood was everywhere smashed by shell-fire and littered with dead – a German sniper hung over a branch horribly resembling a scarecrow, but half the trees had had their branches shot away, leaving fantastic jagged stumps like a Dulac picture of some goblin forest. It was the type of all woods blasted by really heavy shell-fire, Bazentin, Delville, and the even more uncanny woods one knew east of Ypres in the autumn of 1917. Along the west edge ran a trench, from the side of which in places protruded the arms and legs of carelessly buried men, and as our men moved up that night to attack dozens of them shook hands with these ghastly relics. All the old "rides" through the wood were blocked by fallen trees and great shell-holes, and over all hung the overwhelming smell of corpses, turned-up earth and lachrymatory gas. The sinister aspect of the wood was intensified that night by the incessant whistling and crashing of shells and the rattle of machine guns and illuminated by the German flares, Very lights, and the flash of bursting shrapnel.

Before dawn the 6th and 7th Battalions had carried the German front line – a trench running between the two woods – and Bazentin Wood beyond that, while owing to their right flank being exposed, they cleared also the village of Bazentin-le-Petit (though not in their area), but the cost was appalling. Co-operation between artillery and infantry was then in its infancy, the "creeping barrage" not yet being developed, and it was hard for the infantry to keep up with their own barrage or alternatively to avoid walking into it. Seven machine guns were captured in the trench alone, but only after they had done deadly work, especially on the 7th Battalion, which lost fourteen officers killed. The enemy were not wholly cleared from the wood, and incessant appeals came back for bombs and small arms ammunition, which were taken forward by parties of the 9th Battalion, under the Brigade bombing officer. During my second visit to the line that day, in company with General Hessey, we had just found Colonel Haigh of the 9th Battalion in a trench known as Forest Trench, when that particular trench became the object of a heavy bombardment as part of an abortive enemy counter-attack on the troops on our right, and for an hour we crouched in what remained of the trench while a stream of shells came roaring or screaming straight at us. When

the shelling weakened the Brigadier walked along the trench
ordering a general movement forward to occupy the north
side of the wood, and from an orchard near Bazentin village
we saw the enemy waves running back. Passing along to the
west side, and just as we reached a light railway, we ran into
heavy rifle fire from a German "pocket" left behind in the
north-west corner of the wood, which subsequently cost us
a good many casualties.

The following day as the result of an unfortunate misun-
derstanding the Brigade were ordered to withdraw, though,
in fact, there was no-one at hand yet to relieve them. The
wearied troops streamed back, leaving only a company of
the 1st East Yorks, belonging to the 64th Brigade, who had
come up to reinforce our line. I was standing in Mametz
Wood, when the Brigade Major called me to collect everyone in sight, and take them to the front line, while he himself seizing a horse from a gunner rode round sending back
the battalions. I got together about eighty men, and joined
them onto the returning battalions, then wandering round
Bazentin Wood found the Brigadier sitting in a shell-hole,
meditating gloomily over the risk which had been incurred.
He gave me a note for General Headlam, commanding the
64th Brigade, who we understood to have his headquarters
in Bazentin village on our right. On reaching the village
I found it empty and being heavily shelled, so after trying
the cellars turned south and eventually found General
Headlam in a shell-hole. Villages made easy locations on the
map, and were usually death-traps; for the former reason they
were often laid down in orders as headquarters for brigades
or battalions, and for the latter reason as often the headquarters found shell-holes in the neighbourhood to be more
congenial. From the point of view, however, of the solitary
liaison officer, the game of hide and seek under shell-fire had
its drawbacks.

I rejoined General Hessey on the west side of Bazentin Wood, and spent that night there with the 7th Battalion. The following morning we established a fixed headquarters in a German dugout, the entrance to which had to be cleared first of a heap of corpses, but that same night the Brigade was relieved and marched back by way of Fricourt Wood to the back areas.

It had been a gruelling experience for the Brigade, which had lost 2,000 casualties out of about 3,300 effectives. A very large proportion of the casualties were fatal, particularly among the officers, and of my own old battalion most of those I had known best had been killed or wounded. Of the others, I grieved particularly over Colonel Mignon of the 8th Battalion, one of the most charming of the many fine men I knew through the War, who was killed leading a bombing party like a subaltern, and I remember vividly seeing him lying on his back still clutching a rifle. In the later stages of the War commanders of brigades and battalions were constantly enjoined to stay at their headquarters while a battle was in progress, and to make full use of attached officers in my own position, which has sometimes given rise to malicious criticisms among those who only came out in the later stages, but during the early Somme battles colonels and brigadiers were, as far as my experience goes, seldom to be found in dugouts.

The most startling experience of this first battle, apart from the carnage, was the total breakdown of communications. It came to be accepted as a general rule that in battles all touch with units, whether in one's own line or on the flanks, had to be personal, and though runners could carry messages, reliable information could only be obtained by personal contact with the officers in the different areas. This was the primary reason for the attachment to all Brigade and Battalion headquarters of "Intelligence Officers," though in normal trench warfare we were expected to make ourselves useful in a variety of other ways, especially in organizing a systematic service of observation, sniping, and provision of up-to-date maps.

From *39 Months with the "Tigers" 1915-1918* by D.V. Kelly, MC, formerly Captain, Leicestershire Regt. Ernest Benn Limited. 1930.

MEDICS AT WORK: 3RD–5TH SEPTEMBER 1916

'Men being mown down like ninepins'

A concomitant of heavy fighting was that the medical services were kept busy. Sgt. James A. Boardman, one of the stretcher bearers of the 6th Battn. The Cheshire Regiment (T.F.), describes working on the Somme on 3-5 September 1916 after an attack. His battalion did not actually take part in the attack, but relieved the assaulting battalions in the front line on the evening of the 3rd.

September 3. Zero. At last the guns crash. Hell! what a row. You can't hear yourself speak. What an inferno! Wherever you look you see shells bursting. Glancing at the enemy trenches all you can see are lumps of something going up. The sky is one mass of flames. Mingled with the bursting shells you can see the colours of the different kinds of rockets which Jerry is sending up as signals. Added to all this is the whistle and rattle of the machine gun bullets. The first wave goes over. What a sight! Men being mown down like ninepins. The second wave moves on. A third near by. Then another. The enemy is retaliating with a vengeance. We take cover and wait for news. We now get busy. The first lot of wounded arrive, those who are able to walk being first.

We hear that our lads have taken the Jerry first line and are hanging on like grim death. In some cases we have taken two and even three lines, but by teatime are driven out of them by the heavy counter-attacks of the enemy. The casualty list must be a very large one as the wounded have been pouring in since before 6 a.m. The artillery continue to blow hell out of one another throughout the night.

September 5. Weather holds good. Wounded still coming in. The stream of wounded has never ceased since it started yesterday morning.

The last few days on this sector has been hell on earth. About 9.30 a.m. we got a message to attend some wounded who had been collected in during the night. We took tea for them and re-dressed them.

The M.O. asked me to take a message to the nearest Company Head Quarters, which was "C" Company. Here I got on the 'phone for some stretcher bearers. As I was returning I was told that a wounded man was lying in a shell hole in front of the line. I went out and got him safely in our lines. It was only just in time, as when I got in the trench the machine gun bullets began to whiz by. I thought little of it at the time, but I learnt later that I had been recommended by the C.O.

We eventually got all the wounded clear, and returned to our own Aid Post for a well-earned rest, but we did not get much as the wounded were coming in all the day. The shelling is still very heavy and too close to be comfortable.

At night we got the order to move up to the Advanced Aid Post. Our snipers had gone out to search for wounded. They brought in 17 and it took us all night to dress them. They were in a fearful condition. We gave them tea and food which they ate ravenously. It would be about 2.30 a.m. of the 5th when we got back to our own Aid Post again for a rest, but there is no rest for the wicked. Wounded men were still coming in at intervals all day and night. We were relieved about midnight by the Black Watch, and went back to a place called Englebelmer.

From *War History of the 6th Bn. The Cheshire Regiment* compiled by Charles Smith. The Bn. O.C.A. 1932.

BATTLE OF FLERS–COURCELETTE: 15TH SEPTEMBER 1916

'indescribable racket and uproar; the tearing explosions of shells; the pungent fumes of phosphorous from the high explosives, and the curses and shrieks of mutilated and frightened men.'

On 15 September 1916 the next big attack on the Somme took place and the German 3rd Line of defence fell. The day goes down in history as the first occasion on which tanks were used in action; forty-nine – all that were then available – were employed. The capture of Martinpuich by 15th (Scottish) Division is described by 2/Lt. D.W.J. Cuddeford of the 12th (S) Bn. Highland Light Infantry. His battalion was actually in reserve, but on the day of battle he commanded an ammunition carrying party of twenty men, keeping the front-line troops supplied with SAA, bombs, etc. He crossed the battlefield from front to rear three times during the day and is thus able to give a much broader picture than most participants. Four tanks were allotted to assist the 15th (Scottish) Division, of which just two materialised; one proceeding to break down on its way to the assault position. Of the other, the history of the 15th (Scottish) Division relates:

The "male" tank did not cross the British front line until after the infantry had started, and even then it does not seem to have been of much assistance. Eventually it reached the south-west corner of Martinpuich after the 46th Brigade had taken its final objective. It then returned to its base to refill.

It is not perhaps surprising, then, that Cuddeford's account does not men-
tion the tanks at all, despite his privileged viewpoint. He does, however,
describe the creeping barrage, still in its infancy but clearly identified as
an important factor in the attack, despite inevitable casualties from our
own guns (in modern parlance, 'friendly fire'); also he comments on the
German defences, deportment of German prisoners and his 'Jocks" liking
for portable souvenirs.

As the darkness gave way to a wan sort of half light, zero
hour arrived and hell was let loose with a vengeance. Our
watches had all been synchronised the night before, and on
the exact stroke of the second the whole of the 4th British
Army, together with the French armies on our right arose and
went forward. Simultaneously, the thousands of guns massed
behind opened out their barrage. The line of bursting shells
jumped forward at the rate of fifty yards a minute, and we,
being the first wave of the attack, had to regulate our pace
so as to keep just fifty yards behind this barrage, according
to the new mode of advance that had been brought into use
about that time.

I wonder how many people at home, who in 1916 read in
their newspapers all about creeping barrages, realise exactly
what advancing under a creeping barrage meant to the leading waves of infantry. Fifty yards is a very short distance to
be from a line of bursting shells, whether German or British.
If the line of shell fire could possibly have been kept absolutely exact, according to the orders issued by the Staff (who,
of course, would not be there!), there would still be plenty
of splinters coming back; but even supposing the artillerymen to be infallible in the gun-laying (which they were not)
many guns were worn and inaccurate, and the shells fell
short.

I don't think I'm exaggerating in saying, at least as far as
our own brigade was concerned, that in the early part of the

attack quite a third of the very heavy casualties we suffered were caused by our artillery fire. However, the fault did not lie entirely with the artillerymen; many of our men would insist on pressing on too fast. In any case, I daresay the system answered the purpose for which it was devised, though it was altered later on.

Fifty yards a minute was our rate of advance, a mere snail's crawl, and as we went on, the men of the first line of the attack threw forward smoke-producing bombs ("pea-bombs") to create a mask of smoke screening the advance. The effect was most weird. A haze of smoke hung over the whole scene; here and there added to by the black greasy smoke from the heavy howitzer shells which the Germans soon started putting over. It was still not quite light, and as each shell burst the brilliant flash of the explosion lit up the underside of the pall of smoke that hung over everything.

It did not tally in the least with my preconceived notions of a full dress battle. As a boy I was very fond of battle pictures, and I always had an intense admiration for the bewhiskered gentlemen in gay uniforms they depicted careering along on dapple-grey chargers like rocking horses; all waving encouragement with their swords to one another to get on in front. The enemy too in those pictures always seemed equally well dressed and "genteel." The reality was something very different. A modern artist who aspired to paint a truly realistic picture of a big attack in the dawn on the Somme would not require many colours; grey mostly, for the mud, the sky, the figures, and the landscape generally; with small dabs of red showing here and there as the light brightened. He might make it more realistic if it were possible to paint in the indescribable racket and uproar; the tearing explosions of shells; the pungent fumes of phosphorous from the high explosives, and the curses and shrieks of mutilated and frightened men. War makes far from a pretty picture in the reality.

We carried the German front positions without much opposition, though with fairly heavy casualties from machine gun fire from beyond, and there I established my first forward ammunition dump in an enemy position shown in our maps as Bacon Trench, after which I returned with my party to our depot at the head of Highland Alley for another cargo. I found the dugout in which we had formed our depot; a sort of big "cubby hole" built into the wall of the trench and supported by timbers, now chock-a-block with wounded men who had taken refuge there. Also several others suffering more from acute fright than wounds. The two men I had left on guard over the depot were quite unable to keep those people out.

However, we pulled them out as quickly and gently as we could to make working room for ourselves; but it was only with great difficulty we were able to get the boxes of S.A.A. and bombs brought out and lifted up over the top of the trench, on account of the stream of walking wounded, German as well as our own, which all the time kept pressing down the narrow trench. Many of the wounded Germans seemed half demented; some laughing inanely, others crying; and I noticed more than one of our own men who had lost their wits and were shedding tears like children. It is painful to see full grown men lose their nerve to that degree, but it seems that the shock of wounds, or of seeing wounds inflicted, has that effect on some people.

However, I got my carrying party mustered again, and we set out a second time for supplies with our friends, the King's Own Scottish Borderers. Although the open ground was clearer of men by this time; the wounded and returning parties keeping to the trenches mostly; the Boche artillery in the meantime had got very busy and was now shelling our erstwhile front line area very vigorously, I suppose with the object of preventing our reinforcements coming up. We had to pass through this enemy barrage, and I lost six men out of my small party in doing so. I pushed on this time to a position just in front of the Factory Line, an intermediate German system of trenches running from in front of the village of Martinpuich to the old sugar factory near Courcelette on the left. Hard fighting was going on in the neighbourhood of Martinpuich when we got there; machine guns clacking away in every direction. We had a tough job in getting up with our ammunition supplies this time, in fact it was easily the worst trip of three I made to the front line that day.

The German casualties must have been very heavy. At one part, where the Factory Line crossed a sunken road leading out of Martinpuich, I saw what I expect was a record collection of dead and nearly dead Boches. The bank of this sunken road nearest our lines was honeycombed with dugouts, and evidently the Germans had organised this position as a strong-point in their defence. The lane outside the dugouts nearest the trench for a distance of about twenty yards was covered with dead or wounded Germans; not just scattered here and there, but literally in heaps, so that one could not have counted them without pulling them apart. They had evidently been caught by our shrapnel fire as they came up out of the dugouts. It certainly was a ghastly sight, and though I had already seen a good deal of that sort of thing during the short time I'd been in France, I must confess that for a moment I felt a return of those qualms of horror which I expect everyone, unless he is a butcher by trade, must feel at the beginning.

One could not help feeling surprise at the Germans crowding so many men into such an open position, which would obviously be shelled by our artillery in an attack. I subsequently noticed several times that the Germans seemed to show a decided partiality for sunken roads, the very positions our artillery would be likely to mark down for special attention. These sunken roads, which abound in Picardy and Artois, make admirable defensive positions according to the old code of field defences, but they have the disadvantage nowadays that the enemy is just as well aware of their importance and their exact location as you are, and accordingly concentrates his artillery fire on them. In these days of rapid-fire field howitzers and trench mortars they are too easily marked down, and not worth holding in case of a serious attack. In time, from our own experience, and from noting the effect of our artillery preparation on the Boche positions, we discovered for ourselves the principle of "avoiding the obvious."

For all his heavy casualties that day, and the comparative ease with which we carried his front line system of defences, the Boche here and there put up a very stout resistance, which increased the farther we advanced, as is always the case in these operations. In the Tangle Trench on the outskirts of Martinpuich, I remember seeing a German officer who with his men had apparently made a good hand-to-hand fight of it against the K.O.S.B.s. At the time I came up it was all over, and there were eight or nine Germans lying in the trench all bayoneted. The officer himself, though badly wounded in more than one place, judging from the mess he was in, was sitting up in the midst of his men and in quite good English shouting for assistance; at one moment imploring our boys, and at the next offering money to any of our stretcher bearers who would take him back to a dressing station. One couldn't help feeling sorry for even a German in his plight, but I'm afraid nobody took the slightest notice of him, except to tell him that he could "bloody well wait" until our own wounded had been attended to. Besides, I don't suppose he would have any money left in his pockets by that time, though the poor fellow didn't seem aware of the fact. Our "Jocks" were great at collecting souvenirs; a man didn't need to be dead before they had cleaned him out.

The third trip I made with ammunition was in the late afternoon to replenish the same dump in the factory line. By that time the whole of the village of Martinpuich had been captured and our line established all round the front of it, but bending back on the right to the Star Line (the British name for the front trench of a strong German intermediate position running from Martinpuich to High Wood), and on the left to the road between Martinpuich and Courcelette, which latter village also had been captured by the Canadians. The haul of prisoners from Martinpuich was a very big one, and included the complete staff of a German brigade (what they call a "Regiment"). The German brigadier himself was a typical fat and dumpy Hun, and he looked very cross. The officers of his staff, however, didn't seem to mind so much, in fact most of them appeared relieved at getting well out of it.

The prisoners were coming back across the open in big batches in the late afternoon, often without any escort. Souvenirs were to be had in plenty; pickelhaube helmets etc. galore, but I don't think we had time to collect many just then. These things haven't much interest at the time for people going forward into the thick of it, who are not sure they will come out of the business with their own lives much less loaded with souvenirs. By this I am referring to helmets and such like bulky articles. There was never a "Jock" of the H.L.I., as far as I saw, too busy to relieve a live, wounded or dead German of such portable gear as might be worth the taking. Wristlet watches in particular were cheap in our battalion, and German paper money was at a discount.

The only thing I had to eat all that day, in fact since the afternoon of the previous day, was a jam sandwich given to me by a Lieutenant McFarlane of the 10/11th H.L.I. as we passed over Bacon Trench on our last trip to the attacking line. Towards dusk, as we were returning, I saw poor McFarlane's body lying just where I had last spoken to him.

I also found that our ammunition dump in Highland Alley had been blown up by a Boche shell, and the guard I left over it both missing; probably blown to bits and buried in the debris. At any rate we never heard any more of them. The Boche had certainly got his rag out by this time, and he was giving our back areas a disgraceful pasting with his artillery.

From *And All for What? Some War Time Experiences* by D.W.J. Cuddeford. Heath Cranton. 1933.

PATROLLING NO MAN'S LAND: 11TH NOVEMBER 1916

'Pte J. Kirk, who was in the front line at the time, states that he vividly remembers the figure of Capt. Slacke looming over his sentry post and calling out the pass-words, 'Is Mrs. May in?' and then in the next breath, 'For God's sake get the stretcher-bearers!' He then went back into No Man's Land and never returned.'

Patrolling No Man's Land was a nightly responsibility of the front-line troops. Their job was to search for signs of enemy activity, such as digging of new trenches, check on the condition of their own defences – chiefly the barbed wire – and generally to get to know the surroundings. The 12th East Surreys in 47th (London) Division spent nearly a year – October 1916 to September 1917 – in and out of the southern part of the Ypres Salient near Voormezeele. By the end of this time they knew the ground intimately, but when the following incident took place they were evidently feeling their way around in a relatively new environment.

The 11th of November 1916 marks a tragedy in the history of the Battalion. The day had been quiet and everyone had prepared for a restful night, when suddenly the stillness was disturbed by bombing and machine-gun fire. No orders out of the ordinary appeared to have been issued from Battalion H.Q., and the Adjutant, who was in the H.Q. dugout at Dead Dog Farm at the time, was at a loss to understand what was taking place. Some little time later Sergt. C. Turner of B Company, entered H.Q. dugout and gave a report of what had happened. Sergt. Turner stated that at 10.0 p.m. Acting Capt. C.O. Slacke, O.C. B Company, who had recently returned from leave, had taken out a patrol consisting of 2nd Lieut. J.F. Walton and four others to reconnoitre the enemy wire on the left of No. 1 Crater. On arriving at the wire the patrol was heavily bombed and fired on with machine-guns, as a result of which one man was wounded. Stretcher-bearers were sent for, and on their arrival the party was again fired on by machine-guns, sustaining more casualties and being dispersed. In consequence, Capt. Slacke was missing, believed wounded, 2nd Lieut. Walton was wounded and missing, and four other ranks, including Ptes. Budd and Brenton, stretcher-bearers, were missing. The matter was reported to the Colonel, who at once began to investigate. Patrols went out to try to locate the bodies without success. Pte J. Kirk, who was in the front line at the time, states that he vividly remembers the figure of Capt. Slacke looming over his sentry post and calling out the pass-words, "Is Mrs. May in?" and then in the next breath, "For God's sake get the stretcher-bearers!" He then went back into No Man's Land and never returned. From the account of one of the survivors it appears that, when 2nd Lieut. Walton was wounded, Sergt. T.G. Mackenzie, who was with the patrol, got the assistance of Lce-Cpl. A. Kitchen and Pte. T.J. Young in order to bring him in. It was then discovered that Capt. Slacke was also wounded. This little party endeavoured to get both the officers back, but it was found that 2nd Lieut.

Walton was again wounded (this time mortally) and that Capt. Slacke had disappeared. Two of the men were known to have been killed. The firing became such that Mackenzie and his gallant assistants had to get back to the trench. The next day instructions were issued to the observation posts in the sector to scan No Man's Land thoroughly for any vestige of the bodies. No trace was ever found of them. It sometimes happened that, when men were missing on patrols and captured by the enemy, he exhibited a board in his front line trench giving us details. It did not happen on this occasion, neither were any of the missing reported as prisoners of war. In Capt. Slacke's case it was presumed that he fell into a large shell hole and was drowned. Any doubt that may have existed as to the fate of the missing on this occasion can soon be satisfied if one looks on the panels of the Menin Gate. For their services, Sergt. Mackenzie, Lce.-Cpl. Kitchen and Pte. Young were subsequently awarded the Military Medal. The loss of both the officers was serious to B Company, as they were the senior company officers and generally popular.

From *The History of the 12th (Bermondsey) Battalion East Surrey Regiment* by John Aston and L.M. Duggan. The Union Press. 1936.

A New Kind of Gas: 11th November 1916

'I had not gone far before I started to vomit and spit'

Recently commissioned 2nd Lieutenant H.E. Howse joined the 2nd Bn. Royal Berkshire Regiment in France on 7 November 1916. The next day the battalion marched to the trenches at Les Boeufs. Howse lasted just two days and nights in the line before being gassed, as described in a letter he wrote on 18 November.

This time last week I was in the trenches. We were having fine weather, and except for some heavy shelling there was very little doing on our part of the front, chiefly owing to the fact that the earth was literally a sea of mud after the recent long and heavy rains. I was comfortable, more or less, housed in a deep dugout, and was having a chat with none other than C.W., whom I met with his company in the same trenches as we held. It was very pleasant, this sudden and unexpected meeting in such a strange place, and we had a long chat and smoke together down in the bowels of my dugout. And over our mugs of coffee, with shells bursting harmlessly overhead, we discussed the latest news from Walmer, and the tidings we had received of friends, some in various theatres of war, others gone on a long journey, *neque redibunt.*

Well, on Saturday night we were relieved, and I had taken two platoons of men out of the trenches, and was moving towards another trench slightly to the rear, when we suddenly heard shells whizzing about us and bursting in a peculiar manner. Of course, when an ordinary shell bursts, it kicks up the dust a lot and makes a huge noise – "whiz-z-z-z-z – C-R-A-S-H!" but these shells were coming "whiz-z-z-z-z – flop," with not much noise, and very little explosion. Very soon we found out the reason. They were gas shells. There was a pungent smell in the air. I ordered all the men to put on their gas helmets, and as soon as I had seen to this I put mine on, but at night when you have a lot of men to look after, you must take your thing off to shout and give orders. So that I got a good whiff of it. I got the men into the trench, but the dear old Bosche continued to bombard us for over five hours. Luckily – miraculously – no one was hit where I was, and my company escaped with only a few casualties. The Bosche wasted a lot of ammunition.

Anyway, I felt all right next day, and I sent you one of those printed post-cards, and also a note to Mr. Mason. On

Monday morning I had to march my company to X– , about two hours before dawn. Then the fun started. I had not gone far before I started to vomit and spit. Then I knew what was up. This new kind of gas the Bosche is using has no effect for twenty-four hours, when it starts to turn you inside out. I reached our destination, and then the men started to collapse. All Monday they were bad, so that I had to send several to the aid post. The doctor of a neighbouring battalion ordered me to go back to a dressing station as I was "cyanosed," whatever that may mean. Anyway, I couldn't leave the company without an officer – this wasn't the company I had with me when the gas came, but another one I took over when its officers were knocked out – so I waited till the afternoon, when an officer came and relieved me.

Thence I went by means of Shank's ponies, stretchers, motor ambulances, clearing stations and Red X trains, till I reached this delightful spot on the French coast.

From *A South African Student and Soldier: Harold Edward Howse 1894-1917* edited by Professor W.M. Macmillan. Cape Town: T. Maskew Miller. nd (c.1918).

A DAY IN THE LIFE... 24TH NOVEMBER 1916

'in the Division and the Battalion it is a criminal offence to let slip any opportunity of killing, capturing, or annoying the Boche!'

An eerily realistic account of a day in the life of an infantry company holding the front line in the Wieltje sector of the Ypres Salient at the end of 1916. It is quoted in the history of the 1/4th Loyal North Lancashire Regiment and seems to have been written by Captain F.S. Baker, commander of 'D' Company.

The day begins at "Stand to", about an hour before dawn, when the Officer and N.C.O. on duty go round rousing every one with a hoarsely-whispered, "Wake up, there-Stand to!" reinforced by a shake as each man comes slowly up out of the wells of sleep and stumbles to his feet, rubs his eyes, grabs his rifle, and mounts the fire step. The Company Commander rouses the signaller, or vice versa, and every one sniffs the cold night air and hopes that "Jerry" won't come over this morning.

Slowly the darkness thins; faces become visible, then sandbags, then duck-boards, then the screwposts supporting the wire in front; suddenly a lark stirs, mounts up and bursts into his fervent song – the dawn has come, and the Company Commander gives the word "Stand down," which is passed along and acted on promptly, so that in a minute only the sentry on each post is left on duty. For we no longer hold the line continuously – our numbers are too small – but with a certain number of sentry posts, each consisting of an N.C.O. and, when possible, six men – more than often four – some posts being Lewis gun posts, others bombing posts, others riflemen only. This line of posts, weak as it is, is strung out between and in front of a series of "strong points" containing machine guns and an infantry garrison lodged in deep mines, while behind us is the support Company ready to come up in case of need, and reserve troops further back; in addition we have the guns, which we can always switch on in a few seconds by telephone or sending up a rocket; all these things give us confidence, weak though we feel ourselves to be.

About this time there appears in the trench an Officer from the reserve Company, followed by sweating men carrying knapsack food-containers and dixies. The word "Breakfast up" is hardly needed, as already a man from each post is waiting with both hands full of mess tins to draw the bacon and tea for his post – bread and dry stuff was issued by the

Company Quartermaster-Sergeant the night before. The sentries are excluded from the ensuing munching until such time as a chum, his meal swallowed, is available for relief; never for an instant, by day or night, must that vigilant watch over No Man's Land cease.

The Officers crowd into the Company Headquarters or crawl into their own "caboosh" and eat their food in privacy, the same food as the rest but on a plate, sometimes with porridge and eggs, privately purchased, in addition – the Army issues the same ration to all ranks, but extras can be bought at canteens in Ypres.

After breakfast comes cleaning and inspecting rifles, while the Company Commander, who has already had a look round and detailed the day's work to the Company Sergeant-Major, completes and sends down by runner to Battalion Headquarters his Trench State and account of ammunition expended; then adjusting his tube helmet and box respirator and tightening his belt carrying his revolver and glasses (it is a standing order that everyone must wear his equipment all the time in the front line), he sets out to inspect his lines, finding, if he knows his job, a cheery word for all and sundry, and receiving often better than he gives, taking stock of everything, strafing slackers, and generally tuning up for the day, well knowing that, if he misses anything, the Commanding Officer or worse still, the Brigadier, will spot it and strafe him!

Each sentry post has its standing orders pinned up on a board, with a duty roster showing each man's work through the 24 hours, and ensuring that each gets eight hours in which he may try to sleep, and a sheet for intelligence, which is collected by the Intelligence Officer every morning when he visits the sniping posts.

"Dinner's Up" is the signal for a general break and a repetition of the breakfast scene, but the food is stew or roast meat and potatoes or rissoles. At 1.30 p.m. casualty returns and special indents have to be at Battalion Headquarters, and at 3.30 p.m. a report on the situation and direction of wind (this latter with reference to possible gas activities). Having to render this report in the middle of a strafe, some sorely-tired Officer is said to have written, "Situation – Wind vertical!"

Long before this we have all washed (or dabbed) our hands and faces in shell-hole water and shaved as best we can, and an inspection of box respirators has been carried out by the Officer on duty; feet are also inspected and rubbed with whale oil to guard against trench-feet, then work is resumed till tea, after which it is time to stand-to again for another hour.

Then the night routine begins; the men who have worked all day "get down to it," while the wirers begin to slide over the parapet with their rolls of barbed wire and posts; the patrol puts on boiler-suits and cap-comforters – each man leaving behind any possible identification, and slides off into the waste, fitfully lit by enemy flares, in front of us.

The Officer and N.C.O. on duty start their tour of the line, candles are lit in Company Headquarters and correspondence is dealt with, while the Company Commander has another good look round while waiting for the patrol to return; when they come in the leader's report has to be reduced to writing – often no easy matter when an unfortunate reference to "enemy seen" raises a perfect hail of questions from higher authority, truculently asking why they were not instantly gone for and spitted! Picture Second Lieutenant Snooks, on patrol for the first or second time with three men, sent out to examine enemy wire, shivering and squirming his way across No Man's Land, all eyes and ears, suddenly hearing guttural voices and seeing six or more figures looming big in the haze. Of course, he ought to bluff them and bring them in – that is what you would do, Reader, wouldn't you? – but he doesn't; he remembers that he was told to examine wire, not to make trouble, so he crouches motionless in the mud till they pass, and thinks he has done the right thing – till he sends in his report. Then, all at once, the Brigadier, the Colonel, the Company Commander send for him, and ask him abruptly, and with degrees of rudeness befitting their respective ranks, what the – he meant by letting those Boches escape! Needless to say, he never repeats the mistake! And in time he learns that in the Division and the Battalion it is a criminal offence to let slip any opportunity of killing, capturing, or annoying the Boche!

About 10 p.m. is "tea-up," and the rum issue is mixed with this or with the breakfast tea at the discretion of the Company Commander. The patrol and other men coming in cold and wet need theirs at once, followed by a walk down to the Brigade drying room, where they can sleep in blankets before a brazier while their clothes are dried.

With the patrol's return operations usually close for the night, and about midnight, having dealt with the last batch of chits which a thoughtful and zealous runner has seen fit to pick off the Adjutant's table and deliver, asking searching questions about the "number of sandbags laid" or "the number of screw posts, long, salved" the day before, or the name of a man used to operating an electric light plant or minding pigeons or mixing cocktails ("nil returns to be rendered!" which means "If none, say so"), the Company Commander, who alone has no allotted sleeping time, takes off his tin hat, loosens his belt, and sleeps. At 3 a.m. the Officer on duty, who does a four-hour spell, sends in another "situation and wind report," and waits for the hour when he can stir up everyone else for "stand-to," strolling from one post to another and keeping an eye on things in general and the Boche in particular.

It is very quiet, probably raining a little; nothing on the move, except rats. What brutes they were, those rats of the Salient! huge mangy brutes the size of a cat, a few patches of fur on their otherwise bare pink bodies; getting under your feet, running over your face as you lay trying to sleep, eating through haversacks to get the biscuits within, scurrying, scratching, gnawing all night long!

From *The War History of the 1st/4th Battalion The Loyal North Lancashire Regiment 1914-1918*. Published by the Battalion History Committee. 1921.

4

1917: Year of Arras and Passchendaele

'The bullet struck him in the belly, and as usual in the case of these abdominal wounds he rolled about clawing the ground, screaming and making a terrible fuss. Certainly, to have one's guts stirred up by a red-hot bullet must be a dreadful thing'

Before the frequently neglected battle of Arras (its relative success denies it the immortality of the Somme or Passchendaele) opened on 9 April 1917, Lt. D.W.J. Cuddeford, now commanding a company of the 12th HLI benefited from the protection afforded by the ancient Arras caves, or cellars, of which there was an extensive network under the town capable of holding huge numbers of troops. As part of the training for the offensive the officers were able to study a plaster cast relief map of the area, enabling them to memorise important features or landmarks. On the day, the task of the 12th HLI and the rest of 46th Brigade in 15th (Scottish) Division was to support those attacking the first two German lines then leapfrog through to take the final objective. Even in one of the most successful advances of the war there were gruesome sights aplenty, with which the troops coped by finding humour in the situation. This piece is also notable for the author's experience of coming face-to-face with German field artillery firing at him and his men over open sites at point-blank range.

Zero hour was at 5-30 a.m. as I have said, but it was earlier than that when we commenced to move from the cellars to the front. The first part of our subterranean journey was very slow, as we could only proceed in single file through the narrow and tortuous passages that had been constructed from cellar to cellar, but when we reached the main sewer the going was easier, though still slow and in single file. Many jokes were passed among the men as we made our way along that salubrious emergency thoroughfare. In the good old days troops went into battle with colours flying and bands playing, but there is not much romance in advancing to the attack through a city sewer!

However, we eventually reached the long flight of dugout stairs that took us up to the fresh air. When we emerged among the factory ruins above, it was still rather dark and raining, and as the attack was now well started the din of the guns had reached crescendo, though not many enemy shells were coming over our way. From there we proceeded for some distance along an old communication trench; then we crossed the railway cutting, the steep muddy banks of which presented rather a difficult obstacle for our heavily laden men; and so on through the streets of the Fauberge on the other side to the cemetery, through which we passed by a fine new communication trench that had been constructed a few weeks before by our own pioneer battalion, the 9th Gordons. The yellow skulls of many former citizens of Arras grinned at us from the walls and heaped-up parapets of that trench as we pushed our way by.

So far we had suffered no casualties, and it was not till we were winding through the streets of the Fauberge that we saw the first dead man that day; an English infantryman who had just been killed by shrapnel. He lay sprawling across the sidewalk, with a rivulet of blood running to the pavement kerb. Some of the reinforcement draft that had recently joined us were fresh conscripts, and as we filed past the dead man I glanced back to observe how these new lads took the sight. One or two of them were making forced jokes, but others sheered round the corpse with white faces and sidelong glances, as if it was something to be avoided.

On clearing the cemetery, we left the communication trench and extended over the open in "artillery formation," that is, in line of platoons in single file columns at wide intervals. In that order we continued the advance across our own and the German front line trenches into his support area, which by this time had been captured by the 44th Brigade in front of us. While getting over that open ground, however, a distance of more than a thousand yards, we had a bad gruelling, for the enemy artillery just then laid down a fierce barrage that caused us a large number of casualties. In that short space of time, even at this early stage before our own part in the attack had commenced in earnest, our casualties included half the company signallers and stretcher bearers, the men we could least afford to lose. From the intensity of the enemy barrage, and the promptness with which it opened on us as we emerged to the open ground, it was obvious that the 44th and 45th Brigades had not yet succeeded in penetrating to their second objective on Observation Ridge, where the Germans must still have had observers directing their artillery fire on us.

Apart from the hot barrage just mentioned, we encountered practically no opposition at this stage, although we found several pockets of Germans in shell holes and side trenches that had been overlooked by the troops that went over before us. In this way we pushed on to the main support trench of the enemy front defences, a thickly wired trench named in our maps Hermes Trench (the "Black Line"), which according to Operation Orders was our assembly point for the second phase of the operations, that is, for our long two mile advance against the formidable Himalaya Trench and Orange Hill.

Here in Hermes and the adjacent trenches we had a lengthy wait until the scheduled hour for the continuation of the attack; the time of waiting being spent by us in reorganising our forces, which had been somewhat mixed up, and in putting in some consolidation work on the position; also in searching around the trenches and clearing the dugouts. This enemy support trench was a very deep one, much deeper than any German trenches we had seen on the Somme, and from the strength of its construction it seemed to have been intended as the main line of defence in the enemy front system. Like all other trenches we had passed over so far that morning, it was badly damaged by our artillery preparation for the attack, which, as was evident also by the number of dead and wounded Germans lying about, had been very thoroughly carried out.

Some of the German wounded we sent back to our own lines in care of prisoners that were routed out from the dugouts, and whom we utilised as emergency stretcher bearers, so many of our own stretcher bearers having become casualties themselves, but I am afraid a good number of the more seriously wounded died from lack of prompt surgical attention, although we did what we could for them with the means at our disposal. As usual in the case of high explosive artillery fire, the wounds were mostly rather ghastly; I remember one young German soldier there who had been disembowelled by a shell splinter. He was lying on a fire step with his intestines looped up in a bag formed by his undershirt pulled over them, and as we moved about in the trench he eyed us with an air of mild interest, as if we were the first British soldiers he had ever seen. Of course, he and others in a like condition, of whom there were many, were beyond our help, even had there been a sufficient number of stretcher bearers left with us to attend and evacuate the enemy wounded as well as our own. The man who was wounded at an early stage in these shows was fortunate, for there was a chance of him getting quickly back to a dressing station, whereas the hope of being safely evacuated diminished the farther an advance progressed beyond our own lines.

In our search through the dugouts in these trenches we found many things of interest, besides a number of live Germans who were still taking refuge in them. In one big dugout, which seemed to be a Battalion or Company Headquarters, the occupants had evidently been in the custom of doing themselves well, judging by the number of empty bottles lying about. Amongst these we discovered one or two full bottles of cognac and "rhum" which of course we promptly "salved," as well as a large quantity of cigars of the usual German "army issue" kind. Our commanding officer joined us as I was squatting outside that dugout in the midst of several dead Germans, writing a situation report and smoking one of these cigars, as were most of our men in the vicinity at the time, and I think he rather disapproved of this general cigar smoking during business hours as rather unsoldierlike!

We resumed the attack simultaneously with the 12th Division on our right, according to the pre-arranged time-table, at, I think, 11 a.m. Our advance on this occasion, as already mentioned, was to be a non-stop one against the third objective consisting of the German back system of defences, Himalaya Trench and Orange Hill, to reach which we would pass through the 44th and 45th Brigades in front of us, which by this time should have captured and well consolidated the second objective. We had no sooner got going over the top, however, than machine gun and rifle fire opened on us from several parts of Observation Ridge, and especially from the Hart Work, an enemy strong point two or three hundred yards on our half right. It was at once evident that our 44th Brigade had failed to capture the second objective, or at any rate the right hand part of it. As a matter of fact, from then on for the rest of the day we saw practically no men of the 44th Brigade, from which it would seem that that brigade had veered too far to the left in their advance during the morning, thus leaving a considerable gap on the ridge that was still fairly strongly held by the enemy.

Before we had proceeded any distance, the enemy fire became so hot that our attack was held up, and we were forced to take cover in shell holes and in the remains of an old support trench, while on the right the 12th Division likewise were brought to a standstill. The situation for us was untenable. Practically the whole battalion was packed into that old trench, which being shallow and in many places almost levelled by shell fire, afforded very little cover, crowded with men as it was. To remain where we were was out of the question, as it was only a matter of time before the enemy artillery would grasp the situation and concentrate fire on the trench, and when that happened nothing was more certain than that we should be pounded out of existence. As it was, the German machine gunners and snipers were taking their toll of us, and it was plain that our only course was to push on. I therefore suggested to the Commanding Officer (who, with his H.Q., had followed our advance to that point) that I should lead forward my company in widely extended formation to test the real enemy strength, to which proposal he acquiesced, though rather doubtfully.

It is extraordinary how even in times of such confusion and turmoil little incidents stick clearly in one's memory long after other things are forgotten. Among the victims that fell to the German riflemen just then was a young lad in MacLean's platoon; I think he was one of our remaining bantams. He was only a boy, obviously not more than about seventeen years of age, but he had always refused to be sent back to the Base Depot along with the other "under ages". The bullet struck him in the belly, and as usual in the case of these abdominal wounds he rolled about clawing the ground, screaming and making a terrible fuss. Certainly, to have one's guts stirred up by a red-hot bullet must be a dreadful thing, and that a bullet is really hot after its flight through the air is well-known to anyone who has tried to pick up a newly spent one. However, they got the boy back into the trench, opened his clothes and put a bandage around his middle over the wound, but of course we could see from the first it was hopeless. A little later, as I was squeezing my way along the crowded trench passing the word to "A" Company to be ready to go over on the signal, I noticed the lad laid out on a blown-in part of the trench. By then he was lying very still, and I thought he was dead, but as I passed he half opened his eyes and said something to me. I had to stoop down to catch what he said; it was "Good luck to you, sir!"

When I gave the signal for "A" Company to lead on, not only "A" Company but the whole battalion as well went over, and the 12th Division on our right also joined in the advance, which thus became a general one all along the line instead of merely a single company reconnaissance in force as intended! The advance was made without any covering barrage from our own artillery, but as we approached the crest of the hill the enemy fire slackened, and the position was taken with less difficulty and fewer losses than we anticipated. A number of the Germans managed to make their escape down the trenches on the reverse slope of the ridge, and the remainder we dealt with. One cannot but have admiration for an enemy machine gunner or sniper who sticks to his post till the last, that is, if he fully realises he has no chance of escape; but the enemy who continues to deal death and wounds to advancing troops from his own comparatively safe shelter until they are almost on him, in the expectation that when unable to carry on that work any longer he has only to put up his hands and surrender, has no cause for complaint if things do not turn out for him quite as expected.

Something of a surprise awaited us as we pushed on over Observation Ridge, for there on the reverse slope, not more than two to three hundred yards directly in front of us, were two batteries of German field guns that opened point-blank fire on us as soon as we appeared in view. It was something new and certainly very uncomfortable to find ourselves so close up to the muzzles of enemy guns in action; the range was so short that the flash of the guns and the explosion of the shells amongst our men seemed instantaneous. We were in extended formation, of course, but in the few minutes we were under that deadly fire several men were killed and a number terribly wounded. I remember catching a glimpse of my new batman, Don, with a gash in his neck that looked as if his head were almost severed, and beside him, standing stockstill in his tracks and looking at me in a helpless sort of fashion, as if he wanted to know what I was going to do about it, was our mess cook with a spurting red mass of flesh on his shoulder where his arm had been. For the second time that day – and we had to decide quickly this time – we found our safest direction lay right ahead; in fact our only course in that situation was to rush the guns, which we did. We "ca'ed the feet from them," as our Clydesiders put it, and I think we got most of the Boche artillerymen, including at least one battery officer, whose spurs and shoulder straps are still in my possession. They belonged to the 42nd Field Artillery Regiment.

After silencing the German batteries, we moved on across the narrow valley named in our maps "Battery Valley" (for obvious reasons, as we had just discovered!), but we had scarcely commenced the ascent of the opposite slope than a runner from Battalion Headquarters overtook us with a message that our artillery was about to open a covering barrage for our advance from a line running approximately along the bottom of the valley. We had already got beyond that point, but as there was no sense in remaining to be pounded by our own artillery we retired a few hundred yards to behind the promised barrage line. We had not long to wait, in fact we had scarcely cleared the arranged line before the barrage opened and we turned to resume the advance. Our "B" Company I noticed did not retire far enough, and for some distance they went on right under our own artillery fire, which apparently they mistook for enemy shelling! However, the covering barrage, although no doubt meant with the best of intentions by our gunners, was very scrappy, we having now advanced to beyond effective range from our field artillery positions, and before we had gone much farther it fizzled out and was lost altogether. In any case it was unnecessary, as there were no enemy defences worth mentioning between where we then were and our third and main objective.

On reaching the crest of the opposite side of Battery Valley we got our first view of that objective, Himalaya Trench, about a thousand yards away on the slope of Orange Hill. It certainly looked formidable, with immensely thick belts of bristling barbed wire in front of it. The Boche also got his first view of us just then, for his machine guns began to chatter at us as soon as we appeared over the crest of the ridge. However, at that moment we were cheered by the sight of one of our tanks (the first and only one we saw that day) crawling along the front of Himalaya Trench from the direction of Feuchy Village on the left, and vigorously using its guns against the enemy machine gun emplacements. The tank did not get very far before it was brought to a standstill by a well directed enemy shell, but it was wonderful the confidence these mechanical monsters inspired in us infantrymen, and we pushed on across the intervening ground with all the haste our heavily laden men could make.

As we advanced over that long stretch of open ground machine guns opened up on us from all points in front, and the German snipers also made the best practice they could, but as we were in widely extended formation and our numbers were already woefully thin, they did not make so much execution among us as might be thought. I think myself that the machine gun, although undoubtedly an extremely useful weapon in warfare, is often overrated. Its burst of fire of ten to twenty bullets either hits the one mark or is wasted on the empty ground, whereas the distributed fire of a section of fifteen well trained independent riflemen is much more likely to hit several marks. Nevertheless, it is improbable that we could have got into that extremely strong position so easily as we did, but that in our advance we came upon a small open cable trench leading up to the main trench under the many belts of uncut barbed wire, along which small trench and under the wire we crept in single file into the front trench of the system, and so gradually cleared the way for the rest of the battalion. Why the Germans did not put up a bigger defence is still a mystery to me. This triple line of trenches, that he had so strongly fortified at his leisure so far behind his front line, protected by numerous belts of barbed wire, and with an admirable field of fire that commanded the approach up the slope of Orange Hill for at least a thousand yards was a position that might have been held by a comparatively small number of troops in the face of an army. They must have had the wind up badly. Anyhow, we got into it with remarkably little opposition.

I remember that as we made our way one by one into the Himalaya line from that little cable trench, near where we emerged into the main trench there were four badly wounded

German soldiers propped up in a row and being attended to by two German "red-cross" men. The latter calmly went on with their work with merely an interested look at us as we pushed in, but the wounded men were in a bad way; in fact, I saw all four lying there dead a few hours later when I re-visited that part of the captured trenches. When we first came upon them, however, there was one which caused a great deal of mirth to our troops. He was a long lanky fair-haired fellow, and he had been struck by a bullet just under the nose. As he sat propped up against the side of the trench, with his eyes closed and his funny little round German forage cap perched on the extreme crown of his head, his old-fashioned "lug-hook" spectacles had toppled down to the tip of his nose, and in struggling to breathe through the great gash in his nose and palate the poor devil was making a loud snoring noise. Not a very comical sight perhaps, according to civilised ideas, but our men at the time seemed to think it was. And yet those men in their ordinary life at home before the war were probably kind husbands and brothers. War certainly is brutalising. I daresay when nerves were so highly strung it was a case of laugh or cry – and most chose to laugh. Anything was looked upon as a diversion and a relief for the moment.

Another instance of the same kind occurred an hour or so later. My second-in-command, Lieut. MacLean, with our two orderlies and his batman worked along to the right towards an artillery track crossing the trenches, beyond which we knew the enemy were still in force. Their snipers had again become very active, and I spotted two of them edging round in the trenches behind us. Having no periscopes with us, I shouted to the others to keep down until we could see what those Boches were up to, but McLean's batman, Rodgers, must needs look over to see for himself. He got one – smack in the middle of the forehead, and he sagged down into a crouching position at the bottom of the trench, the blood trickling down his cheek from the little black hole in his forehead. We of course could see he was stone dead, but as we sat looking at him in consternation for about half a minute, he suddenly heaved a great gusty yawn! That made us laugh – it seemed so funny to see a dead man yawn!

Grim humour! – as in the case of the man who had his brain-pan carried away by a shell splinter. "Gosh!" remarked one of his comrades, as he surveyed the grisly sight– "I didna think Geordie had as many brains!"

From *And All for What? Some War Time Experiences* by D.W.J. Cuddeford. Heath Cranton. 1933.

MESSINES RIDGE: 7TH JUNE 1917

'It can honestly be said that the troops were eager to go "over the top."'

The attack on Messines Ridge was a precursor to an offensive at Ypres; the Ridge extended southwards from the bottom of the Ypres Salient and had been heavily fortified. Had it still been in German hands during the Third Battle of Ypres (commenced 31 July 1917) it would have enabled the defenders to enfilade British gains. So, the battle for the ridge had no grand motive; plans were not even laid for a breakthrough to take place, even if the opportunity arose. It was a skilful 'set-piece' attack; the training and artillery preparation as thorough as one could hope for. In addition, twenty-one mines were to be fired under the German lines (nineteen exploded, in fact; one of the remaining two did likewise during an electrical storm in the 1950s and the whereabouts of the remaining mine is unknown!). In all, over one million pounds of explosives were packed into these mines, which along a nine-mile front averaged approximately two immense eruptions per mile. The attack was to penetrate between one and two miles and was a complete success. The following piece describes the rôle of the 11th Royal West Kents, Lewisham's own Service battalion, which was raised and trained during the second half of 1915 but had by now seen much active service, including the battle of the Somme.

On the evening of the 6th June, 1917, the Eleventh Queen's Own, less details, moved up the overland track by platoons and took up their position in Old French Trench ready for the attack.

It can honestly be said that the troops were eager to go "over the top." This eagerness was due to several factors. The harassing time at Dickebusch Lake, the heart-breaking fatigues and the constant, though not heavy, enemy retaliation, made the men long for some sort of relief, some change of occupation; made them long to *do something* and get on with things. Again, there seemed every prospect that this show was going to be a huge success – there were the mines all along the line, which would blow many parts of the German front sky-high; there was the encouraging fact that our artillery had so heavily and so constantly pounded the enemy positions, that few trenches could have remained formidable obstacles. The weak nature of the German retaliation too, was an encouraging indication that our artillery was dealing efficiently with the opposing batteries. The news that, when practice barrages had been put down, the troops in the line had followed them over and had made successful raids in daylight, meeting no opposition, and capturing many prisoners whom the strain of the bombardment had numbed, and had then withdrawn without so much as a casualty, put all ranks in high fettle. But above all, there was the ardent desire to wrest from the Bosche the ridge from which he had, since the previous November, dominated our line, watched our every movement, drained his water down to us, strafed us with his detestable "Minnies" and given us endless work in making our line habitable and bullet-proof.

What was this attack meant to accomplish? To what end had these tremendous preparations, spread over many months, been designed? Why was it necessary to make a frontal advance against so strong a 'position, a position which, in places, was fortified and guarded more strongly even than the Somme?

The reasons were many and involved, but there seems little doubt that the crux of the matter lay in the success of the enemy submarine campaign, which, it seemed, would, before many months passed, achieve its object of starving our country into submission. It was necessary, therefore, to strike a blow at the seat of his submarine operations on the Belgian Coast – Zeebrugge. To do this efficiently, the army must be in a position to co-operate with the Navy and an advance must be made to bring the army within striking distance of the Belgian Ports. No such move could hope to be successful without the occupation of the high ground facing Ypres and no attack on the hills of the Salient could be effective unless the Messines-Wytschaete Ridge, which gave observation over the whole area, was in the hands of the Allies. The enemy knew the importance of this ridge and had fortified it in a most scientific manner. Parts of it, such as the Dammstrasse, were immensely strong, and at every point of importance were sited concrete pill-boxes and emplacements.

The Battalion's role was to follow behind the 123rd Brigade until the Dammstrasse had been taken and then to go through them and take first Oboe Trench and then Oblong Reserve in Ravine Wood, an advance of some 500-600 yards. The Brigade was to attack with the 12th East Surreys on the right, the 15th Hampshires in the centre, and our own Battalion on the left, with the 47th (London) Division on its left, the latter having the White Chateau among its objectives. In the Battalion itself, the order of battle was a four-company front divided equally between the companies in the order, from right to left, of A, B, C, D, an arrangement which worked most successfully.

So, with every detail of the advance worked out to a degree which serves as a model for an advance with limited objectives, General Plumer's Second Army lay eager and waiting for the explosion of the nineteen miles which were to herald in Zero Hour.

"Up she goes, and the best o' luck." – One wonders how many voices uttered that remark at 3.10 a.m. on the Seventh of June, 1917. On the nine miles of front covered by the attack on the Wytschaete-Messines Ridge, nineteen mines were sprung, many of them larger than any yet exploded on the Western Front. Some had been in course of preparation for more than a year, some were but recently finished; all warranted the time and labour and risk involved in their construction. It was no small satisfaction to those who had struggled up the trenches from the dumps, with boxes of ammonal or pit props, had sweated underground shifting countless sandbags of soil from the bowels of the earth, had manned for hours the air and water pumps at the head of the shaft, to see their efforts successfully culminate in an explosion which rocked the whole area, sending up earth, concrete emplacements, dumps and mangled forms in one huge fountain of flame and smoke, leaving a huge gaping crater to announce for all time, "Here was War."

It is said that Mr. Lloyd George, who at the time was Prime Minister and Head of the War Cabinet, went out to Hampstead Heath and heard the mines go up. One can imagine that his trip was not fruitless, for near at hand the effect was truly terrifying. What must have been the feelings of the enemy, who did not know, as we did, what was coming and who had already been subjected to the fiercest bombardment yet put over by the Allies? It is marvellous that he put up the resistance that he did; it was only his front line troops, who, with their nerve gone, and their morale crushed, surrendered without making some semblance of a fight.

Nothing untoward had happened during the tiring trek over the dusty overland route up to the assembly area and few casualties had been sustained. One of them, however, cast a gloom over "A" Company, for they lost the man who was carrying the rum ration, due to be issued during the period of waiting for Zero. Fortunately, a fresh supply arrived from some unexpected quarter before it was time to go forward.

Once assembled, the troops were issued with bombs, S.A.A., flares, tools and with the chewing-gum designed to ward off thirst during the advance, while the Company Officers foregathered at Battalion Headquarters for the synchronisation of watches and the C.O.'s final instructions.

All was quiet and apart from an unusual number of coloured lights sent up from the enemy line, there was nothing to indicate that he suspected trouble. In fact, prisoners taken during the attack, said that their information was that it was to take place on the 10th June, and dispositions had been made accordingly. One suspects that this was the result of an arranged "leakage of information" on the part of our High Command.

A few minutes before Zero, the Eleventh, waiting with the other attacking troops of the Brigade in the Old French Trench area, were fetched out of the dugouts in which they had been resting, in case the explosion of the mine at St. Eloi, a few hundred yards away, should cause the dugouts to collapse or the trenches to cave in. All were ready for the attack, the culminating moment of much training, many fatigues and difficult re-organisation. In the latter respect, one must remember that by this time each battalion was a collection of specialists, each platoon, even, having its section of Bombers, Lewis-Gunners, Rifle-Grenadiers and Bayonet-men respectively. As 33 per cent of all specialists had, in accordance with the orders for the attack, to remain out of the line as "details," together with a certain proportion of Officers, Warrant Officers and Senior N.C.O.'s, so as to provide a trained nucleus in the event of the Battalion being cut up, the formation of the sections and the allocation of the duties of their members was thereby considerably altered. Especially was this so in the case of the Lewis-Gun teams. The training for the attack had, however, included much practice at "the other fellow's job" and little difficulty was envisaged as to the successful outcome of the new scheme of things.

In view of the boggy nature of the approach to the enemy line, the use of tanks was limited. One cannot imagine a tank negotiating with any likelihood of success the front line area between the Mound at St. Eloi and the Canal. The Mud Patch, for instance, would have proved a veritable burial ground for them. A few were, nevertheless, allotted to the Divisional Front for use in the later stage of the advance and the presence of one, at least, at the opportune moment, was a great aid to the Battalion advance.

So far, we have made little mention of aeroplane activity in connection with the attack. In point of fact, our 'planes had, during the weeks of preparation for the advance, established an absolute ascendency over the enemy airmen. They were thus able to "spot" many enemy batteries and to supervise with success the counter-battery work of our artillery, the result of their efforts being reflected in the silencing of a large proportion of the enemy's guns when the attack commenced and in the consequent diminution of his retaliation. During the "show" itself, our 'planes cruised up and down, watching for enemy concentrations which might indicate counter attacks, receiving messages from the infantry signallers and reporting the position of the attacking troops to Headquarters from the flares lighted on the attainment of certain objectives.

For the first two hours after Zero, the Battalion had to remain in the Assembly Area while the 123rd Brigade, including our own Tenth Battalion, completed the first phase of the attack, the capture of the Red and Blue lines – the enemy forward trenches and the Dammstrasse respectively. The former proved but little obstacle, but the latter, consisting of a line of concrete pill boxes, cleverly sited on the edge of a sunken road running parallel to the front, proved more formidable. Known to be a position of immense strength, strongly garrisoned and with a marvellous field of fire, the Dammstrasse had been subjected to especially severe treatment by our artillery, but its defenders were not going to surrender so splendid a position without a struggle. It speaks well for the courage and dash of our sister brigade that it fell "according to plan."

At 5.10 a.m., the Eleventh left the assembly area and moved forward in artillery formation with a precision of which a regular battalion might have been proud. The enemy artillery fire, though not heavy, was harassing, but few casualties were sustained, even when his barrage was met as the old "No Man's Land" was crossed. The Tenth had, apparently, not been so fortunate, for a number of bodies of their officers and men were lying about at this point. The going was extremely difficult over the enemy forward lines, which the full brunt of our artillery bombardment had transformed into one huge collection of shell craters. By 5.40 a.m., the Battalion was formed up in two waves just behind the Dammstrasse, ready for the advance, the companies on a two-platoon front with the left of "D" resting on Oar Lane. Just in front, were the 11th Queen's, busily consolidating the ground that they had just won. After a wait of 50 minutes, the Eleventh moved froward in front of the Dammstrasse so as to be close up under the barrage. This pause looked like proving costly, inasmuch as the left of the Battalion, which had had to extend outwards in order to join up with the 140th Brigade of the 47th Division, was being enfiladed by a machine-gun just in front of that Division's line. Colonel Corfe thereupon signalled a Tank, which had by this time arrived upon the scene. It took but a few minutes for the Tank to move forward and dispose of the annoyance in an effective manner.

1. Men of the 1st Bn. Rifle Brigade manning a primitive breastwork-type trench in Ploegsteert Wood, December 1914.

2. Men of the 1st Rifle Brigade in Ploegsteert Wood, 1914. The photograph shows the widening variety of 'uniform' resorted to during the winter months, including sheepskin coats and balaclava helmets.

3. Sandbagged parapet of a British front-line trench at Fauquissart, near Aubers Ridge, about May 1915.

Above and left: 4 and 5. Men of 1 / 6th West Yorks in trenches north of Ypres, August 1915. In the above picture a periscope is being used to view No Man's Land. To the left, a sniper – his head camouflaged – is guided by another man using a simple periscope.

6. Rare photograph of the Liverpool Scottish assaulting at Hooge on 16th June 1915. The photograph was taken by Pte. Fyfe of 'Z' Company, who was lying wounded. The German front-line trench is on the right with an artillery flag planted on the parapet. British barbed wire entanglements can be seen on the left and a shell-burst in the background.

Above: 7 and 8. Conditions in front-line trenches during the first two winters of the war were almost unendurable. Trench foot and frostbite were, unsurprisingly, prevalent.

9. 1st Battalion Queen's Westminster Rifles in front-line trenches near Houplines early in 1915. These were known as the Mappin Terraces, after the famous monkey enclosure at the Regent's Park Zoo.

10. Machine gun section of 1st Battalion Queen's Westminster Rifles wearing early gas masks in the trenches near Ypres in 1915.

Above: 11. Hohenzollern Mine crater near Loos. Photograph taken in March 1916. When a new mine was exploded both sides rushd to occupy it as a strongpoint. The Germans were the acknowledged masters of the art, but the crater shown in this photograph was occupied by the British and extensively sandbagged by this time.

Left: 12. Essex Sap, a grisly front-line post on the Hulluch Road near Loos, much fought over in October 1915.

13. Trench Headquarters Dugouts of 1st Bn. The London Rifle Brigade at Voormezeele, near Ypres, from November 1915-January 1916. This was a relatively quiet period but marred by incessant rain and the effects of a German gas attack nearby on 19th December 1915.

14. A front-line post at Festubert, circa 1916. Note the dugout entrance and camouflaged periscope.

15. 'Funk Holes' – shelters dug into the sides of the trench for sleeping. While such excavations were often frowned upon as the side of the trench could cave in, the British never dug such elaborate and comfortable deep dugouts as the Germans, although by the end of the war Allied dugouts were deep underground.

16. Gommecourt Wood, June 1916, with British barbed wire entanglement in foreground. Objective of the diversionary attack on 1 July 1916.

17. Scaling ladders are placed in the trenches in preparation for 'Hopping the bags'.

18. Assaulting troops wait for the order to attack. Officers check their watches ready to blow their whistles at Zero.

Above: 19. Over the Top! This photograph shows the Highland Brigade attacking at Martinpuich on the Somme, 15th September 1916.

Right: 20. The attack continues, the men rush across No Man's Land.

Below: 21. Some troops are detailed as 'moppers-up' – their job is to search out Germans hiding in dugouts who might otherwise disrupt the advance.

22. Outpost line is established in the captured German trench, to await the almost inevitable counter-attack.

23. Sentry (and several sleeping companions) of the 8th Bn. South Lancashire Regiment in a captured German trench at Ovillers on the Somme, July 1916.

24. Both sides fired flares at night to light up No Man's Land, especially if enemy activity – a raid, patrols or night attack – was suspected, or the sentry with the flare pistol was windy – contemporary parlance for jumpy.

Right: 25. Steel Observation Post tree used in the Ypres Salient, 1917. The tree had an internal ladder and a slit for observation, facing the enemy on the opposite side to the door. Such trees would be brought up during the night and would replace the remains of genuine trees, so that the landscape did not alter from the German perspective.

Middle: 26. Derelict tank on the Ypres battlefield, 1917. This example was utilised as an Observation Post.

Below: 27. An old front-line trench at the Ypres Salient. Photograph taken in 1917 after the fighting had moved from this spot.

Above: 28. The Grand Palace, Ypres, 1917. Remains of the Cloth Hall with British Army hut and vehicles.

Left: 29. A mine crater in the Ypres Salient.

Below: 30. Overgrown sandbag dugout near Ypres, 1917.

31. Brothers in distress. Two destroyed Mark IV tanks on the Ypres battlefield, 1917. The one on the left still has its 'unditching beam' attached. This iron reinforced beam could be attached to the tracks by chains and used to haul a bogged-down tank out of a trench or other obstacle.

32. More abandoned tanks in the Ypres Salient, 1917, showing the waterlogged ground that so hampered the British offensive that summer and autumn.

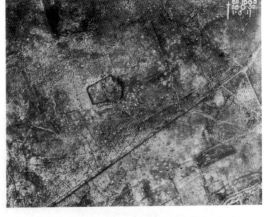

33. Aerial photograph taken on 1 May 1917 of the Dammstrasse (the road running diagonally NE from left to right on the picture). The moated emplacement north of the road is Eikhof Farm.

34. 'Cheddar Villa', a large German pill box at St Julien. Once captured was used by the 1st Buckinghamshire Battalion (and no doubt other regiments) as a company headquarters, also housing a platoon and the Regimental Aid Post, despite the rather large entrance which, of course, faced the Germans.

35. Gas was first used by releasing it towards the enemy lines when the wind conditions were deemed to be favourable. Later, with greater effect, it was mainly released via gas shells. Here a team of signallers are able to continue to operate their equipment during a gas bombardment by wearing gasmasks.

36. The trench mortar bomb (or German Minenwerfer) was a lethal trench weapon. Fired from a transportable projector, with its high trajectory it could all too easily come whistling down on unprepared infantrymen.

37. Gunners' War: everyone in the front line lived with the constant fear and attendant stress of artillery bombardment, especially, as seen here in September 1917, in the ever turbulent Ypres salient.

38. Men of 'D' Company, 7th (Service) Bn. Royal Sussex Regiment waiting for orders during the Battle of Arras, April 1917.

39. Tea and tobacco evidently cheer up these inhabitants of a front-line post at Croisilles in January 1918, despite the snow on the sandbags.

40. The German soldier was a rightly respected foe. His stormtroopers were brave and well-trained in minor tactics and use of ground. Here German soldiers are seen advancing to the attack.

41. German attack develops with stick grenades as they encounter barbed wire in No Man's Land.

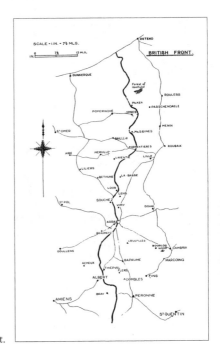

42. The Western Front.

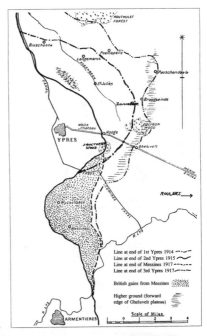

43. The Ypres Salient.

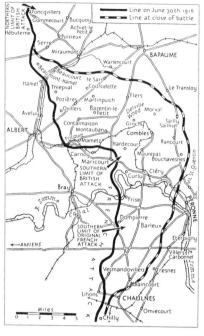

44. The Somme region.

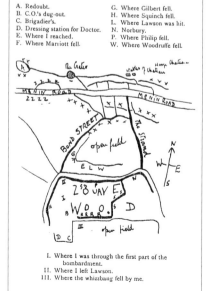

A. Redoubt.
B. C.O.'s dug-out.
C. Brigadier's.
D. Dressing station for Doctor.
E. Where I reached.
F. Where Marriott fell.

G. Where Gilbert fell.
H. Where Squinch fell.
L. Where Lawson was hit.
N. Norbury.
P. Where Philip fell.
W. Where Woodruffe fell.

I. Where I was through the first part of the bombardment.
II. Where I left Lawson.
III. Where the whizzbang fell by me.

45. Liquid Fire attack at Hooge.

When, at length, the barrage moved forward at 6.50, the enemy retaliation was remarkably light, although machine-guns from positions in the various woods showed great activity. One, particularly, sited at the North-East Corner of Pheasant Wood, was remarkably well handled and for a few moments seemed likely to hold up the advance, practically enfilading the assaulting waves from the right. Appreciating the situation and realising that its capture was essential to success, Captain Maltby, O.C. "C" Company, took across a party, including 2nd Lieut. J.H. Greenwood and Sergt. C.A. Roberts (acting C.S.M.) and rushed it, in spite of its crew continuing to fire at point-blank range. Three of the Germans were killed and the remainder taken prisoners. Capt. Maltby's prompt and effective action was of great import. Had the assaulting troops not been able to keep up with the barrage, its protection would have been lost, and the enemy garrison would have had time and opportunity to resist more effectually. Instead the advance progressed in accordance with schedule. Within a quarter of an hour Oblong Trench had been captured, its occupants being taken prisoners after slight resistance. Pte. H.G. Oliver showed great initiative at this point. It was due to his courage and dash that the resistance of a determined group of Germans in a section of the trench did not give more trouble. Rushing forward, he killed two of them, where-upon their comrades thought it wise to surrender. Pte. Oliver's action won him the Military Medal.

"B" Company, under Capt. Stallard, who was not sup-posed to go over with the Battalion, but who, after repeated requests, was eventually allowed to do so, disposed in sum-mary fashion of the task of capturing the strong point at the junction of the tramway and Oboe Trench. Sergt. J.W.J. Barnham, of "D" Company, helped greatly in this. With only a few men to help him, he rushed the post, taking 20 pris-oners and then set about the work of altering it, to form a strong point facing the enemy. Later, his C.S.M. becoming a casualty, he took over those duties successfully, showing a splendid example of coolness and courage to the men, fully deserving the Military Medal which he afterwards received.

To another party of "B" was allotted the role of digging a communication trench back from Oboe Trench to Oar Lane (from which point the 11th Queen's were digging forward), a task which they accomplished in quick time. Unfortunately, Captain Stallard, who had led his men forward with splendid courage and utter disregard of personal danger in face of the hostile machine-gun fire, received a shrapnel wound in the chest, whilst leaning against a tree stump, studying his map, but his place was ably taken by 2nd Lieut. Drumgold, under whom the consolidation and garrisoning of Oblong Trench was effected.

At Oblong Trench, the second wave joined up with the first and the whole, less "B" Company, went forward to the Black Line – Oblong Reserve. Here the opposition was stronger, the defenders continuing to fire until the line reached the trench, when most of them surrendered, whilst a few scrambled back towards the rear. The Battalion's "bag" of prisoners from Oblong Reserve amounted to about 40. The barrage now halted (7.30 a.m.) while the task of mopping up and consolidating proceeded, interrupted occasionally by "shorts," from which a number of casualties resulted. The enemy also shortened his range and, though not intense, his shelling and machine-gun fire was troublesome.

The Eleventh still had more work to complete. In order to assist the 47th Division on its left, it was directed to clear the Lane running across the front from Delbske Farm to Englebrier Farm, a few yards beyond Oblong Reserve. There were a number of dugouts and machine-gun posts in this Lane, from which the ground to the left could be swept with fire. It was important, therefore, to render these posts ineffective. Patrols and Lewis Gun were sent forward to do this. No resistance was forthcoming and the dugouts were quickly mopped up.

The other Battalions of the Brigade had been equally successful, but the 47th Division on the left had met with sterner opposition. Their objectives had included the huge pile of white masonry which had once been Chateau Mahieu, but now universally known as the White Chateau. Used as a Headquarters by the Bosche, strongly fortified and with much underground accommodation, it was a tough proposition and did not finally fall until some hours after the 41st Division had reached its objectives. Further opposition was encouraged at "The Stables," but was eventually overcome.

The Battalion was not to remain long in undisputed occupation of its gains. It had settled down to dig in under cover of Lewis Guns pushed forward, when, suddenly, two Germans came out of the wood and gave themselves up to "D" Company, at the same time giving them to understand that a counter attack was forming in the wood. Captain Fraser at once jumped up and, calling to his company to "down tools", ordered them to charge the wood at the point of the bayonet. "A" and "C" could not let them go alone, so they, too, dumped their picks and shovels, picked up rifles and were soon up alongside "D."

"What's us going to do now, sir?" said a stout little Cockney to his Company Commander.– "You're in a bayonet charge," was the reply.– "Gosh! won't my old woman be proud of me after this," said the little fellow, as he brought his rifle to the "high port."

A splutter of machine-gun fire from inside the wood was answered by a ragged volley from the men of the Eleventh, and thereafter the affair took on somewhat the nature of a rabbit shoot. Many casualties were inflicted and 25 prisoners taken to

swell the already considerable "bag" which the Battalion had
collected that day. The various trenches in the vicinity were
quickly cleared, but casualties were being received from our
own artillery, due, to a certain extent, to the use of the new
"106 fuse," which, like its German "sensitive" counterpart,
had a very wide danger-zone. In spite of this, Captain Fraser
insisted on digging in on the spot, for he maintained that
the "Queen's Own" had never given up a yard of its gains in
all history. There followed a vigorous argument between the
three Company Commanders, the two maintaining that not
only were casualties being incurred unnecessarily, but also that
the tactical position was very poor.

Finally the two prevailed and, withdrawing to the former
position, the three companies continued to consolidate on
the line they had already started. The little trip had cost them
nearly half the casualties sustained throughout the attack.

Colonel Corfe was soon on the scene and approved of the
course taken, but he had some very caustic remarks to make
about liaison and co-operation with units on the flanks, for
the Hampshires on the right were nowhere to be seen. It
was not long, however, before "A" Company had extended
outwards and joined up with them. As usual, Lieut. Salmon,
whom we had lent to the Divisional Observational Section,
was up on the spot. The two Company Commanders were
well pleased when Salmon confirmed their opinion of the
suitability of the spot chosen and the unsuitability of the forward position, for we always looked on him as a splendid
judge of country.

The attempted counter-attack had given opportunity for
one man especially to prove his worth. Lying out in front, with
his Lewis Gun covering the work of consolidation, Pte. R.E.
Hicks was suddenly confronted by a large party of Germans
trying to rush his gun. Cool and collected he continued to
fire, until they were almost on top of him, by which time he

had made casualties of all but a few, who then considered discretion the better part of valour and surrendered to him. Pte. Hicks' little episode resulted in the award of a well-deserved Military Medal.

The day wore on with little further excitement, apart from the sight of a German Battery galloping into action on the slope beyond Oosttaverne. If only one could have telephoned back to our guns! But other eyes had seen and in a short time a noise like express trains passing over-head and columns of black smoke appearing on the distant slopes, heralding the silence of the battery for good and all. The men suffered rather from thirst in spite of the chewing gum and careful planning of water-dumps. The ground was dry and the shelling threw up clouds of dust which, added to the reek of the fumes from the shells, quickly parched the throat.

Busily working with pick and shovel, the troops received a welcome surprise, then, in the arrival of Lieut. Donnet with dixies of hot tea. Donnet had been attached to Division, in charge of water supplies for the attack, but with ever a soft spot in his heart for the "boys" of his old Battalion, he had not let the opportunity pass of bringing them what comfort he could. Incidentally, he had received a slight wound in the foot, but, with his usual disregard of self, continued at duty for several weeks, before he was finally forced to go to hospital. During those weeks he dispensed hot tea to hundreds of West Kent men from his water-dump at Voormezeele, as they passed on their way up to or back from the line.

About 3 p.m., the roar of our guns increased, units of the 24th Division came through and moved forward towards the final objective:- Rose Wood–Olive–Trench–Opal Reserve.

Our forward posts were now called in, for the responsibility of watching for counter attacks no longer rested with the Battalion, but the position was still under enemy observation from the left, as a party who went forward to forage found to their cost. They did not return empty-handed, though, "C" Company's Sergeant-Major having discovered a black kitten which he bore back triumphantly on his shoulder. The shelling, too, consisting chiefly of heavies, continued desultorily, but the Eleventh settled down to await relief, with a complacent sense of self-satisfaction.

All objectives had been reached, the situation was secure, so now was the time for the Colonel to light up that well-seasoned, gurgling pipe of his, which never seemed to burn without frequent resort to the match-box. So badly, in fact, did the Colonel fill his pipe, that there was always a distinct shortage of matches in Headquarters' Mess. No one ever said anything, but we all made a fairly accurate guess that the bulk of the weekly ration found its way via the C.O.'s batman (whose ability to "scrounge" was of no mean order) into the C.O.'s pocket.

Safely ensconced in front of the Dammstrasse in the battered pill-box which now served as B.H.Q., "Jimmy" had already lighted his usual "Dubec." The Colonel produced matches and pouch, and felt for his pipe. A fervent ejaculation announced that it was missing. "Signaller!" he shouted to the little dark fellow on duty as "writer" for the show. "Sir," replied the signaller, from the scant cover where he and the runners were crouching low to allow the machine-gun bullets to pass on instead of through.

"I've lost my pipe. I think I left it in the shell-hole where Captain Fraser had his company headquarters early this morning. You know the spot?" "No, Sir, but I'll try to find it."

What a hope! To discover one certain shell-hole in a wide area absolutely pitted with them! However, off went our little signaller, not giving a thought to the fact that for so small a thing as a pipe he was running considerable risk of making a widow of that young wife of his. It was a case of dodging from one shell-hole to another, for the Bosche was still sniping from the left. Time after time he found it necessary to lie "doggo" as the bullets skimmed the edge of the shell-hole or went with a thud into the earth nearby. For five hours this sort of thing went on and still there was no trace of the particular spot where the erring pipe was supposed to be. At last, he plucked up enough courage to go back to the Colonel and report failure, taking care to omit mentioning the fact that he had been unable to discover the elusive shell-hole. While he was delivering this carefully worded sentence, designed to soften the blow to the C.O. and to alleviate the wrath which might possibly fall upon himself, he was interrupted with, "Oh! It's all right, Signaller, you needn't have worried; I found that I was lying on it."

From *The History of the 11th (Lewisham) Bn. The Royal West Kent Regiment* by Captain R.O.Russell, MC. Lewisham Newspaper Co. 1934.

Raid at Neuve Chapelle: 11th–12th June 1917

'casualties were so heavy that it was realised that every remaining man would be required for carrying in the wounded'

The Raid was the principal offensive action outside of large-scale attacks intended to gain ground. A Raid was not intended for this, but was a quick in-and-out penetration of the opposing lines with the purposes of capturing prisoners (to identify the unit opposite) and, incidentally, to cause casualties and damage. Some officers and men perceived in them opportunities for blood-letting, glory and medals; for others they were merely another way of losing one's life. The adversarial nature of trench warfare, and the dictum that one must always have 'the upper hand,' dictated that when one was raided, one promptly made a retaliatory

Raid. Raids were always prepared with meticulous precision, but still they were inevitably hazardous affairs. In the following example the unreliability of Portuguese allies had much to answer for.

In the early morning of June 3rd the Germans raided the Portuguese in the vicinity of the Duck's Bill Crater and extracted ten prisoners. Hence we were not surprised to hear next day that we were to carry out in reply a raid on a large scale. The details were rapidly arranged, and the party selected spent its time practising the raid on ground near Rue Bacquerot, a mile behind our front-line trenches.

The party consisted of about two hundred and forty men under ten officers, with Major Stickney in command. The plan was to advance from the Birdcage Craters in a south-east direction, with the right on the German front line and the left a hundred yards inside his territory (which was believed to be held by isolated posts only), to kill or capture any Germans met, and to do as much damage as possible to the German trenches.

Two or three nights before the raid Lieutenants Ryan, Gifford, Martin and Bridger went up to the line for a final reconnaissance. They penetrated some considerable distance beyond the enemy front line, and were then suddenly challenged in German. Several shots were fired at them, but they got back safely to our lines with a very useful knowledge of the enemy ground.

Zero hour was fixed for 12.30 a.m. on the night of June 11/12th. The afternoon of the 11th was spent busily at La Fosse in settling the many necessary details and then the party was inspected by the General. In a short speech he intimated that our raid, besides having great importance of its own, was necessary in order to divert a little enemy attention from the battle that was then going on at Messines, and that on receiving instructions that his Brigade was to make the raid, he had selected the Hallamshires, feeling confident that they would succeed.

The party was then packed into motor lorries and drove off. If the enemy had any spies at all on our side of the line, he must have been aware that something was on foot, for the string of about ten lorries, packed with black-faced men, passed through four or five villages full of open-mouthed civilians. Near Epinette Dump they picked up bangalore torpedoes and the sappers who were to fire them, and then made themselves comfortable near the foot of the communication trenches and rested for an hour or so, as there was plenty of time to spare before they could go up to the front line. The Portuguese troops, in the part of the line concerned, had been withdrawn, and Captain P.N. Johnson, with B Company, took over in their stead. When it was dark enough, the raiders moved off up the winding communication trench and began to file out over the top to take up the positions of assembly. A good deal of water-logged ground was anticipated, and, therefore, each of the four front-line platoons carried a specially-made bridge for crossing any impassable places.

At 12.27 a.m. everyone was in position, and the seconds dragged slowly along until 12.30, when the whole front appeared to break into flame, and down came the barrage. The raid had been practised so carefully that when the time came all were in the positions laid down – i.e., fifty yards from where the barrage should have fallen. This distance has been proved many times to be perfectly safe, and it had the obvious advantage of allowing our attacking troops to be on top of the enemy when the barrage lifts before he has time to recover himself. Unfortunately, however, in this case one of the batteries was not shooting accurately, and, within five minutes of zero, one of our shells burst just behind Lieutenant Ryan and a shrapnel bullet passed through his thigh. Next minute a shell burst amongst a Lewis-gun section, killing or wounding every man and blowing the gun to pieces. Other platoons fared little better. In spite of these difficulties, and now very much reduced in strength, the raiders pressed on, and twenty minutes after zero the left company (Captain E.M. Holmes) sent down two prisoners, while soon after 1 a.m. the right company (Captain S. Brooke) sent eleven more to Headquarters. By this time casualties were so heavy that it was realised that every remaining man would be required for carrying in the wounded. Of Lieutenant Ryan's platoon of thirty-one men there remained only three unwounded. Major Stickney then sent every available man from the supports and also the men of the right party who were returning, up to the left to assist in clearing the casualties. Lieutenant O'Donnell was found very seriously wounded and was carried back, but died on reaching our lines. The work of clearing the casualties was continued until dawn arrived, and made it impossible to remain out any longer, but by this time all of the wounded and most of the dead had been brought in. Padre Elgood had been out during the whole of the time helping to carry the wounded to our lines.

The enemy retaliation was not very serious. He trench-mortared his own front line mercilessly, but most of the party were well past it by the time he began to shoot. The raid was a success from a military point of view, as we had achieved our object and secured thirteen prisoners, one of whom was a "Hauptmann." The cost, however, had been very great. We lost twenty-eight men killed and fifty-five wounded; and of the officers, O'Donnell was killed and Ryan and Williams were wounded.

The inaccurate artillery fire which had caused most of our casualties was traced to a Portuguese battery. Our own artillery officers had registered the guns of the Portuguese accurately, and every possible precaution had been taken by our artillery commander, but, despite this, the Portuguese altered their ranges at the last moment without reference to our C.R.A., and thus caused the loss of many valuable lives.

From *The 1/4th (Hallamshire) Battn., York and Lancaster Regiment, 1914-1919* by Capt. D.P. Grant, MC. Printed for private circulation. [1931].

A Working Party: 14th-15th July 1917

'Blighty is the place for me!'

During the build up to the Third Battle of Ypres – very often referred to, wrongly, as Passchendaele – the nightly labours of the fighting area increased in intensity. With more men in the area there was the need for more provisions; with the guns firing their bombardment there was the need for more shells; and with a battle in prospect there was the need for more trenches. In this piece Lieutenant T.H. Floyd, who had recently joined the 2/5th Lancashire Fusiliers, describes one of many nights spent in attempting to improve the defences, and the enemy's – rather successful – efforts to prevent them from so doing.

Up about 2 a.m. Twenty-eight more men in B Company reported sick with gas, but they were not sent to hospital. The M.O. said that they would be excused duty to-night and must report sick to-morrow morning. We had a little more gas in the afternoon. I think a German heavy exploded one of our gas dumps near the Canal Bank. A dense cloud of vapour rose in that vicinity, and we felt the smell slowly drifting towards us in the almost breathless calm of a bright summer afternoon. Giffin, who was the senior officer present at the time, ordered respirators on. But it did not last long, so we went on with our tea.

In the evening Giffin and I were on a working party with Sergeant Clews, Sergeant Dawson and forty-five other ranks.

We proceeded to Potijze Dump and drew tools; thence to Pagoda Trench and carried on with the making of a new trench branching off that trench. All went well for the first three quarters of an hour. Our guns were pounding the German trenches the whole time – the first preliminaries in the bombardment preceding our offensive. But the Germans do not always allow us to have all our own way in these matters; they always retaliate. And, by Jove, we did get some retaliation too! At 10.50 p.m. quite suddenly, a heavy shell exploded just near us; and a regular strafe commenced. I was standing near a shell-hole at the time, so I immediately crouched where I was; the men digging at the trench at once took refuge in the trench. In a few minutes I mustered sufficient courage to make a dash for the trench. I got there just in time, for, soon afterwards, a shell burst almost where I had been. They were dropping all round us, both in front of and behind the trench. Only the trench could possibly have saved us. And it was a marvel that no one was hurt as it was. I honestly expected every moment to be my last; it was a miracle that none of our party were hit. If we had remained out in the open I firmly believe that the whole lot would have been knocked out. It seemed as if it was never going to cease. I never went through such a disagreeable experience in my life before. Then, to crown it all, gas shells began to be mixed with the others. There was soon a regular stink of gas; I smelt it this time all right. We got our respirators on, which added to our discomfort. This went on for quite a long time. Then it also began to pour with rain and we were all drenched. The night was pitch dark. Every now and then the exploding shells around us and far away, the burning dumps near Ypres and the star shells along the line, lit up the whole panorama with an effect like that of lightning. The water and mud grew thick in the trench; and still the shells fell thickly all around. We were thankful for the discomfort of rain because it saved us from being gassed.

July 15th. About 1 a.m. Giffin decided, the shelling having slackened a little, that we had better get down a mine-shaft near; so we stumbled along to it in anything but a happy frame of mind. Everybody was cursing. Despite our discomfort, however, the humour of the situation under such circumstances cannot fail to strike one; I could not help chuckling. Eventually we got down the mine. It was horribly damp and dirty down there, but the atmosphere was much clearer; there was no smell of gas. That was a relief. And we felt much safer here! No heavies could reach us at such a depth as this. But it was all darkness. We remained in this subterranean sanctuary for three hours, standing on a water-covered floor, amidst dripping walls, in the darkness; above us, all the time, we could hear the dull thud and feel the vibration of the bursting shells. For want of anything better to pass the time away the men began to air their opinions about the war to each other. 'We're winning!' 'Are we heck as like; Billy's winning. Judging from t'newspapers you'd think t'war was over long since! They keep telling us he's beat; but they want to come out 'ere and see for 'emselves. ...They say t'last seven years'll be t'worst!' Such was the conversation which was going on. Others had a sing-song. 'Hi-tiddle-ite! Take me back to Blighty; Blighty is the place for me!' rang out with great enthusiasm from the darkness under-ground.

When we did go upstairs again daylight had dawned. We left the mine at 4.20 a.m. Giffin went, with one or two men, back to the trench to replace the camouflage; he told me to get back to the Ramparts with the remainder as quickly as possible. I did so. We went along the road all the way from Potijze to Ypres. We were literally chased by gas-shells; we had to run in respirators as fast we could go; we came round by the Menin Gate and got back into the Ramparts, safe and sound, about 4.45, very thankful that nobody in our party had got hurt. Other battalions out on working parties had had a good many casualties. One party of the King's Own had had one killed and eleven wounded by one shell on the Canal Bank.

When I got back to the Mess dugout I found Captain Andrews, Dickinson, and Allen all sitting there. They had not been to bed. They had had a deuce of a time. The shells had been falling here as well – also the gas. But due precautions against gas had this time been taken! Captain Andrews declared that the rain had saved the lives of hundreds of men. Giffin got back soon after me. He is feeling the gas. We all got to bed about 6 a.m.

From *At Ypres with Best-Dunkley* by Thomas Hope Floyd. Bodley Head. 1920.

THIRD YPRES: 31ST JULY 1917

'I might just as well be blown to bits in the open, trying to get back to safety, as lying in this shell-hole'

Lieutenant T.H. Floyd commanding a platoon of 'B' Company, 2/5th Lancashire Fusiliers, took part in the first day of the Third Battle of Ypres – an experience of which he wrote the following lengthy account on 3 August from a hospital bed in England. His commanding officer was an almost unbelievably unpopular 26-year-old fire-eater, Lieutenant-Colonel Bertram Best-Dunkley, of whom he heard shortly after joining the battalion: 'They enquired whether we were going to the Club; and when we replied that we were, they exclaimed: "Don't; the C.O.'s there!"… apparently Colonel Best-Dunkley had now returned. Everybody was very fed up at his return.' And shortly afterwards when the battalion moved by train: 'It was rumoured that Colonel Best-Dunkley was going to travel by a particular carriage. You should have seen how that carriage was boycotted! Nobody would go into it. They preferred to crowd out

*the other carriages and leave the tainted carriage empty. It was most
noticeable. I do not think there is a single person in the Battalion who
would not rather travel with the devil incarnate than with Colonel
Best-Dunkley.' Then at Third Ypres: 'All this time our interests
(and, perhaps, our fears!) were centred upon one man, the unpopular
Colonel who, few of us guessed in those days, was destined to win
the V.C. on "the day," going down in a blaze of glory which should
ever associate his name with that battle.' Colonel Best-Dunkley was
mortally wounded on 31 July 1917 and died of wounds on 5 August.
He was posthumously awarded the Victoria Cross.*

I will now endeavour to tell you the story of the Third Battle
of Ypres. As you are aware, we were preparing for this battle
the whole time I was at the front. It was part of Haig's general
plan of campaign for 1917. When I first arrived in the Prison
at Ypres [used as billets], the day before Messines, Captain
Andrews had me in his cell and explained to me the plan
of campaign. He opened some maps and explained to me
that Plumer's Second Army was, very shortly, going to attack
on the south of the Ypres Salient with the object of taking
Hill 60 and the Messines ridge. If that attack should prove
successful *we* should, a few days afterwards, do a little 'stunt'
on a German trench named Ice Trench. We were issued with
photograph maps of this trench and many conferences were
held with regard to it. Further, he explained that this was only
a preliminary operation: the main campaign of the year was
to be fought on the front between Ypres and the Sea, and Sir
Hubert Gough was coming to Ypres to take command. Well,
the Battle of Messines was fought the following morning;
all Plumer's objectives were gained; it was a perfect 'stunt';
but, still, our Ice Trench affair was cancelled! We left Ypres
soon afterwards and went into rest billets at Millain and then
training billets at Westbecourt. Hunter-Weston's VIII Corps
became a reserve corps behind the line and we, Jeudwine's 55th

Division, were transferred to Watts's XIX Corps which became part of Gough's Fifth Army – that famous general having arrived in Flanders. While at Westbecourt we – Stockwell's 164 Brigade – practised the Third Battle of Ypres in the open cornfields and amongst the numerous vegetable crops between Cormette and Boisdinghem. When we got back to the Salient we understood Haig's plan to be that Gough's Army should smash forward from Ypres, that there should be a French Army on Gough's left, and that Rawlinson's Fourth Army should land upon, or push up, the Belgian Coast at precisely the same moment as Gough struck north from the Ypres Salient. That plan commended itself to me as highly satisfactory. But one always has to reckon with an enemy as well! I do not know whether Armin got wind of it or not, but he effectively thwarted Haig by doing precisely the kind of thing I expected he would do. Rawlinson's Army was engaged and driven back at Nieuport, thus disorganizing his plans; and Ypres – the other flank – was intensely bombarded with high explosives and gas shells on that never-to-be-forgotten night of July 12-13. The gas casualties in Ypres who were taken to hospital on July 13 were, I was told, 3,000! A much higher figure than I thought at first. A day or two after these events Gratton came to see us at the Ramparts and casually informed us that the Coast idea was postponed: the battle was going to be fought north and south of Ypres only. The Coast landing was going to take place later if the third Battle of Ypres should prove a success – of which, of course, no patriot could entertain any doubts! Rawlinson was not ready. Nieuport was to me sufficient explanation for that. And Beatty was not ready! That I do not understand. I was very disappointed, indeed, when I heard this news, as I was not very hopeful as to the chance of success in any battle fought in the centre. A flanking movement is, in my opinion, the best policy; and the original idea would have meant, if a landing had been effected, a triangular advance which would have left before Armin only two alternatives – retreat or surrender. But attrition seems to be far more in Robertson's line than strategy! So the Third Battle of Ypres has begun. And, unless things change very quickly, I am bound to say that it is not a success. So much for the general idea.

During our twenty days in the Ypres Salient, from July 1 to July 20, we suffered very heavily in casualties; and when we came out we were certainly not strong enough to go into battle. So while we were at Valley Camp, Watou, we were reinforced by large drafts. And, in accordance with the above plans, we left Watou on the night of July 25 and marched to Query Camp, near Brandhoek, but on the left of the main road. Here we remained awaiting 'XY night.' 'Z Day' was the day on which the battle was to take place. On 'XY night' we left Query Camp and took up our positions in our concentration trenches near Vlamertinghe. My platoon and Allen's platoon were in a trench on the right of the Vlamertinghe-Ypres road, across the field stretching from the road to the railway. Sergeant Brogden's platoon (6 Platoon) was a little further on. Dickinson was in command of B Company. We had our Headquarters in a little wooden dugout (this refers to the officers' quarters) in the centre of the field behind the trench. Battalion Headquarters were at the Café Belge – a house on the right of the road close by. 'XY night' was the night of July 29-30. We got a little sleep during the morning.

For the last fortnight the artillery had been preparing the way for us, raids had been taking place, and conflicts in the air had been of frequent occurrence; the Royal Engineers had been constructing roads and other means of advance; miniature railways were running up to the front line; and the road from Watou, through Poperinghe and Vlamertinghe, to Ypres was simply thronged with transport. The weather had been fine and hot. On 'XY night' troops were swarming round

Vlamertinghe and there was every sign that a great push was about to commence.

During July 30, in our little wooden dugout here, Dickinson held conferences consisting of Allen and myself with Sergeant Brogden, Sergeant Baldwin, Sergeants Stokes and, of course, Sergeant-Major Preston and Quartermaster-Sergeant Jack. Did it occur to us that within twenty-four hours we should all be scattered to the winds – some killed, others wounded? I expect it did. But it did not worry us. We smiled and discussed plans. During the day Colonel Best-Dunkley looked in and chatted most agreeably; he was in a most friendly mood. Padre Newman also looked in.

At 8.55 p.m. I marched off with my platoon along Track 1, leaving Goldfish Chateau, the one building in that region which stands intact, on our right, along Track 6, touching Ypres at Salvation Corner, along the Canal Bank and through La Brique, where the Tanks (commanded by Major Inglis) were congregating ready to go forward on the morrow, to Liverpool Trench. We reached Liverpool Trench, the assembly trench from which we were to go over the top on the morrow, about 11 p.m. ...D and B Companies were in Liverpool Trench, and C and A Companies in Congreve Walk – the other side of Garden Street. It was a dull, cloudy night. The guns were continually booming. Our howitzers were flinging gas-shells on to every known German battery throughout the night. The enemy replied by shelling Liverpool Trench and Congreve Walk – especially the latter. One shell burst right in the trench, took one of Verity's legs almost clean off, and killed his servant Butterworth. The shells were bursting all night. All our trenches were simply packed with troops ready to go over the top at Zero. Lewis's 166 Brigade filled the trenches in front of us. The 55th Division occupied a front from the west of Wieltje to Warwick Farm. Half of this frontage was occupied by Lewis's 166 Brigade on the left, and Boyd-Moss's 165 Brigade occupied the other half on the right. Stockwell's 164 Brigade occupied the whole frontage in rear with the object of passing through the front brigades and penetrating into the enemy's positions. The 2/5th Lancashire Fusiliers were the left front battalion of the 164 Brigade. Colonel Hindle's 1/4th North Lancashires were on the right. We were supported by the Liverpool Irish as 'moppers up'; and the North Lancs were supported by the 1/4th King's Own Royal Lancaster Regiment in the same way. In our battalion, D Company, commanded by Captain Bodington, were on the left front. On their right were C Company, commanded by Captain Mordecai. In rear of D Company were B Company commanded by Second-Lieutenant Talbot Dickinson, M.C.; and on our right were A Company commanded by Captain Briggs. The front companies comprised the first two waves; the rear companies the third and fourth waves. The first wave of D Company contained Beesley's platoon on the left; and behind Beesley's platoon was that of Telfer. Then came Sergeant Brogden's platoon of B Company, with Allen on his right. My platoon occupied the whole company front behind Brogden and Allen. My orders were to advance to the 'Green Line,' and when I got there I was to take Lance-Corporal Tipping's rifle section and four Lewis Gunners on to reinforce Allen at Aviatick Farm where he was to dig a strong point in front of the front-line when the Gravenstafel Ridge was reached. Two of my sections were detached: Corporal Livesey took his bombers with Brogden's platoon to mop up a dugout beyond Aviatik Farm, and Lance-Corporal Heap was sent with his rifle grenadiers to 15 Platoon. On my left was a platoon, commanded by Sergeant Whalley, of the 1/6th Cheshires. They belonged to the 118th Brigade of the 39th Division of Maxse's XVIII Corps – so, you see, I was on the extreme left of Sir Herbert Watts's XIX Corps. It was Cuthbert's 39th Division that was to take St. Julien. We were to go through Fortuin and leave St. Julien just on our left. On the right of our division was the 15th Division. Behind us, in the Watou area, was Nugent's 36th (Ulster) Division, ready to go through us in a day or two. The 15th Division is entirely Scottish. So much for Gough's dispositions for the battle.

Zero was fixed for 3.50 in the morning. As the moment drew near how eagerly we awaited it! At 3.50 exactly I heard a mine go up, felt a slight vibration, and, as I rushed out of the little dugout in which I had been resting, every gun for miles burst forth. What a sight! What a row! The early morning darkness was lit up by the flashes of thousands of guns, the air whistling and echoing with shells, the calm atmosphere shaken by a racket such as nobody who has not heard it could imagine! The weird ruins of Ypres towered fantastically amongst the flashes behind us. In every direction one looked guns were firing. In front of us the 166th and 165th Brigades were dashing across No Man's Land, sweeping into the enemy trenches, the barrage creeping before them. I stood on the parados of Liverpool Trench and watched with amazement. It was a dramatic scene such as no artist could paint.

Before the battle had been raging half an hour German prisoners were streaming down, only too glad to get out of range of their own guns! I saw half a dozen at the corner of Liverpool Trench and Garden Street. They seemed very happy trying to converse with us. One of them – a boy about twenty – asked me the nearest way to the station; he wanted to get to England as soon as possible!

The Tanks went over. As daylight came on the battle raged furiously. Our troops were still advancing. Messages soon came through that St. Julien had been taken.

Our time was drawing near. At 8.30 we were to go over. At 8 we were all 'standing to' behind the parapet waiting to go over. Colonel Best-Dunkley came walking along the line, his face lit up by smiles more pleasant than I have ever seen before. 'Good morning, Floyd; best of luck!' was the greeting he accorded me as he passed; and I, of course, returned the good wishes. At about 8.20 Captain Andrews went past me and wished me good luck; and he then climbed over the parapet to reconnoitre. The minutes passed by. Everybody was wishing everybody else good luck, and many were the hopes of 'Blighty' entertained – not all to be realized. It is a wonderful sensation – counting the minutes on one's wrist-watch as the moment to go over draws nigh. The fingers on my watch pointed to 8.30, but the first wave of D Company had not gone over. I do not know what caused the delay. Anyhow, they were climbing over. Eventually, at 8.40, I got a signal from Dickinson to go on. So forward we went, platoons in column of route. Could you possibly imagine what it was like? Shells were bursting everywhere. It was useless to take any notice where they were falling, because they were falling all round; they could not be dodged; one had to take one's chance: merely to go forward and leave one's fate to destiny. Thus we advanced, amidst shot and shell, over fields, trenches, wire, fortifications, roads, ditches and streams which were simply churned out of all recognition by shell-fire. The field was strewn with wreckage, with the mangled remains of men and horses lying all over in a most ghastly fashion – just like any other battlefield I suppose. Many brave Scottish soldiers were to be seen dead in kneeling positions, killed just as they were firing on the enemy. Some German trenches were lined with German dead in that position. It was hell and slaughter. On we went. About a hundred yards on my right, slightly in front, I saw Colonel Best-Dunkley complacently advancing, with a walking stick in his hand, as calmly as if he were walking across a parade ground. I afterwards heard that when all C Company officers were knocked out he took command in person of that Company in the extreme forward line. He was still going strong last I heard of him.

We passed through the 166th Brigade. We left St. Julien close on our left. Suddenly we were rained with bullets from rifles and machine-guns. We extended. Men were being hit everywhere. My servant, Critchley, was the first in my platoon to be hit. We lay down flat for a while, as it was impossible for anyone to survive standing up. Then I determined to go forward. It was no use sticking here for ever, and we would be wanted further on; so we might as well try and dash through it. 'Come along – advance!' I shouted, and leapt forward. I was just stepping over some barbed wire defences – I think it must have been in front of Schuler Farm (though we had studied the map so thoroughly beforehand, it was impossible to recognize anything in this chaos) when the inevitable happened. I felt a sharp sting through my leg. I was hit by a bullet. So I dashed to the nearest shell-hole which, fortunately, was a very large one, and got my first field dressing on. Some one helped me with it. Then they went on, as they were, to their great regret, not hit! My platoon seemed to have vanished just before I was hit. Whether they were in shell-holes or whether they were all hit, or whether they had found some passage through the wire, I cannot say. I only know that, with the exception of Corporal Hopkinson and one or two Lewis Gunners who went forward soon after, they had all vanished. It was one of the many mysteries of a modern battlefield! Allen was going on all right: I saw him going on in front: I believe he got to Aviatik Farm! It was 10.20 a.m. when I was wounded. I lay in this shell-hole for some time. When I had been there about half an hour the enemy put down a barrage just on the line which contained my shell-hole! It was horrible. I thought I was lost this time. Shells were bursting all around me, making a horrible row; some of them were almost in the trench. I was covered with the fumes from one or two of them and also sniffed some gas. I put on my box-respirator. One piece of shrapnel hit me on the head, but, fortunately, I had my steel helmet on my head; so I was all right.

At 11.30 a.m. I decided that I might just as well be blown to bits in the open, trying to get back to safety, as lying in this shell-hole; so I made a dash for it and got out of the barrage. I inquired the way to the nearest aid post, and was told that it was a long way off. But I proceeded in the direction indicated. Before long I met Corporal Livesey returning from his bombing stunt with about half a dozen prisoners and a shrapnel wound in his back; also another lance-corporal, from D Company, who had been on a similar stunt and was wounded in the ear by a bullet. Some of the prisoners were also wounded. So we all walked down together.

From *At Ypres with Best-Dunkley* by Thomas Hope Floyd. Bodley Head. 1920.

The Fog of War: 31st July–1st August 1917

"'Jock' Dunlop, commanding 'A,' smiled, saluted me, led on, and disappeared in a cloud of mud, earth and smoke'"

On the left, or northern flank, of the 55th (West Lancashire) Division attack described above, the 39th Division – which is referred to – attacked. The 39th Division included the 1/1st Bn. Cambridgeshire Regiment whose objective was a feature known as Hill 19, on the eastern side of the village of St Julien, itself in German hands but to be captured by preceding waves. The Cambridgeshires' commanding officer contributed this account of the long and tiring day of battle to the regimental history. His pride in his battalion – shattered in the action – is evident; as is his 'chagrin' at being strenuously bombarded by the British artillery (friendly fire was not headline news in 1917!), and his disappointment when at the end of the action St Julien was evacuated as a result of misinformation reaching Divisional Headquarters.

It was nearing the time for us to start. Officers were leading their men up the steep banks of the Canal to the appointed place for parade, their figures looking ghost-like in the morning mist. Looking towards Ypres I saw some of our artillery crossing the bridges over the Canal at a trot, a good sign. We must have captured the Blue Line.

I climbed onto the top of the Canal Bank, with Nightingale at my heels, and looking towards the north saw the Cambridgeshires drawn up in artillery formation (platoons in column, with fifty yards interval between platoons and two hundred yards between Companies from front to rear). 'D' Company (Raven) was on the right, 'A' Company (Dunlop) on the left, and behind these two came 'C' Company (Jonas) and 'B' Company (Fison). Tebbutt, my intelligence officer, who was to guide our advance, was standing in front of 'D' Company taking a compass-bearing, with his scouts by his side. To the right of the Cambridgeshires about twenty 4.5 howitzers suddenly opened fire, almost drowning out Nightingale's shouted remark 'That's er tidy bunch o' Fritzes, sir... Look at 'em... They're carryin' our chaps.' Through the mist I could just distinguish a long line of German prisoners carrying wounded on stretchers towards one of the Canal bridges.

'Come on, Nightingale... It's time,' and I walked to the head of the Battalion.

We had about two miles to march over the open before reaching the British front line of the morning. Tebbutt moved off through the tall thistles and long grass, now very wet from the dew, and we all followed.

All went well for the first mile. To the left, near Hammond's Corner, several groups of German prisoners were coming back under escort and one of our tanks was making the best of its way forward over the soft ground.

Up till now no shells had fallen near us. I was congratulating myself on our good fortune when a bunch of a dozen threw up fountains of earth a hundred yards in front of us, directly in our path. We halted for a couple of minutes, then moved on into the area which had been shelled, for I guessed the Boche was starting an 'area shoot.' He would not shoot at the same place twice. Therefore, the best thing to do was to march straight towards the place where shells were bursting, wait until the shoot stopped, and then move across the shell-holes.

I suppose it was during these zigzag movements that Tebbutt lost touch with us, for on rising to move forward after one of our halts I could see nothing of him or his scouts. We had been lucky so far in guessing where the Boche would not shoot. After all, he could not see the ground over which we were crossing. He, too, was guessing. It was a toss-up who won, with a shade of odds on us, but for once our fortune was out. We walked right into it. Nightingale stepped in front of me and marched as policemen march when going on duty, the leading man almost touching the man behind him. I was the man behind... A flash and crash, and we were smothered with mud and earth... We pushed on, but not before I had seen Nightingale stagger and put his hand to his face. He was advancing again when, taking him by the shoulder, I tried to turn his face towards mine, but he averted it.

'Are you hit?'

'No, sir,' he answered, still pushing on. He knew my orders, that all men wounded in the advance as far as the Blue Line were to report to an officer and be sent back to the nearest Aid Post... I ordered him to go back with the other wounded; there were seven of them. Only two men had been killed. We had been lucky...

The men were as steady as rocks and full of cheer. When the news reached us that our tanks were in Kitchener's Wood 'D' Company sang, 'Oh! Oh! Oh! It's a loverly war.'

Tebbutt and his scouts rejoined us. He had been like the little boy at the fair, he had 'seen so many other funny things around

him that he lost father.' We saw only two dead Englishmen
and about twenty dead Germans.

The Battalion 'fell in,' and we continued our advance in
accordance with the Brigade time-table.

Things were different now. As we picked our way through
the shell-torn ground to the east of Mouse Trap Farm the
hostile fire increased in density. Fritz was hammering the
Wieltje-St Julien road on our right with his 'heavies.' Many
wounded of both sides and a number of prisoners were
moving down it. Poor devils! It was all very horrible. I waved
my map to signal to the leading Companies to incline to their
left in order to keep clear of the road. I might have given the
signal on a barrack square in good old peaceful England. The
whole Battalion inclined to the left with the precision of a
drill movement.

Away behind us, on Hill Top (so I heard afterwards), two
brigadiers were watching the progress of the battle.

'Isn't it splendid!' ejaculated Bellingham.

'Splendid?... It's magnificent!' said Hornby. 'My
God! Bellingham, my God!... Look, man, look at your
Cambridgeshires! It's glorious! It's glorious!'

They had seen the Battalion approaching the Black Line
– and the Boche had seen us also. We were getting it hot and
strong, guns and machine-guns. But the men never wavered.
The officers led on. A signal, and the platoons split up into
sections in file and headed on for St Julien, now lost in the
smoke of the shell-burst, now coming in view again; shaken
for the moment as shells exploded amongst them, then
reforming, but ever advancing steadily and slowly as if nothing unusual had happened. From our position in the Black
Line, two hundred yards in front, Tebbutt and I watched them
coming, the German trench affording us unexpectedly good
cover. This mere lad, fascinated by what were, to him, novel
surroundings, kept calling my attention to dead Germans,

bundles of brand new steel body-armour, the almost continuous concrete machine-gun emplacements, loaves of bread, and
abandoned rifles in the trench.

Five hundred yards to the north-east, below us, on the banks
of the Steenbeek, stood the ruins of St Julien. Over the tops of
the nearest houses I could see the bush-covered banks of the
Hanebeek (East), from which rose the mound known to us as
Hill 19. To our right the Hanebeek (South) oozed its way through
the bog-land to meet the Hanebeek (East) at the eastern end of
St Julien. To the east of this bog-land the ground rose to a height
a little above that on which we now were, but I could distinguish
the ruins of Fortuin, and further north, Border House.

Our shells were bursting in a line running east and west
beyond St Julien. Could that feeble fire be our artillery barrage
that was to creep to the final objective and cover the Cheshires,
Hertfordshires and the Black Watch in their advance? The
mist was thickening, and I could not be sure if I saw troops
moving near the line where our shells were bursting, but I
knew from my watch that all the other battalions of my brigade must be well over the Steenbeek and Hanebeek (East).
On my right our machine-guns were firing from Canteen
Trench. One of their officers put my mind at rest when he said
that the Cheshires, Hertfordshires, and the Black Watch were
approaching the hamlets, Winnipeg and Springfield, seven or
eight hundred yards north-east of St Julien.

Swinging the Cambridgeshires to the right, so as not to
interfere with the fire of our machine-guns, we entered the
Black Line on the eastern side of the Steenbeek. Here we
had to halt, for Stanway's reserve company of the Cheshires
was preparing to move forward in support of the rest of his
battalion.

My Battalion, still retaining its formation, took cover in
Canvas Trench and shell-holes. My God! how proud I was of
those men! They had been under fire, increasing in density,

for four-and-a-half hours with no cover save a slight mist, and now a few battered trenches and hundreds of muddy shell-holes. Bullets and shells were taking their toll. Fison, of 'B' Company, was wounded and his place taken by that 'Cœur de Lion,' 'Jerry' Walker. When passing a shell-hole I spoke a few words of congratulation to Awberry, who drew my attention to the fact that bullets were coming from our right where the 55th Division should have been level with us.

'Awberry, send a platoon up there to see if it can see Fortuin village,' I said, pointing in the direction he had indicated. But as I turned towards his shell-hole I saw that he was dead, shot through the head. It was Awberry who had led the raid from Hill Top which had resulted in the capture of the German with the fish-hooks. Poor Awberry, how he had hated it all! Two subalterns (Ritchie and Rash) were wounded, and 35 N.C.O.'s and men killed or wounded, and we had not fired a single shot! Yet everybody was cool and collected. Wonderful fellows!

A patrol, sent into St Julien, found two 5.9 German guns with a lot of ammunition. They might be of use to us, so a runner was despatched with a message to the nearest artillery observation-officer giving an exact description of their whereabouts.

The hour for our advance to Hill 19 having arrived, 'A' and 'D' Companies moved forward. 'Jock' Dunlop, commanding 'A,' smiled, saluted me, led on, and disappeared in a cloud of mud, earth and smoke. On my right I had glimpses of two platoons of 'C' Company, under Spicer, running eastward on the crest of the rising ground. What could have happened to the 55th Division? Had it failed? If it had, the position of my right flank and that of the whole of the 39th Division was getting more precarious every yard we advanced to the north-east. Fortunately, Canvas and Capital Trenches had been dug by the Boches against an attack from the east (i.e. the direction of Fortuin). I sent Jonas with his remaining two platoons of 'C' Company to occupy Border House and hold it at all costs. Nothing was to tempt him from his position save a written order from me or my successor.

That was the last I saw of the gallant Jonas. His Company still contained many of the original N.C.O.'s and men recruited from around Wisbech and Whittlesey. They were destined to play the rôle of a breakwater against successive waves of the German counter-attacks. This they carried out to the uttermost, but at the cost of their own annihilation. As is told later, Private Muffett's party withdrew in the evening on the receipt of the written order; repatriated prisoners having also told how two parties of 'C' Company held on to two advanced concrete dugouts. These were full of wounded, but they held out for two days, hoping against hope that further British attacks would carry the line forward again. Eventually shortage of ammunition and the septic condition of the wounded, several of whom were delirious, forced them to bow to the inevitable.

Jonas and the majority of his men have no known resting-place; their names are graven on the Memorials to the Missing and their deeds on our hearts.

In times of stress it is remarkable how trivial things attract a man's attention from greater matters. Prisoners had been drifting through our lines, some terrified, with but one desire, to reach a place of safety, and others defiant. I was speaking to an officer of another regiment when, pointing to an approaching figure he shouted:

'Lor', blimey! Here comes Prince Ruprecht himself.'

The man walking towards us was a German officer immaculately dressed, wearing white kid gloves and carrying a black ebony cane with a silver knob. Addressing my companion, he said in excellent English:

'I am a German officer, and demand an officer escort to take me to a place of safety.'

'Half a mo', Cocky, you won't want these,' casually remarked England's representative as he relieved the prisoner of his automatic pistol, field-glasses and cane, and dropped them into a sandbag held open by an orderly. Then running his hands over the German's pockets he extracted a watch and note-case, adding, 'Nor these.'

Here I intervened. The watch and money must be returned. 'Here you!' said my companion, addressing a diminutive Cheshire private who, with the aid of his rifle as a walking-stick, was limping back towards the place whence he had set out at dawn. 'Take this back with you, and see that he doesn't dirty his gloves.'

A runner brought me news that 'A' and 'D' had reached Hill 19 and that 'C' Company had occupied Border House, killing or capturing its garrison. The German officer was forgotten, and I moved forward to a concrete gun-pit, where Baynes Smith, my acting adjutant, had established Battalion H.Q. about two hundred yards short of Border House. When I got there the first man I met was Nightingale, a patch of field-dressing and a plaster across his nose. He was much engaged with the task of forcing upwards of a dozen prisoners to leave the shelter of the gun-pit for the less salubrious road leading to the prisoners' cage.

For a few brief moments the mist lifted. On the crest of the hill, a mile to our front, we saw German artillery and infantry retiring in disorder, and north of Winnipeg, a crowd of two or three hundred Germans that had surrendered to the Cheshires, whilst the Hertfordshires looked to be fighting around Springfield, but the trees and hedgerows interfered with our view. Not a single man of the 55th Division could be seen north of the Hanebeek (East). Then the fog fell like a curtain and all was mystery again. It was 11 a.m.

A ghost-like figure loomed through the mist. It was a runner from Canvas Trench where Spicer was watching our right rear. His written message conveyed the disturbing information that fifty men of the Liverpool Scottish and one officer had been seen on the banks of the Hanebeek (South) where that stream was cut by the Black Line. These troops were moving westward instead of north-eastward! They had mistaken the Hanebeek (South) for the Hanebeek (East). Had we been able to teach all our officers and non-commissioned officers the proper use of the compass this mistake would have been averted.

The Liverpool Scots were collected by Spicer and put to swell the garrison of Canvas Trench, where they did noble work and got into touch with some troops of the 55th Division holding Fortuin Farm, three hundred yards south of Border House. It was now clear that the whole of the right flank of the Cheshires and Cambridgeshires was 'in the air.' A report on the situation was sent to advanced Brigade H.Q. at Corner Cot.

The question was, 'What does "A" do now?' I thought of my pipe (like Mr Baldwin). I put my hand into my haversack and drew it out. A bullet had passed through the bowl, but, thank goodness, it had not split the wood. Some clay to plug the two holes, and a couple of inches of plaster from my field dressing case, remedied the disaster, and Mr Dunhill's creation was smoking soothingly. As I puffed my pipe in the shelter of the gun-pit my mind ran through all that we had done and what we ought to do. The Black Watch, I knew, had gained most of their objectives, the Cambridgeshires were well advanced in their work of consolidating their positions, but had lost a number of officers and men, how many I could not be sure. The feeble fire of the artillery covering the early stages of the advance of the Black Watch, Hertfordshires and Cheshires, had been explained by my Intelligence Officer,

who said that he had seen many of our guns stuck in the mud.
But why had the 55th Division failed to reach the Hanebeek
east of Border House? Well, it was no good worrying about
the why and the wherefore of it; the fact remained – they had
failed. That was all about it. No doubt they would push on as
soon as possible. I was just about to send a suggestion to the
nearest brigade commander of the 55th that, as our brigade
had advanced right up to the Green Line, he should bring
his reserves into the 39th Division area and attack the Boche
in flank from Border House and Canvas Trench, when an
unexpected change altered everything. Suddenly the German
gun-fire increased. Shells crashed around us. News of a dis-
concerting nature reached me from my forward Companies.
They could see the Hertfordshires and Cheshires retiring.

It was all so confusing. Droves of Germans, their hands above
their heads, crying 'Kamerad, Kamerad,' were running past my
gun-pit. They said they had been captured near Winnipeg,
and they had but one thought, to get to the prisoners' cage.
I wondered how many would get there through that barrage
of shells and bullets.

It was 11.30 a.m. The mist was clearing away. Long lines
of Germans could be seen crossing the Winnipeg-Springfield
road, and one battalion was advancing on Border House and
Hill 19 from the east. If nothing was done to help them,
the Black Watch would be cut off and the Cheshires and
Hertfordshires wiped out. The Brigade signallers had failed
to get a telephone line through to me. (They had about as
much chance of doing that as of finding a snowball in Hell.)
Therefore, it would have to be an infantryman's battle, for I
could not warn our artillery in time. There was just a hope
that the 'gunner' officer at our advanced Brigade H.Q. at
Corner Cot would see the Germans and get through to his
guns. Anyway, with luck, my runners would reach him, sooner
or later.

Walker with 'B' Company was in St Julien. I told him to move across the Steenbeek west of that village and to attack the right of the advancing Boches; at the same time assuring him that Spicer and the remaining two platoons of 'C' Company were moving forward to help him. The crews of two derelict tanks, with half-a-dozen Lewis guns, were willing and anxious to fight anybody. They took Spicer's place in guarding our right flank.

Our gun-pit, with roof and sides of concrete, was open at each end. To protect us from the German side we had piled up a mound of earth, leaving the British, or south, end open. Over the concrete roof, and for five or six yards beyond the concrete sides, the Germans had heaped earth, which was now overgrown with grass. It was not a residence calculated to command a high rent in times of peace, but at that hour many a soldier would have given all he possessed to be allowed to stay beneath its shelter. The floor of the gun-pit was roughly ten feet square. Besides Baynes Smith and Sergt.-Major Pull I had 'Baby Smith' the signalling officer, some runners, and Nightingale, so we had a 'full house.'

As I sat at the southern entrance, anxiously waiting for any sign of life from the telephone, a dismal picture presented itself. Thirty yards away a very gallant officer had, for the last hour, made frantic efforts to extract his tank from a network of barbed wire and a sea of mud. During a momentary lift of the mist the Boche gunners had spotted him and had never ceased to pelt him with high explosive shells. He had sent his crew away to help guard our right flank, but, like a good sea captain, had stuck to his ship – alone. (After he was killed we took the remaining Lewis guns from his tank and mounted them on our gun-pit.) A wounded German boy, with a bayonet wound in the abdomen, had been slowly dying in the mud outside the gun-pit. We could not help him; Hunter, our doctor, was killed. Each one of us would have wished to put a bullet through the poor boy's head to end his agony, but no one had the courage or the right to do it. His pleading eyes fascinated us until, his head falling back into the mud, they stared fixedly at the sky.

Although messages had been received from my Companies, they grew less frequent as time went on. Often, under such circumstances, no news was good news: sometimes it is different, for there may not be anyone left to send news.

It will be remembered that Tebbutt, my very youthful Intelligence Officer, had been with me when we crossed the Black Line. He, with his scouts, had pushed on through St Julien and eventually to Hill 19. There he had done excellent work in supplying the Company officers with such information of the general situation as he had gathered in his wanderings. He mounted a 'salved' German machine-gun and got it manned and in action. His narrative is so well and simply told that I give it in his own words, from the time when the Hertfordshires and Cheshires were being driven back. He writes of the situation on Hill 19:

"Seeing that there were only two subalterns left in charge who, though very cool, had very little military imagination or idea what special measures were needed to meet the contingency, I thought I had better take over the command of the front line. The situation was rather obscure. There appeared to be no one on our right or left. It seemed certain that there must be some Cheshires and Hertfordshires in front, but I did not know if they were merely stragglers or a formed body. It was, therefore, difficult to know if it was advisable to have a barrage put down by our guns in front of us. I could see troops some five hundred yards in front of us, but could not determine who they were. It seemed the best thing to find the Colonel, report the situation, and get his orders... During the last half-hour I had been watching the men rather carefully, as I was not sure how the fact of other men retiring through them would affect them. They were very quiet, and hardly talked at all, but were very steady and obeyed orders promptly. They had dug a good trench. …Telling Corporal Tabor I was going back to find the Colonel, and my servant to go on digging a trench for me (as he had hurt himself going over some barbed wire), I went back over the Hanebeek (East) alone. A little way on I saw Twelvetrees going back, wounded in the jaw. He could not speak much, but he did not seem badly hurt although bleeding quite a lot. He went on while I was having a look round. A few minutes later, when walking back, I was aware of a shell bursting close behind me and of a burning sensation in my left hand, and of the fact that I was sitting on the ground. I picked myself up and, on looking at my hand, found that it was mostly gone, and there was a fountain of blood spurting up from the middle of the back of it. Though a bit dazed, I had enough sense to realise that I must stop this, so I grabbed the wrist with my other hand and was relieved to find that the violent spurts stopped. I started walking back, as I could not take my hand away to get out my shell-dressing, hoping to find someone in the Black Line who could do it up. After walking for a few minutes, getting rather alarmed by the fact that there seemed to be no one about, I heard a shout from behind me and, turning, found the Colonel, Adjutant, Spicer and the Sergeant-Major standing at the entrance of a gun-position some fifty yards behind me. I went back to them. Sergeant-Major Pull started to do up my wound. I remember the Colonel telling him to do something, and him saying that he thought that would hurt me, and the Colonel saying not to take any notice of that, and of saying myself that it was not likely to hurt any more than it was doing at present. The gun-pit was a concrete affair open at both ends, and sunk about two feet below the level of the ground. The Colonel, Baynes Smith, 'Baby' Smith, Spicer and Pull were there. Sitting down by the side were Twelvetrees and a Cheshire sergeant. Spicer gave me some brandy and I sat down. I felt very faint and the Colonel gave me some more. I told them all I could about the situation. I remember Smith sending off a runner rather sharply. Then Spicer was told to go to St Julien to make sure who was in it, with a crowd of Cheshires and Hertfordshires who had been collected there. I thought what a rotten job it would be. The Colonel also told Smith to clear the place out, as it was getting too crowded. I also asked where the doctor was, and heard he was killed. After a bit, a runner came in with a message, and the Colonel said that the Brigadier had gone out and he must go across to Brigade to take over. He told Baynes Smith to take command of the Battalion, and asked him if he was quite sure he understood the situation. His orderly took away the pack I was sitting against, and they both went out. After that Walker came in and talked to Baynes Smith. I thought he seemed a bit shaky (as he has since told me he was). His orderly had been shot by a sniper, going across the open, and he asked for another man to go back with him. He showed Baynes Smith where he thought the sniper was operating from. It was gradually dawning on me that there was little chance of getting any stretcher-bearers to take me down, and Baynes Smith also told me that, if I thought I could manage it, he thought it would be best to try and walk down; so, at last, I determined to have a shot at it. I borrowed a stick from Spicer and took my brandy flask in my hand, so that I could take a sip of it when I felt faint, and started off. Once on my feet I did not feel so bad. There were odd shells dropping about pretty continuously. Before reaching the Black Line, I saw Hill in a shell-hole with Twelvetrees looking after him. Twelvetrees said he was pretty bad, and he looked it. His orderly was dead in the same hole. Passing the Black Line, the signalling officer of the Cheshires shouted out something about a blighty one which annoyed me. I did not cross the Hanebeek (South) at once as I wanted to avoid the Vanheule Farm, which was being shelled. Just in front of me, as I crossed, was a Tommy, and as a shell burst close to us I gave vent to my feelings by saying that I thought it the limit being shelled after being hit. I passed him, and walked up the edge of the wire of the Black Line. I only saw one dead Sussex in it on a stretch of about three hundred yards. I got on to the road just in front of Vanheule Farm. In front of me was another officer whom I caught up and found to be Fison. He was hit in the side and arm and looked very white. I could walk faster than he, but had to lie down every now and again, which he could not do, so we kept passing and repassing each other. We passed some German dead, and I discarded my steel hat for a German one which I thought would make a good souvenir. Later on we passed some pioneers, who were making up the road, who asked us if there was anything they could do for us. I was only anxious to get somewhere where I should be attended to, and get an ambulance. After passing them, my memory fails me till I arrived at Hammond's Corner. I must have been very faint and know I went off quite once. Here there was a sort of aid-post and several doctors, but they were very busy. I lay down and a padre gave me some more brandy. I gathered from him that there was no chance of getting a lift there. This, followed by a '5.9,' which burst about ten yards away and covered me with dirt, decided me to go on to the Canal Bank. The road from there on was pretty crowded. There was a six-inch battery coming up and lots of limbers about. At last I got down to the Canal Bank, crossed it by Bridge 4 and walked into the First Aid Station. There I was promptly very faint, and had some more brandy. I hardly remember having my wound dressed, only asking the doctor if he thought my hand would have to come off, and he said he thought it would. He said that I should be a stretcher-case and, almost at once, I was put in an ambulance and sent off to the Corps' Dressing Station."

It was noon when a battalion of the enemy attacked 'D' and 'A' Companies. Thanks to stout hearts, well-sited trenches, and a number of Lewis and machine-guns salved from tanks, the hostile assaulting troops were almost decimated, save at the northern end of Hill 19, where the Winnipeg-St Julien road ran through a shallow cutting situated fifty yards in front of our trench. The Germans had got into the cutting but they could not get out, for elements of the Sussex, Hertfordshires and Cheshires, still in the north-east end of St Julien, were able to shoot any men attempting to leave the west end of the cutting, and 'D' Company covered the other end. The Boche was a good fighter, and did a brave thing – he attacked, and was wiped out by the Cambridgeshires, who added two Boche machine-guns to their armament store. It was during the progress of this attack that Tebbutt came to Battalion H.Q.

Although repulsed on its left wing, the hostile attack was nearing the north-east end of St Julien. Walker had crossed the Steenbeek, and, keeping under cover of the trees and houses, presently appeared at the north end of the village; catching the Germans' right in enfilade, he inflicted heavy losses, and, for the moment, drove it back. The Cambridgeshires, and mixed troops of other units, together with the Black Watch, were putting up a good fight unaided by our own artillery.

The mist which had left us in doubt as to what was happening now lifted.

Down came the German artillery and machine-gun barrage, crashing, thundering, and whistling on our front line, where we were, and back beyond Vanheule Farm, where we had located advanced Brigade H.Q. Across the whole of our Corps' front and that of the Corps on our right the Boche was advancing in force. He reached the outskirts of St Julien. A runner from 'D' Company brought the news that there were only three officers left alive between 'A' and 'D' Companies, one of whom was wounded, and none in 'C' Company at Border House. They were all running short of ammunition, to replenish which volunteers had been called for to attempt to salve cartridges from the derelict tanks. This perilous work was successfully accomplished.

As our wire to the Brigade was again cut, and every man with a rifle needed, Nightingale and I set off to run the seven hundred yards to Vanheule Farm to get the assistance of our artillery. As may be readily imagined I did not loiter by the way to admire the view. Probably the men I passed thought I was running away. I think they did, for in reply to some shouted remarks I have a recollection of Nightingale bawling back:

'Cowards? Bloody liars! I'll punch yer bloody 'eds when Oi come back.'

We got to Vanheule Farm. When I had recovered my breath I set the machine-guns at work from the Black Line to fire on the line Winnipeg Cemetery-Northern Houses of St Julien. Then I got through to the Brigadier and asked for our artillery to fire on the same line. He told me that most of our guns had been stuck in the mud when the Cheshires and Hertfordshires had advanced against the Green Line. That would have accounted for the feeble creeping barrage. He assured me that the 55th Division had reported the arrival of its leading battalions at the Hanebeek (East), whereas I knew that they had lost their direction and, in the mist, had mistaken the Hanebeek (South) for the Hanebeek (East). One of the Companies of the Liverpool Scots had, in fact, attacked our advanced Brigade H.Q. while the Hertfordshires and Cheshires were approaching Winnipeg and Springfield. I presume it was these contradictory reports that led the Division and Corps to hold back their artillery fire and leave us to fight our battles without the support of our guns. The great advance, which had progressed so much in favour of the British forces in the early morning, was now degenerating into a disjointed fight. I begged the Brigadier to come to his advanced Brigade H.Q. and conduct the battle, and urged that the 116th Brigade be ordered to advance up the line of the Hanebeek (East) to relieve the pressure on my right and the left of the 55th Division. I do not know who, or what circumstances, prevented this plan being put into operation, but I am convinced it would have succeeded. On looking through my diary, I find that I despatched two runners to Brigade with this scheme in writing as early as 11.10 a.m., but they must have been killed or wounded, for Bellingham did not receive it – the fortune of war.

With the Brigadier's promise to turn our artillery on to assist us in the defence of Hill 19 and St Julien I left Vanheule Farm for my journey back to the gun-pit.

It was half-an-hour before our artillery opened fire. I have no idea what caused this delay. The result was immediate. The enemy fell back everywhere between Winnipeg and St Julien. As the Boches left the cover of hedgerows, ditches and trenches, they were cut down by our machine-guns, Lewis guns and rifles. After this, except for desultory fire by snipers, and occasional shells, comparative quiet reigned for an hour. More ammunition and Lewis guns were collected from the tanks for the garrison of St Julien, Hill 19, and Border House. The gun-pit was cleared of all wounded and reconstructed for defence with four Lewis guns on its roof. The Liverpool Scots and Stanway's Cheshires were ready for all comers in Canvas and Capital Trenches. West of St Julien, Walker with the survivors of his own Company, and a few of the Hertfordshires and Sussex, were awaiting developments.

The light had improved so much as to enable us to see the whole length of the ridge which runs east of Winnipeg-Springfield road. Baynes Smith and I were looking at Wurst Farm (five hundred yards east of Winnipeg), where we noticed some movement, when the German artillery opened out in real earnest across the front of the Corps on our right. From Fortuin to the south-west nothing could be seen save smoke, spurts of rising or falling earth, and the white 'woolly-bears' of the bursting shrapnel. Wave upon wave of advancing German infantry were passing to the right of Hill 19, our shells bursting amongst them, whilst the Cambridgeshires, on Hill 19 and Border House, enfiladed them with Lewis guns. Suddenly the position of my Battalion was blotted out of view by an intense bombardment from hostile guns.

By this time I knew that all the officers of 'C' and 'D' Companies were either killed or wounded, and that Sergt.-Major Burbridge had taken command.

The rattle of rifle-fire from Border House and Capital Trench told me that the Germans were across the Hanebeek. The Sussex were falling back through St Julien, but Walker and the Black Watch still held both banks of the Steenbeek west of St Julien. Fearing a complete envelopment of my forward position, I withdrew 'A' and 'D' Companies to the line Border House-St Julien. This was the position when, at 5.45 p.m., I heard that the Germans were at Fortuin and still attacking. The bombardment of our position increased in density. The climax came half-an-hour later, when our own guns opened on our position. Battalion H.Q. came in for rather more than its share. We were being shot at from north, south and east. My telephone-wire was cut. Outside the shelter of the gun-pit the German machine-gun bullets whipped flicks of mud into the air, or zipped by to find a billet about the Black Line. All my runners were dead, wounded or exhausted. I had begun to write a message when one of our shrapnel shells burst overhead, killing Company Sergt.-Major Pull and blowing the writing-pad out of my hand. Having told Baynes Smith to withdraw the Cambridgeshires, except 'B' Company, to the Black Line, I shouted to Nightingale that I was going to Brigade and started to run for it. The first three hundred yards was the worst part of that race against shells, bullets, and time. We ran, threw ourselves into shell-holes to get

our breath, and then ran on again. Every time we got up to run
the Boche machine-gun bullets zipped past us. Automatically
we took to diving from one shell-hole to another. A wounded
Liverpool Scot raised his head and begged us to carry him to
safety. But it was not one life we had set out to save; it was, possibly, three hundred. Poor devil, we had to leave him. Another
rush and I dived into a wet hole. I had lost Nightingale!

'Beg pardin, sir,' came a familiar voice from behind me on
my right. I turned my head, very slightly, for I was terribly
afraid. My heart was thumping as if it would burst. I shouted,
'Are you hurt?'

Two fierce brown eyes looked at me out of a white face
beneath a steel helmet.

'Oh! no, sir; but I was jest thinkin', we ain't both goin' to
get to Brigade – leastways not likely – Oi was jest thinkin'...'
Then he disappeared in a cloud of mud as a shell burst
between us. 'As I was sayin', sir, 'adn't you best tell me wot
you was goin' ter sy to the Brigade?–Jest in case, yer know.'

I told him. Then we did the run-and-tumble turn until we
reached Canteen Trench, from whence we ran, or walked, to
Vanheule Farm. Fortunately, the telephone to the Brigadier
was through. Thus it came about that our guns were told that
we did not want them to shoot at us as we did not like it.

Some food, and two bottles of German soda-water,
consumed under the thick stone roof of what had probably
been Vanheule Mill, revived us. After a pipe and a talk with
Brown, Nightingale and I started back for the gun-pit. The
hostile shelling was not so severe. Our guns had found some
other target and the mist was again thickening. We passed the
Liverpool Scot. He was dead.

When we reached the gun-pit 'A' and 'D' Companies were
falling back towards the Black Line. Baynes Smith and two
men were lying on the roof firing Lewis guns. Taking his pipe
from his mouth, 'Baynes' turned half round and said:

'There's no sign of anybody coming back from Border House, although Burbridge says he sent an orderly through with a verbal message for "C" Company to retire.'

All the wounded had been sent back to Canteen Trench. And although we waited for a quarter-of-an-hour, no one came back from Border House.

'Did "C" Company ever get that message to withdraw?' I asked 'Baynes.'

'I expect so, sir,' replied the imperturbable adjutant, and continued shooting.

Then a runner, with a bandaged head, came over from Canvas Trench. He brought a written message out of his pocket, handed it to me, and collapsed to the ground.

'There's firing at Border House,' said 'Baynes.'

I read the message:

'I received a message, by orderly, to retire, but as Captain Jonas, before he was killed, said we were not to retire without written orders from the C.O., I am holding Border House. There are only three of us left alive, and two of those chaps is wounded. I am holding Border House until I get written order to retire. (signed) Private Muffett. 7.30 p.m.'

I asked for volunteers to carry a written message to the gallant defender of Border House ordering his retirement. Spicer and the wounded orderly crept back to Canvas Trench, and after many hairbreadth escapes delivered my order to withdraw.

Throughout the day Muffett had held the advanced post with his Lewis gun. Every time he ran short of ammunition he made a trip across the open to an abandoned tank and replenished his store of drums. Targets at long range did not interest him, he 'preferred to wait and make sure.' He was one of the two men I recommended during the war for the V.C. (he was awarded the D.C.M.). A fine Lewis gunner and a natural soldier, Muffett was prominent again during the Somme battle in March, 1918. Clayton, for whom he worked in peace time, persuaded him after the war to try to enlist in the Regular Army. He possessed the strength of a horse and abnormal powers of endurance, but the recruiting authorities rejected him as being 'under the required standard of physique.'

It was nearly 8.30 p.m. when Baynes Smith fired the last drum of cartridges and slid off the roof of the gun-pit. We threw the Lewis guns into a water-logged shell-hole, and those of us who had not been hit – 'Baynes', Nightingale and I – each helping a wounded man, set out for Corner Cot.

It took me nearly an hour to get my man in safety to Canteen Trench. The poor fellow had lost a lot of blood, and had to rest every hundred yards. I remember that he never said a single word until we reached the trench. Then he just took my hand and, grasping it, whispered, 'Thanks!'

I found Baynes Smith talking to the adjutant of the 13th Sussex – an able and stout-hearted officer who was full of information and sound ideas. By the time we had got the units composing the Cambridgeshires, Cheshires, Hertfordshires, Sussex and Liverpool Scottish sorted out and distributed along Canteen and Canvas Trenches, and had linked up with the 55th Division at Wine House, it was dark. Firing had ceased and all was quiet.

We all wanted sleep more than anything else, but there was to be no rest for me that night. The adjutant of the Sussex confided to me the disturbing news that his C.O. had sent a report to his Brigadier to say that the Germans held St Julien. It was then 1.30 a.m. on 1 August. The Sussex commanding officer, like many others in a similar position, was prostrate from exhaustion, and could give me no clear information. I at once informed my Brigadier that Walker (with 'B' Company and part of 'C' Company) was still holding the whole of St Julien, in the centre of which a medical officer had an aid-post, in a cellar, full of wounded men. We collected a party of Sussex and Cambridgeshires and set to work to carry the wounded out of St Julien, and to drag two captured German guns out of the village. Whilst this work was in progress, a message from the Division reached us. St Julien would be subjected to an intense bombardment by our artillery at dawn! It was the fog of war again. Of the lot of us, the Sussex adjutant was the only one to keep his head.

He said, 'We must get your men out, sir, and the wounded, and leave the guns.'

This brought me to my senses. It was pouring with rain. Walker and his men, together with the Sussex, brought all the wounded back, and the village, for the retention of which we had fought all day, was abandoned.

The G.H.Q. official communiqué stated 'that the Germans had recaptured St Julien' !

It was still raining heavily when, about noon, I received orders to withdraw the 118th Brigade from the line, leaving the position in charge of the 116th Brigade.

Of the 19 officers and 451 other ranks of the Cambridgeshires who took part in the battle, 16 officers and 286 other ranks were killed or wounded.

From *The Cambridgeshires 1914 to 1919* by Brig.-Gen. E. Riddell, CMG, DSO and Col. M.C. Clayton, DSO. Cambridge: For the Regiment. 1934.

A QUIET DAY AT CUINCHY: 15TH SEPTEMBER 1917

'nothing whatever exciting'

While battle raged in the Ypres Salient, just ten miles down the road at Cuinchy the 2nd Bn. Oxfordshire & Buckinghamshire Light Infantry — obstinately referred to as the 52nd LI by its officers and men alike — was engaged in holding the line in what was then a very quiet sector. While Lt. J.E.H. Neville wrote home that 'nothing whatever exciting' was happening, in the same letter he recorded that his Platoon Sergeant and a brother subaltern whom he had known at Eton had both been badly wounded.

There has been nothing whatever exciting on our piece of front, and of fighting, as little as ever. Also there is not so much patrolling these days. Up till a little while ago, there was a patrol out every night, but, nowadays, only when there is some definite object to be attained.

Yesterday I had my Platoon Sergeant, Boddington by name, sniped through the head, but not killed, thank God. He was damned lucky, the bullet, hitting a sandbag, ricocheted into three pieces, of which one hit him in the nose and the other two split his helmet. The latter undoubtedly saved his life. He had been looking over the top at two Boches, who had just thrown a bomb, and he was getting direction to throw a rifle grenade at them when the sniper pipped him. I had been doing exactly the same thing a little further to the left, and had heard the bullet sing over my head soon after popping down behind the parapet, after getting the direction of the brutes. The Sergeant lost a lot of blood, but seemed quite cheery when I bid him good-bye in the Aid Post.

Ames, who was next for leave, has had his hope ditched by a Divisional Order which states that no officer, who is out for the first time as an officer, can get leave until he has done five months in the country.

Just as I had written those last words, a Sergeant came in and said, "Beg pardon, Sir, Mr. Ames has had his leg blown off." I seized my helmet and rushed upstairs to find him lying stretched on the firestep. His right leg was shattered above the ankle. All he said was, "Isn't this bloody." So he has got his leave after all!

From *The War Letters of a Light Infantryman* by Captain J.E.H. Neville, MC. Printed privately by Sifton Praed & Co. 1930.

HELL IN POLYGON WOOD: 30TH SEPTEMBER 1917

'his body, doubtless blown to pieces, was not found'

The weight of artillery firing out of the Ypres Salient during the 3rd Battle was immense, but if anything the amount firing into it was greater, because the Salient, a relatively confined space chock full of men, animals and materials of war, was surrounded on three sides by the Germans. Every square yard was within range and nowhere, and no-one, was safe from some airborne hazard, as Captain D.V. Kelly, a staff officer of 110th Infantry Brigade describes in this account of attack and counter-attack in Polygon Wood. The piece also contains an account of the death of Lt. Col. P.E. Bent of the 9th Leicesters in an action which resulted in his being awarded a posthumous Victoria Cross.

All roads and tracks except the Menin road had been totally obliterated, and the Army rapidly replaced them by plank roads for vehicles and "duckboard" tracks for foot transport. The enemy had concentrated every available gun and used ammunition with lavish prodigality, constantly smashing the new tracks which were as constantly repaired.

As the infantry line was pushed forward, each advance at great sacrifice, huge masses of artillery followed behind, the guns bunching together wherever a piece of relatively dry and unbroken ground could be found, and to the guns came, often twice a day, melancholy trains of pack mules and horses, their bodies caked with mud and loaded with ammunition, the weary drivers on foot urging them on amid shells crashing right and left, and shrapnel bursting overhead. Our massed guns – the crews often exposed without shelter day and night for several weeks – and wooden tracks – off which it was seldom possible to step on account of the condition of the ground – were visited at frequent intervals by bursts of shell-fire, always including a proportion of gas-shells. The

"mustard" variety of gas-shell, already referred to, was difficult to distinguish from the more harmless kinds unless the
stuff splashed one, when it caused severe blisters, but had two
unpleasant characteristics – it lingered some hours and rose
in vapour under the influence of the sun if there was any, and
it contaminated clothes, so that persons thus affected could
infect a whole dugout. The other types in fashion were lachrymatory ("green-cross"), chiefly intended to make the gunners
wear masks, and the "blue-cross," which I think affected the
heart and lungs, causing coughing and hoarseness.

It was into this inferno that on September 30th a party of
officers from the Brigade came to reconnoitre Polygon Wood,
and had a foretaste of the prevailing conditions, as nearly every
member of the party suffered in some way from shell-fire.
That night the relief of the Australians in the newly-captured
Polygon Wood took place, the Brigade headquarters moving
into Hooge crater dugout, a noisome hole under what had
been Hooge Château, of which building not a stone could
be found. The crater itself was an old one blown when the
German front line had run there, at the side of the Ypres-Menin
road, and alongside the site of the château. Besides accumulat-
ing a great mass of artillery, the Germans had concentrated
all available reserves of troops – now greatly swollen by the
Russian collapse – opposite us, and each gain we made was
followed by heavy counter-attacks by fresh troops.

It was hardly therefore a surprise when early in the morning
of the 1st October – just as our relief was complete – a great
counter-attack was launched to recapture Polygon Wood. It was
accompanied by the heaviest enemy shelling I had encountered
– a series of barrages distributed in depth over several miles
of ground and maintained, with only occasional short lulls
throughout the day. I got halfway up to the front line, but not
having had definite orders to make contact, and knowing that
whatever happened reinforcements could not get through such

fire, I abandoned the attempt. My professional conscience was worried at the time, but it was really the sensible course.

The Brigade, as usual, stuck it out, and one dramatic incident I give as I heard it from the Adjutant and a company commander of the Battalion concerned. Colonel Bent, V.C., of the 9th Battalion was in a "pill box" on the west side of the wood when a runner came in saying "S.O.S. gone up from (the reserve) company." "Then we'd better get on," said the Colonel, and went forward with his headquarter personnel. Collecting the reserve company and everyone available, the Colonel led a counter-attack, and, struck down in the moment of victory, was last seen – for his body, doubtless blown to pieces, was not found – waving his pipe and calling, "Go on, Tigers!" This very gallant officer was, I think, only twenty-four at the time and was a civilian, but was so devoted to his work as a soldier that when granted ten days' leave he was back in less than a week with his Battalion.

From *39 Months with the 'Tigers,' 1915-1918* by D.V. Kelly, MC, formerly Captain, Leicestershire Regt. Ernest Benn Limited. 1930.

STOICISM IN THE FACE OF WOUNDS: 17TH OCTOBER 1917

'My left arm is off below the elbow'

Lt. N.V.H. Symons, MC, of the 2/8th Bn. Worcestershire Regiment, describes to his mother how he came to be wounded in No Man's Land on 17 October 1917 in advance of the front line near the River Scarpe.
Dear Mother

I know that it will be a great relief to you to know that I am coming home, for good, in a day or two, and yet shall not be a wreck or cripple for the rest of my life.

My left arm is off – below the elbow, which next to a foot is the amputation I mind least.

On Wed morning about 5 o'clock I was out in No Man's Land posting some snipers to do an hours shooting in the half light when we suddenly came on a German sap 15 yards away. The first thing I knew about it was a rifle going off point blank and I turned round and cursed the sniper who was with me as I thought he had let off his rifle. As I turned I saw the earth at his feet kick up and then a bullet came at my feet and I looked and saw the Huns within a handshake distance firing. Luckily they were either so flurried or such putrid shots that they did not hit us, anyway I was in a shell hole almost instantaneously. But the second I got in I saw a hand grenade just falling in my hole so I dashed off and got into another 5 yards further away.

As I ran they threw 6 at me which burst in a shower all round and I felt my left hand go numb as I fell into the crater and when I looked at it there was only a red pulp with splinters of bones and tendons in it on the end of my arm.

They threw some more but did not land any in my shell hole luckily.

The first thing I decided was that my only chance of not being captured was to stay still till night and then try and crawl back before they came out and got me.

Then I got out my field dressing and poured the iodine over the jelly and put on the dressings as well as I could and then bound my arm to my stick with my tie. As soon as this was done I ate my maps with all the H.Q.'s etc. marked on them and also pages out of my note book with invaluable information on them and then settled down to wait for dark.

Oh blessed morphia! I took one tablet in the morning, afternoon and evening, and while it does not send you asleep it banishes pain and consciousness of present surroundings and puts the most agreeable reflections and thoughts through your head for about a couple of hours.

About 8 o'clock the Huns called out something in German, and I peeped up and saw my man lying on the ground. I suppose he made some response or movement too, for they at once threw another bomb at him which luckily did not go off.

Later I heard them marching by me and then a command – a rush – a scuffle – and laughter so I imagine they either bayoneted him or captured him. They must have thought the bomb had killed me as they did not worry me any more, tho' I looked up again and saw their sentry peering through the wire in my direction.

I prayed to God to let me not be captured and resigned myself to his keeping and then prayed (a) for a fog or (b) for a hot day and he sent the latter and I was quite warm in the sun in my hole though it was cold above ground.

When it was quite dark I crawled out and found it a pretty awful game as my wound had got firstly stiff, I had lost pints of blood.

I just managed to get into our Sap when I collapsed and was delirious for some hours till I woke up in the Field Ambulance miles back.

The next morning I was brought on here and within an hour had my amputation. I am remarkably fit with a temp of only 100° and feel rather prouder of my constitution than I did.

I am going down to the Base today and ought to be crossing to England pretty soon.

My arm is quite comfortable compared to what it was before the operation and except for considerable soreness and a feeling as though my hand is still on and is very numb everything is all right.

Sister is just going to dress me so good bye.

Much love
Jerry
Original letter in the compiler's collection.

GASSED AT TOWER HAMLETS: OCTOBER 1917

'This was the most sinister place I ever saw'

William Linton Andrews, now a Company Quartermaster Sergeant (CQMS) in the 4th/5th Black Watch (the original 4th and 5th Battalions were combined in the spring of 1916) describes taking rations up to the front line during the later stages of Third Ypres and comments on the tenacity of the wounded.

After one turn in the front line we had two hundred casualties from gas alone. Going into a headquarters dugout to make a report, I stumbled over a man in the dimness. He murmured weakly, "Sorry, quartie, it's all right." I knelt down, thinking he was dying, and found his face was black. He murmured, "It's all right, quartie, I'm getting better." He had been gassed, but he was one of our veterans, and would not leave the battalion. He was allowed to lie there, and after a day or two he was able to crawl about again. Almost everyone of us had a whiff of gas about this time.

To get rations up to the Tower Hamlets section we took the carts to Mount Sorrel, where shelling rarely ceased, and then carried our stuff on the shoulder, by ghastly battle scenes, on a duck-board track overlooked by the enemy at Comines. No matter how fierce the shelling became, it was impossible to leave the duck-boards, for the crater area was a waste of churned-up mud, in which lay many of our dead, with the inevitable litter of an advance, such as mules with their bellies torn out, abandoned boxes of bombs, broken rifles, headless corpses, legs, and arms.

Coming back on the first night we had to run the gauntlet of many gas shells. There were so many casualties that it was thought best to go up in the morning when mist baffled the German observers at Comines, but we were always in danger at Mount Sorrel, and in that evil valley of the dead, Bodmin Copse. This was the most sinister place I ever saw. The ground had been smashed into a swamp in which many wounded were drowned. The track was broken every few yards. In one shell hole were a machine-gun crew who came down head-first into the mud; their legs were still sticking up from the slime.

I heard an extraordinary story of a wounded man's tenacity for life. It was said that, though he had both legs shattered, he rolled in from No Man's Land, passed our front line without being noticed or noticing it himself, and reached a battalion headquarters, a mile from where he was hit.

The tenacity of some of the wounded was, indeed, astounding. A man would struggle towards safety when almost unconscious. Thus my friend, C.Q.M.S. Campbell, when wounded in High Wood, and paralyzed down one side, crawled six hundred yards among the many dead, and having left a wounded chum planted rifles and spades every yard or two to guide stretcher-bearers back. He hardly remembered doing it, but was told afterwards that he had planted a straight row of rifles showing the way clearly as a line of white tape, and his chum was brought out.

From *Haunting Years: The Commentaries of a War Territorial* by William Linton Andrews. Hutchinson. nd (c.1932).

DELIGHTS OF THE YPRES SALIENT: 10TH NOVEMBER 1917

'We had not been in supports ten minutes before 'Jerry' found us'

Private William Sharpe, serving with the 2/8th Lancashire Fusiliers, describes his first vivid experience of going 'up the line,' near Passchendaele during the foul autumn of 1917 as the battle for that place ground to a dismal, belated halt. He was later a prisoner of war and in 1919 he wrote his memoirs, which he called 'The Answer,' in anticipation of his young son's inevitable question, 'What did you do in the Great War, Daddy?'

After all this drilling & stunts we were eventually warned for 'The Line' – and the warning consists of a big reminder of the punishment for deserting or cowardice... I had diorhea [sic]... but I did not report sick on account of that action being considered 'cowardice'... we were issued with emergency rations, Bombs, Bomb Bags, three days ordinary rations & well loaded up generally & in the pouring rain we started to march to supports... along a duck-board track – for there is not a spare yard of ground in front of Ypres that is not pitted with a shell hole... I will never forget this march, pouring down with rain, we made fairly good progress until it became dark & THEN fellows fell off the duckboards into shell holes & had to be got out, & suddenly the duckboards would be broken & the whole company would have to wade waist deep in mud & try to regain the duckboards, again we had to get off the boards to allow troops that had been relieved to come along in the opposite direction, again stretcher cases would have to be made way for... Smoking had been prohibited from our leaving Ypres – but I never enjoyed a smoke more than one I had under my waterproof cape – it was the one crumb of comfort in a night of misery...We had not been in supports ten minutes before 'Jerry' found us... the result of a shrapnel shell bursting 10 yards away was two casualties. An officer (2/Lt Evans) having two legs shattered & a private named Sargent... having an arm shattered & after dressing him as best I could, I took the gas guard with very mixed feelings...

W.A. Sharpe's manuscript journal is held by the Imperial War Museum, London.

RUNNING THE GAUNTLET OF BOURLON WOOD: 23RD NOVEMBER 1917

'I made my way back along that shell-swept, blazing road once more always dodging, every nerve strained listening for the shells and trusting in Providence.'

Communications during a battle were at best unreliable and almost always broke down. Telephone lines, where used, were liable to be destroyed by shellfire even if buried. In any case, in newly gained territory wires would be absent and communication between front-line positions and battalion headquarters relied on runners carrying messages across the battlefield, and then returning with the reply if one was called for. In this piece, H. Gregory of the 119th Coy., Machine Gun Corps (40th Division) describes his role as a runner during the desperate fighting in Bourlon Wood during the Battle of Cambrai.

We set off for the ravine at 4 a.m. All the guns were mounted, and the Infantry were in the same ravine, ready to go over the top at 5 a.m.

About 4.30 a.m. I was told that I had been put down for company runner, and that I had better get back to Headquarters before the bombardment opened, so I now left them and made my way back.

When we were going up to the ravine we had noticed a lot of dark objects lying about near some houses, but it was too dark to see what they were. It was now a little lighter, and I found that the forms we had seen were dead Germans; there would be about 30 of them. They had all been killed with the bayonet, defending the position.

Just as I arrived back at Headquarters the bombardment opened. Thousands of guns seemed to blaze out in all their fury. The flashes as the guns were fired, and the explosions as the shells burst in the wood, the rat-tat-tat of the machine guns, made it appear as if the world was tumbling to pieces.

The enemy now opened out with his Artillery and machine guns, and they sent shells over by the thousand. It was a veritable duel. The shells screamed, and the machine gun bullets swished in all directions.

We took cover at Brigade Headquarters, which had been a church. The Brigadier and his staff used the deep cellars.

The Machine Gunners went over the top with the infantry at 5 a.m. A lot of our men were killed before they left the ravine, as the enemy put his shells right into the middle of them, but the rest went forward with the Infantry.

We runners were kept at Headquarters until midday, ready to take dispatches up to the wood when needed.

At midday a lot of prisoners were brought to Headquarters. They had evidently gone through it, several were on the verge of collapse, as white as ghosts, their teeth chattering, and shaking all over with fear.

The wood had been like a raging furnace, and it seemed impossible for anything to live in the midst of all that fire, as the shells seemed to cover every inch of the place. The bombardment was as intense at midday as it had been when it started. The roar was deafening, and the screaming, shrieking shells, as they went both ways, made it seem as if there would not be anything or anybody left by the time they had finished.

About 1 p.m. I was called to go over with my first dispatch. They could give me no information as to where I should find the Officer that I wanted. A barrage was lying between the two opposing forces, and only open country to go through. This was going to be very dangerous work, and great care would have to be used to get through. I made across country until I got to the end of the road in front of the wood at the left-hand side. I was safe so far, but as I looked on that road it was a blazing, screaming, shell-bursting barrage all the way along, and if ever there was an inferno outside of Hell it was this road. It was one mass of flame the whole length, and I had to go near midway. As the shells came hurtling over, they cut the trees down with a crash. This was an added danger.

But I had to get on somehow. I took my courage in both hands, set my teeth, and made a start on that death-defying journey. As the shells came over, I dodged them as best I could, keeping my eyes open for a falling tree, and dodging from behind one tree to another.

I at last reached my destination. Sad news I received when I got there, as the men told me of the Officers, N.C.O.s, and men who had been killed long before they had reached the wood. Nearly half our company were gone, and the other half must carry on somehow. The Infantry had fared just as badly.

After delivering my dispatch, and getting one to take back telling of the plight they were in, I made my way back along that shell-swept, blazing road once more always dodging, every nerve strained listening for the shells and trusting in Providence.

I eventually arrived back at Headquarters, and on giving my message to our Commanding Officer, his face turned an ashen grey. The Company in the wood had suffered terrible casualties.

The first day I went up to the wood through this blazing barrage four times, and I was walking hand in hand with death every second of these journeys. I banished fear, and set my mind on getting through each time.

The intense bombardment was kept up all that day and all through the night. We knew now that we were in for the toughest proposition of our lives, and those who came through this trying ordeal must consider themselves lucky.

Our men had done that which they had set out to do: that was to get into the wood. The question now was could they hold what they had got with the depleted force?

This great struggle was kept up without ceasing for three days and nights.

The second day I made five runs up to the wood with dispatches, each time having to go through the blazing and howling barrage.

I had already been up four times on the second day; it was about 9 p.m. and I thought that I had finished for that day. I had taken my boots off, and was making ready for sleep in the cellar, when the Sergeant Major came. He said that he was very sorry, but there was another message to go up to the wood. When a Sergeant Major says he is sorry, he means it, for they were not used to throwing needless sympathy about. He detailed another man to go with me; this was always done at night.

We set off at 9 p.m. and it was 6 a.m. next morning when we returned. It was an utter impossibility to get on that road that night; not a flea could have got through the barrage that the enemy put on it. We got through about 4.30 a.m. next morning, when it had quietened down a little, and got back to Headquarters at 6 a.m. It had taken us nine hours to get through and back again; but we were safe, that was everything.

Things were now getting serious in the wood: every gunteam was considerably reduced, fresh casualties were coming down during the day, and reporting at Headquarters; all the Headquarters staff were rounded up and taken up the line to fill the gaps.

On the second day here, we had double runners day and night, as it was not considered safe for a runner to go alone. I was going up to the wood this afternoon with a man who had been detailed to accompany me. He was a Cockney, and usually a jolly chap, but the joviality had departed from him since we had been here.

As we went on our way shells came hurtling over the place, exploding with a ferocity that chilled the blood. We were crossing a field when a shell came over. I thought that shell was for us, if we did not move quickly, and shouted, "Down!" We both dropped flat, and the shell exploded about four feet to my left. We had only just dropped in time. We got up considering ourselves lucky that we had escaped.

From this time my companion got "windy." He was for turning back, saying we should never be able to get through the barrage. I told him there was only one way we had to go: that was to the wood.

He started arguing; he had now got the "wind up" badly. I did not intend him to put the "wind up" me. For argument I got hold of my rifle by the muzzle and told him that if he mentioned going back again I would split his head in two. He could see I was in earnest. That finished the argument. Drastic measures had to be put into operation at times like these; the men's lives in the wood depended upon runners getting through. If we had failed them, we were betraying a trust.

We sheltered in the houses at the corner of the road at the left end of the wood. The shelling died down a little, so we made our way along the road, dodging the shells as best we could. There were two rows of houses a little farther down the road, and as we drew near to these we could hear somebody moaning in terrible agony.

The doors and windows of these houses were out, and as the noise continued, we thought that the moans must be coming from these. We looked into the parlour of each house as we came to it. In one of the houses, as we looked through the window, a sight met our eyes that was enough to chill the heart of anyone. Four Germans were lying on the floor; two of these were already dead, lying in pools of their own blood. One of them had a terrible gash across the chest; he had been bandaged by some of our men. The other was

wounded in several places. They had gone to their last rest.
The other two Germans were not long for this world. Their
moans were terrible, as they begged us with their eyes to do
something for them; but they were passed [sic] human aid.
They were both lying in a pool of blood, their faces were
pinched and drawn, they already had that ghastly look of
death on their faces, the pallor of which there is no mistaking
when once seen. The moans were now becoming fainter and
fainter; before long they would be gone. We turned away from
this sight with a sickly feeling; they were human beings like
ourselves.

We went on our way to our gun position, handed over our
message got another to take back with us, then we made our
way back along the road. As we came to the houses where
we had seen the four Germans, we could not hear any moans
now, all was quiet. We looked through the window: they were
all dead; their sufferings at an end.

We got back to Headquarters, and while waiting for other
messages, I made some porridge in my dixie. We had had
practically no food since the action started on the 23rd. We
had to get a little when we could, rations were not coming
up so well, as the transport could not get up.

This afternoon, while I was making porridge on a small
fire that I had made with a few sticks, a shell came over,
which sounded as if it would drop on the house we were
in. All except myself made a dash for the cellar, which was
at the bottom of two flights of stone steps. The entrance to
the cellar steps was facing the front door. I rushed to the
fire for my dixie. I was nearly famished, and I did not want
to lose my porridge. After grabbing this, I rushed for the
cellar steps, and went down those two flights of steps in
about three jumps.

As I dashed down the steps, I noticed a man lying about
half-way down the steps on his stomach, head downwards, I

leapt over the top of him, and gained the cellar in safety. The shell crashed with a deafening roar just outside the door.

We looked at the man on the steps; he did not move. We wondered who he could be; then we found we were one short.

I had now eaten my food, and we decided it was safe to attend to the man on the steps. We shook him, but no sign of life came from him. We called him by name, but received no answer. We lifted his arm; it dropped like a stone. He was dead. The shell must have caught him as he went down the cellar steps. We carried him upstairs between us, took him outside, and laid him down in the road. On turning him over we discovered that his face was completely smashed in, nothing but a pulp of flesh and blood. It was a shocking sight.

The men in the wood were having a hard struggle. Rations had not been able to get through. They could not get any rest or sleep. It was attack and counter-attack all the time, and the bombardment was kept up unmercifully.

It was by this time a nightmare of the worst description. At night every little rustle of the trees made the men think the enemy were on top of them, and with missing so much sleep they could hardly keep their eyes open. Each time I went up into the wood the men looked more tired and haggard than on the previous journey.

A sharp look-out had to be kept all the time. Some of the men looked a sorry sight: they had not had a meal or a wash since the attack started, and with the constant strain of watching day and night their eyes looked hollow and dim.

On the second afternoon, as I arrived at one of the gun positions, a Sergeant of the Infantry came into our gun position and told us that they had only twenty men left out of his battalion. He was just ready to drop from sheer exhaustion. Another N.C.O. came down later the same afternoon, and told us that they had only eighteen men left of their battalion, and that he was the only N.C.O. They were both going down to Headquarters to see if they could get help, as they said they could not hold out much longer.

He told us that the enemy were coming, and they had practically no men in the front line positions. On hearing this, the Officer who was with us, ordered us to fix our bayonets in case they were needed. We had got four machine guns in this position, which had been cut into the side of the road. We waited like grim death for the enemy, ready to fire. He did not come, as it happened, so after an hour or two, we decided that he was not coming our way.

The third day we were in Bourlon Wood, was the worst of the lot. The Artillery fire was intensified to such an extent that it was impossible to increase it. The guns boomed all day, the shells screamed and crashed with terrible ferocity, and the road in front of the wood was a road of fire.

I went up from Headquarters seven times on the third and last day we were there, and according to all the rules of warfare I should have been killed or wounded many times over; but my confidence that I should come through all right never left me during the whole of those terrible experiences.

On this last day, as I went along the road in front of the wood, I had been dodging falling trees and exploding shells all the way, when I came to two tanks which were trying to get out of the way of a German aeroplane which was trying to drop bombs on them. As I was passing these I nearly got trapped as they were turning round, and another danger was the dropping bombs.

On another run up to the wood on the last day, as I got to the ravine where the attack commenced on the 23rd, I came across two of our Machine Gunners sitting on the side of the bank. When I reached them, I asked them what was the matter. They were as white as sheets, and looked scared to death. I knew there was something wrong. They said they had been lost all night and wandering about in the wood trying to find their gun position. I told them I was going there, and they could come with me. They did not seem to like the idea of going into the wood again, but I told them the consequences that would follow if they did not return with me, as I should be compelled to report it to the Officer. At last they decided they had better return with me, so we went forward on our way, and soon arrived at our position. They told the Officer that they had been lost, but the truth was that they had become scared, and got the "wind up" to such an extent, that they had deserted their gun.

One incident that happened on the second day, and occurred just outside Headquarters, was the saddest thing that anyone could imagine. Two limbers with eleven badly wounded men from the wood, were being brought down to the Hospital on the main road. The men were all bandaged up: head wounds, arm wounds, and leg wounds.

They were singing as they came down the road in the limbers, which were drawn by two mules. When the limbers got to within thirty yards or so of the hospital, a tremendous shell came hurtling over and exploded, crash, right under the two limbers. The men and limbers were scattered about in all directions, all being killed instantly. The mules lay dead in a pool of their own blood, while the limbs of the unfortunate men were scattered about all over the road: legs, arms, and head being severed as with a scythe. The limbers were splintered to matchwood. These men, only a few seconds before, were happy in the thought that they would soon be in "Blighty." This was the sad ending to their high hopes. War demands a terrible price!

On the third day that we were here, I had been up the wood with a message. The enemy were now continually shelling our Headquarters. High explosive shells, which swept right up the road, came over in torrents. They seemed to sweep everything before them with a swish that went for a hundred yards.

I was returning to Headquarters during the afternoon, when I came across the Major commanding our company. He had just returned from the wood; his face was white and drawn with care and worry, for he knew the terrible casualties our men had sustained, in fact, by now our lot were nearly wiped out.

"Well, Gregory," he said, "this is awful, isn't it?"

"Yes, sir, it is," I replied.

We walked on together. He seemed as if he wanted me for company; to be able to talk was a lot in times like these, and these are the times when every station in life is equal. The common danger is apparent to all. We went up the road to Headquarters, talking together. Shells were dropping in the road as we went up, but we got back safely.

We heard after tea that day that we were being relieved in the wood, after three nights and three days of Hell. When I think of it now, it is a night mare, even after all these years; that furnace of raging fire where men had to endure. How they lived through it God only knows.

The Guards were coming up to relieve our men at 11 p.m. that night. One of our Corporals came down to Headquarters to say that the men must be relieved, they could not stand any longer, they had reached the end of their endurance. The Sergeant Major told him that all were being relieved at 11 p.m. that night.

The Corporal had been in charge of a gun team in the wood, and had had no rest or sleep all the time, and very little food. His eyes were strange and wild-looking, in fact he looked just like a man going out of his mind. The continual strain of watching and listening, had been too much for him; he was on the point of total collapse.

I spoke to him, but he did not seem to know me. The Sergeant Major gave him a cup of rum and told him to lie down until the others came back from the wood, and as he need not return, he could sleep. The man laid down, and in a few seconds was fast asleep.

I asked the Sergeant Major to give me a cup of rum, as I was feeling just about done, and at the end of my strength.

I was going to fill my water bottle in the yard that night at about 10.30, so that we should have all ready, and as I got to the door a great shell came whistling over and crashed in the backyard. On hearing it coming I made a sudden rush for the cellar, and was down at the bottom of the steps and in safety in no time. I would do without water; better to be thirsty than to get killed now, after all that we had been through.

I did not move out of that cellar again until our men arrived down at Headquarters about midnight, and it was not long before we left the place behind us.

We marched about ten miles back that night to the Hindenburg Line.

From *Never Again: A Diary of the Great War* by H. Gregory. Stockwell. [1934].

CAMBRAI – THE GERMAN COUNTER-ATTACK:
30TH NOVEMBER–6TH DECEMBER 1917

'As soon as it got dark, we collected some bits of men, put them in a sandbag, carried out the recognisable bodies over the top and dumped them in a shell hole, and Billy Barnard said the Lord's Prayer'

*The 2nd Division was one of those which bore the brunt of the coun-
ter-attack that followed the dramatic gains of the British offensive at
Cambrai. Captain J.E.H. Neville, then a subaltern in 'B' Company of
the 52nd LI, describes conditions during the period of British retrench-
ment. His battalion was not heavily engaged but suffered casualties nevertheless. During the period Neville assumed command of 'A' Company
when the company commander was wounded, and he described his*

*feelings: 'The responsibility of that rearguard was the worst part of it,
and the knowledge that if I floated, one hundred men's lives would be
on my head.'*

The 5th Brigade was, luckily for us, in reserve when the
enemy attacked the Division. We woke up to the tune of a
barrage which we could see plastering our front line. I said
to myself, "Now we are for it," and at noon the 52nd moved
up to support either of the two Brigades in the front line,
according as help was required.

We stayed at Lock 7 for some time and then orders were
received for the Regiment to counter-attack the Sugar
Factory on the Bapaume-Cambrai road. (As a matter of fact
this factory had never been captured by the enemy, though it
was being pasted to hell.)

We moved forward again, soon after, into Hughes Support
trench, which ran parallel to the Hindenburg Line. Here we
remained from 5 p.m. till 2 a.m. The trench had been evacuated by some reserve troops of the 47th London Division, who
had left their packs stacked high in the bays of the trench.
We were packed like sardines, my platoon occupying half a
traverse only. Some very heavy stuff was coming over at odd
intervals, and one 8-inch shell laid out 20 men. As you know,
you can hear these very heavy birds coming from a very
considerable distance; they seem to take ages to arrive, and
there is always a second during their flight, when you know
whether they are going to fall near or far from you. I heard this
particular bird from afar, and felt relieved that he was going to
plant himself away from us. Then I began to doubt my sup-
position; a second later, it was touch and go, and then I realised
that it was probably going to blot me out. I lived through one
agonising second of uncertainty. There was no way of escape;
we could not dodge the brute, as we were far too cramped
for space. With a tearing, rushing, mighty roar as of an express

train screaming at top speed through an enclosed station, it crashed in the next bay from me, right in the middle of my platoon! I darted round the corner and found a shambles. It had fallen plumb in the centre of the trench, a magnificent shot from the enemy's point of view. Among the killed was Serjeant Archer, Platoon Serjeant of No. 7, and a damned good chap. The only man who escaped untouched of all the men in that bay, was sitting on the top of a pile of packs, at the foot of which the shell had landed. The packs were utterly destroyed and he was lifted off his perch but unhurt!

As soon as it got dark, we collected some bits of men, put them in a sandbag, carried out the recognisable bodies over the top and dumped them in a shell hole, and Billy Barnard said the Lord's Prayer over their remains. I think it was probably the only prayer he knew for certain!

By 2 a.m. we were pretty hungry, as we had had nothing to eat since 7 a.m., but we moved forward again in the moonlight to Kangaroo Alley, a trench behind the Arras-Cambrai road. There was only desultory shelling at the time, and we were extraordinarily lucky in that respect.

We stayed in Kangaroo Alley till the evening of December 1st, when "B" Company went up to the front line for 48 hours. The trench was very shallow and broad, and the weather was excruciatingly cold, so much so that sentries could only watch on the fire step for half an hour. We were in the front line from the evening of the first till the evening of the third, and had no casualties. Messages came with annoying regularity whenever we sat down to a meal in the dugout, to say that the enemy were massing for an attack. Thereupon, we all went to our battle stations and stood-to-arms, waiting and ready for him, but he never came; not that he would have got far if he had tried. By the time we had "stood down," our meal was naturally stone cold. On the nights of the 1st and 2nd there were bombing attacks on our left, made by the 6th Brigade to try and extricate a Company of the 13th Essex which had been cut off at Lock 5 and Moeuvres and surrounded, when the Boche attacked on the 30th. This gallant handful of officers and men were still holding out in spite of their predicament, and were annoying the enemy with great success, by sniping over the parapet and parados. I am afraid the bombing attacks failed in both cases and the Essex had to surrender when their ammunition was exhausted.

We watched these attacks from our front line. It was very thrilling. We could see the shrapnel bursting over the enemy trenches, and the smaller flashes of flame from Mills bombs. The darkness, meanwhile, was continually lit up by Verey Lights which burst high in the frosty night and fell into the rolling clouds of smoke. They were rather grim firework displays.

We went back into support from the night of the 3rd till 2 a.m. on the 5th, when the front line was evacuated, and we were left as the front line for 48 hours. "A" and "B" Companies were in the front line, the former holding Lock 6, where Dick Warren was in command, while we held about 400 yards of Kangaroo Alley on the right. This was a very long stretch and meant posting one man in every other bay for battle stations.

We had a very quiet time until the morning of the 5th, when Fritz showed a lot of activity. We could see tin hats worming towards our line on the left, where there was a trench along the canal bank. At our end, this trench had been blocked and a bombing section posted under No. 8665 L/Cpl. Tilbury. We sent back this information to Headquarters, and Seale came up to see if he could get at them with his trench mortars. This he did, and discouraged the Boche a lot by lobbing over a few really good shots. However, early in the afternoon they started to creep forward again, and the bombing post was kept busy until at about 3 p.m. a whizzbang barrage came over. I was sitting in Company Headquarters with

Billy Barnard when it opened. I rushed upstairs and along the trench to the right to get to my platoon area. The shelling was pretty hot, the damn things bursting first in front of me and then behind me, so that I expected to catch one all to myself in each bay. However, I reached my platoon safely and found the men "standing-to" in battle order. Scarcely had I sat down on the fire-step for a breather when an orderly popped his head round the corner of the trench and told me I was wanted at Company Headquarters as the Captain was hit. So back I had to go, running the gauntlet of the damned whizz-bangs. I found Billy B sitting on the top step of the dugout nursing his left knee. He had been hit by a piece of shrapnel. The stretcher-bearers were just contemplating the removal of his great bulk, when a man of the bombing post on the left reported that the enemy were in the trench. Billy B got up at once and hobbled down the trench towards the Canal, which was our only covered line of retreat and, incidentally, towards the post which had reported the entry of the enemy into our trench! As it happened, the lad who brought the message was not telling the truth, thank God! He was a bit windy, for the Corporal had only told him to tell Billy B that the enemy were massing in the trench immediately opposite his post.

Billy's departure left me in command of the Company to carry out a rearguard action and a retirement later. I was taken by surprise, and had the wind up badly that I should make a mess of it.

All the afternoon, rumours came round that the enemy were massing at different map references. One report stated that the Lock had been captured on our left. This came just after Billy was wounded and put the wind up me badly. Thank heaven, it was also false, but all the same it was most alarming.

We held this position until the evening of the 6th. A message from Regimental Headquarters reached me early in the afternoon stating the time at which we were to withdraw, and I issued all orders accordingly so that there should not be any confusion or noise. But 20 minutes before that time, the Boches attacked Lock 6 and got into it, so that "A" Company on my left, which was responsible for the Lock, was compelled to retire immediately.

I had had no idea what was happening, until a terrific explosion rent the air and bits of the Lock sailed through space. It had been mined by the Sappers and was to have been blown up by a time fuse after "A" Company had evacuated it, and when it was hoped that there would be a big covey of Boches making themselves comfortable inside the Lockmaster's quarters.

A few minutes after the explosion, Dick Warren sauntered into my trench and told me that he had given the order to the Sappers to blow the mine, and that when it went up, there were about 20 of the enemy in it. So the covey was caught after all!

My left flank was now completely in the air, and the enemy was in a marvellous position to enfilade the whole length of my trench.

My original line of retreat down the Canal bed was now cut off, so I sent three platoons down a road running towards our rear led by Windross, the only other officer left in the Company. This road was completely exposed and liable to be swept by machine gun fire at any moment, and I had visions of heavy casualties. The enemy, however, did not fire and the platoons got away safely. By this time, the other two platoons were ready in the trench, so I sent one off and a minute later sent out the last platoon, and marched in the rear of the Company with my Headquarters. We got back quite safely without a single casualty, which was extremely lucky considering how Fritz had plastered the road the night before.

The 2nd Division saved the whole of the ground won on November 20th in the Bourlon Wood-Moeuvres area by hanging on so long. There were six enemy Divisions against the 2nd, and the front-line troops on November 30th inflicted such severe casualties that all the six German Divisions are now out of the line recuperating. The 52nd had none of the hard fighting or perhaps I should not be able to write this.

From *The War Letters of a Light Infantryman* by Capt. J.E.H. Neville, MC. Sifton Praed & Co. 1930.

A Very Near Miss: 23rd December 1917

'My escape was almost as miraculous as the sight of a Sapper wiring party!'

The more one reads about the First World War, the more one realises that luck had a major part to play in the survival chances of any of the front-line protagonists. Lieutenant Neville of the 52nd Light Infantry neatly proves this point.

We had a very quiet time in the line; but I had a very narrow escape. There was a particular trench junction on our front which the Boche shelled at five minutes to every hour. I was making my way back to call my relief, and reached the trench junction at 10.50 p.m. Just as I reached it, an orderly came up leading a party of Sappers, commanded by an officer, who said he had come to put out wire on our front. I forgot all about the time in my amazement at seeing Sappers in the front line, let alone going to do a job of work in No Man's Land. The officer wanted to know where the wire was to be put out, and I hadn't the foggiest idea. We were discussing it, standing at the trench junction, facing the parapet, when, suddenly there was a terrific explosion and a sheet of flame seemed to envelope me. The next thing that I knew, was that I was sprawling full length on the ground, just clear of the pieces of frozen earth that were falling all around. I felt myself all over, thinking I must be dead, picked up my tin hat and ran round the corner. There was not a graze on me. The explosion came from a whizzbang, which burst on the parados immediately behind my head. I saw the shell crater, the next morning. How it missed my head, Heaven only knows. Of course I never heard it coming; you never do hear the one that hits you. That shell must have arrived punctually at 10.55!

My escape was almost as miraculous as the sight of a Sapper wiring party!

From *The War Letters of a Light Infantryman* by Capt. J.E.H. Neville, MC. Sifton Praed & Co. 1930.

5

1918: Darkest Before the Dawn

Tunnel Catastrophe: 4th January 1918

'the bodies of our men were found in the various bunks wearing their gas helmets'

On 2 January 1918 the 2nd Bn. Green Howards, Princess of Wales's Own Yorkshire Regiment, took up residence in Hedge Street Tunnels, an extensive dugout system capable of housing a whole battalion and more, although like any dugouts the narrow tunnels were liable to become congested and the atmosphere disagreeable. The Tunnels were south of the Menin Road near to Tower Hamlets and, at that time, were used to house the support battalion to that in the front line. Two days after they entered the Tunnel – days during which only officers and messengers might have actually left the Tunnel – fire broke out within its confines. The result, and the attendant heroism of members of the battalion, is recorded in an account written by the quartermaster, Major E. Pickard.

Went up to Hedge Street Tunnel about 11 a.m. to arrange details for the move next day with the C.O. Very cold, ice

was lying thick on the ground. I had never been down
this particular tunnel previously and I was much surprised
at the intense heat in the tunnel and mentioned the fact
to Birch. The tunnel was very well built and had bunks all
along the length of the main alley-way. It was strongly tim-
bered and in the various messes the woodwork was covered
with hessian canvas; this I thought was very dangerous in
case of fire. I stayed some hours and fixed up everything
for the move and then returned to the transport lines at
Reninghelst and left by lorry shortly after to arrange billets at
Wallon Cappel.

The 20th Division was due to relieve our division, but
failed to arrive, and the relief of our Battalion was therefore
delayed one day. Shortly after the time we should have been
relieved had the 20th arrived in time, a fire broke out in
the Tunnel, and from what the Medical Officer, who was
with Headquarters at the time, stated, it appears that about
midnight, looking up to the ceiling of the Tunnel, he saw a
streak of flame. He at once gave the alarm, and everybody
was roused and told to get out of the Tunnel as quickly as
possible. Before many seconds had elapsed the Tunnel was
one mass of flame and black smoke. Lieutenant Picken saved
many lives by his brave conduct in staying at the bottom of
the stairs and pushing and guiding the men which way to
go, as it was impossible for them to see. The C.O. (Major
Birch) was seen to be moving about, and it was thought that
he would be able to get out; but it appears that as soon as he
learnt that everyone was not out of the Tunnel, he went back
into the flames again to see if he could save anyone. He was
not seen alive again. He and the adjutant – Lieutenant Dean
– and the whole of the officers of 'B' Company – Captain B.C.
Camm, M.C., Second-Lieutenants G.P. Smith, J. Symon and
W. Barber, also one R.E. officer, an officer of the Shropshire
L.I., and a Church of England Brigade Chaplain, and twelve

men of the Battalion were burnt to death. All these men belonged to our Battalion Headquarters staff, many of them were signallers and most of them had been with the Battalion during the whole of the war.

The Tunnel had to be sealed up to localize the fire, and when it was reopened some days after by the 20th Division the bodies of our men were found in the various bunks wearing their gas helmets. Except where was part of a man's body lying in the main alley there were no marks of burning on the bodies, but everything in the main alley was charred up.

From *The Green Howards in the Great War* by Col. H.C. Wylly, CB. Published by the Regiment. 1926.

The Storm Breaks: 21st March 1918

'such HELL, makes weaklings of the strongest and no humans nerves or body were ever built to stand such torture'

Pte William Sharpe, 2/8th Lancashire Fusiliers, was captured near St Quentin on the first day of the German 'Spring Offensive,' when after three-and-a-half years of British attacks the Germans crashed through our lines to a depth of some twenty miles using advanced tactics and helped in large measure by a recent re-organisation of the Allied defences which had left the British thinly stretched on the front where the attack took place, and on this first day particularly they were also aided by the mist which lay over the British lines.

We were again out wiring & later patrolling and at 4.30 am took our usual places for the 'Stand To' – it was a thick misty morning…impossible to see above five to six yards. At 5.30 am there was a distinctive chlorine smell… and we put on our gas masks only to find that it made visibility still worse & many of us, very imprudently & to our later regret removed them. Also had started a terrific barrage... dropping increasingly nearer... we who had been at Ypres began to compare, saying it was getting as bad, but it continued to get even worse & came to a pitch when it seemed impossible that anything could live in it... such HELL, makes weaklings of the strongest and no humans nerves or body were ever built to stand such torture... The barrage was now on top of us & our trench was blown in... About this time, after having sent messages to the S.M., who was in the dugout together with three of the officers during this awful time, we were sent a bottle of rum, but still told to stay where we were... the rum was more than accept-able – but as – amongst all things, there was one who abused it & got 'mad' drunk... Going to a box of Mills bombs he withdrew the pin of one & put it back in the box. Those who saw him do it immediately took cover... the Cpl., for such was this madman's rank, with us. One poor old chap... had not seen what happened & *was killed*. This madman's antics were stopped by being hit on top of the head with a rifle butt... later when he was informed of the event in a German prison camp he cried like a baby – but this did not bring back someone's dear husband... [later:] A few minutes by 10, we hear signs of the wire in front of us being cut & opened out with rapid fire, firing some 50 rounds into the mist, without seeing anything... we followed this with bombs for some 10 minutes & still with no attack, by now, our section... decided to make our way for instructions... to the sunken road & even this could hardly be recognised. The fog was now lifting & the sun breaking through – no sooner had we got into the road than we ran into 'Jerrys' who opened fire with revolvers. A few of the lads bolted... the remainder of us stood still – simply amazed & were again fired at by a German officer – directly afterwards a shell burst... just a few yards away & this I am just certain saved our lives – as we were then told to put up our hands...The whole road was occupied by Germans.They quickly relieved me of my rifle, bombs, equipment etc. & we were simply left... I helped to attend the German wounded & there were some hundreds & some most awful wounds too – they all seemed to be quite decent fellows. [later:] I was told to make my way through their lines as this was their big push... I climbed the bank & what the German had said was true & as far as the eye could see... was nothing but the blue grey uniforms of German troops advancing in well ordered company formation...

W.A. Sharpe's manuscript journal is held by the Imperial War Museum, London.

OPEN WARFARE: 23RD-26TH MARCH 1918

'The officer's face was completely raw, all the skin off his forehead and face hung like an icicle from the tip of his nose, while the skin of his jaw and chin encircled his neck in a grey fold, like an Elizabethan ruff. His hands were raw too, and he gave me the impression of having been lathered in blood. Actually, he and his crew had been flayed in a burning tank'

The German spring offensive gave most of those who were caught up in it their first taste of open warfare, for few of those still serving with the British Expeditionary Force had been with it in the early days in 1914. One of those caught up in the retreat was Lt. Neville of the 52nd, Oxfordshire Light Infantry, who had been with his regiment for fifteen months of constant trench warfare. In his diary he recorded the alien experiences associated with the retreat: lack of communication with anyone who knew anything of what was really going on; disintegrating command structure; lack of provisions (in the end he was tempted to eat bully beef from an open tin found in a

dugout that smelt of 'decay, rats, and putrescent vegetation and food'
and was consequently very sick) and constantly moving. The Germans
advanced rapidly, their highly trained attack troops pushing forward all
the time, making good use of ground cover and light machine guns to
support their attacks, identify strong points and so on. These German
tactics are well described in Neville's account. The offensive opened
on 21 March; on the 22nd the 52nd had moved up, roused from a
period of rest to take its place in the already crumbling line, and the
23rd found them strengthening this line.

The weather was very warm, and digging became thirsty
work. By 2 p.m. each man had dug himself a small hole with
a thin parapet, and work was started to connect these holes
into one trench. All the Companies except "B" had taken over
partially dug trenches, very wide and shallow, such as we had
been digging for the last two months when in Brigade reserve.
They were to prove their uselessness this day; though "B"
Company had to dig like fury, yet we were better off in our
little holes, when once they had been dug deep and narrow.
However, in front of this so-called "prepared" position there
were four rows of wire, both apron and chevaux-de-frise.

At midday a battery of field artillery took up a position in
front of this wire, but before it had been in action half an hour,
it was subjected to indirect machine-gun fire from Velu Wood.
The battery limbered up at once and galloped away, the guns
being drawn by only one pair of horses. It was a very thrilling
sight, and reminiscent of a picture by Lady Butler.

At 2 p.m. from the commanding position of our trench, we
could plainly see the enemy streaming over the sky line, in
pursuit of our troops, who were retiring in good order, covered by machine guns in rear and Lewis guns on the flanks.

We telephoned through to our guns to concentrate on the
enemy masses, but in vain. Not a shot was fired by our guns!
They must have been trekking back.

Through glasses every movement and signal could be spotted, and men could be seen to fall, here and there. There was no shell fire or smoke to obscure the view; it was open warfare in very truth. By 3 p.m. the rearguard troops had passed through our line and retired to another so-called "line" behind, which was non-existent except for rows of wire without a trench behind them. These troops formed a very heterogeneous crowd; men of different regiments, Divisions and Corps, all retiring under unknown officers in many cases. None of them seemed to know where they were going next, nor the line of retirement. It looked a rather sorry rabble, very nearly constituting a rout.

Two officers of the 25th Machine Gun Corps, and six men, all that remained of 50, took up a position in "B" Company's section of trench, and mounted their sole remaining gun. One of the officers came to me for some water and food, as he had been without rations and water for three days. I had to refuse his request for water, because we were already short, and did not know for how long we might be compelled to subsist on our water bottles. I managed to find a tin of bully for him and some neat whisky, for which he was very grateful. He was in a pitiful state; his face was black from powder, his hands bleeding, his jacket ripped from shoulder to wrist by shrapnel, and his puttees and breeches torn to ribbons by wire. He said he had been blown up three times and had had three guns destroyed under his hand. He had lost his Division which had retired early in the morning, and he informed me that he intended to stay with us and see it through. He was rather bitter about certain troops, who, he said, had retired without orders and left him and his guns in the lurch. It sounded bad enough that such a thing should happen, but we were to experience the same very shortly. Such was the disorganisation caused by the rapid advance of the enemy, that orders often did not reach the front-line troops simultaneously, and, indeed, some never received orders at all.

At 3 p.m. we became the front-line troops, and all the gaps in the wire were closed with movable chevaux-de-frise.

The enemy followed up very quickly, and the trench was soon peppered with machine gun bullets. "A" Company on our immediate right had many casualties. The enemy worked a light machine gun forward along the railway embankment which ran through our front, and from a concealed position on top he was able to enfilade the trench. The piece of trench held by "A" Company was on a slope towards the railway embankment, and every movement in the trench could, thus, be spotted by the enemy. Also, as the trench was seven feet wide and three feet deep, there was absolutely no cover; in fact it was a death trap and nearly as bad as nothing at all.

"B" Company was more fortunate. We were just over the crest and the only casualties which we suffered were due to indirect enfilade fire from the embankment.

"A" Company had a forward post in our wire, which was well placed to snipe the enemy as he worked forward. However, this post was spotted by the light machine gun team, and its position rendered untenable. "Bunjie" Littledale, commanding "A" Company, went forward to withdraw this post, and was killed, hit through the heart and neck. Next, Colvill ran the gauntlet of a hail of bullets and managed to get the men back and Littledale's body as well.

The afternoon was quiet; only heavies were in action on both sides; ours dropped some very heavy stuff into Velu Wood, while the enemy contented himself with plastering the Bertincourt-Velu road, about 400 yards behind our front line.

Towards evening, the frost came down, and the shelling on both sides increased considerably, the enemy registering his guns on the Bertincourt-Velu road. Night came on, and with it the awful suspense of waiting for the attack that was certain to be launched against us in the morning. We dug a little and tried to improve our narrow, shallow trench. All round us the enemy's Verey lights twinkled in the sky, revealing the extent to which we were "bottle-necked." They indicated more surely than any map references the line which the enemy held. Our orders were to hold the Switch Line at all costs.

At dusk the shell dump at Ytres was fired; all night long we could hear the distant thud of exploding shells, while occasionally the sky was lit up with a red glare of burning dumps.

The cold was intense; sleep almost impossible, and there was no mail; but rations came up. There was nothing to be done, but to wait and wait for the infernal daylight. However much we might be shelled, there was no chance of any retaliation from our guns. A rearguard is a nasty business.

Diary. March 24th, 1918. At 2 a.m. I was woken up by an orderly from a cramped sleep and told that George Field, commanding "B" Company wanted to see me. He gave me a message to read, the purport of which was that we might have to retire before dawn to another position in rear.

The hours slipped by, but no orders came through, and the suspense grew greater every minute. Dawn came, a glorious spring dawn; we stood-to-arms. No orders. No sign of an enemy attack.

Just as it was getting light, two German officers came forward to reconnoitre our wire and succeeded in finding two gaps made by heavy shells. They were allowed to wriggle through one row, and then No. 8 Platoon stopped any further nonsense by shooting them neatly!

George Field, Wilsdon, and I had some breakfast at 8 a.m., and then went back to our posts, expecting brother Boche to come and maul us at any moment.

However, at 8.50 an orderly came to me with a message, the one word "Corunna," the code word to retire. I went along to Field who gave me orders to retire with No. 8

Platoon from the extreme left. I was the only officer with a map of the area, and I was given the job of leading the Company. I handed over No. 6 Platoon to Sergeant Stevens and led out No. 8.

We started in single file through our wire, behind the trench. There was a stretch of 400 yards before we could reach the Bertincourt-Velu road. No sooner were we all in the open than the enemy opened machine gun fire on us; we carried on steadily; and then, as it were, a thunderstorm seemed to burst over our heads in a deafening roar. The sun, which shone with all his might, was suddenly blotted out by the yellow acrid smoke of shrapnel bursting overhead. The ground shot up all round in fountains of black smoke and earth. Everything on all sides was being heaved into the air. The Nissen huts bordering the road parallel to our line of retreat were flattened in one blast. Hell's fiery furnace was let loose.

I looked round and tried to collect the men together, because they were inclined to straggle, and even as I did so, a whizzbang caught the slanting roof of a Nissen hut a few feet away on my right, and cut away Private Grey's legs. Another man and I tried to lift him, but he was too badly hit, and we had to leave him to the enemy.

We crossed the road and halted behind a manure heap for a breather. Field and Wilsdon came up, and the former tried to shout orders to me; but it was not wise to wait too long in any one place, for five whizzbangs burst on the other side of the midden, showering manure all over us.

And so we retired in small parties to the Bertincourt-Haplincourt road, through some stables, and out again into the open.

Meanwhile, Bertincourt was being plastered with every conceivable type of damnation, and the noise was terrific. I never expected to see any of the Headquarters officers again.

It was a great relief to be free of the roads and buildings, and to be in the open again. The heat seemed to be very intense, and the men were black and dripping with sweat; mostly battle sweat, for the sun was not hot enough to cause such perspiration. We marched on, through the Green Line, up the slope, and past some machine gunners who had dug in to cover our retreat.

During this retirement, it was possible to see to what extent the British were, in fact, "bottle-necked." For miles I could see our troops filtering back across the rolling downs towards one spot, one narrow channel, while machine gun fire came from three sides.

On reaching the ridge in front of the Briastre-Bus road, we met Brett, and there we sorted out 52nd men, recognisable by the Regimental ribbon on their steel helmets, from the rabble of troops of all divisions of the 5th Corps, who were retiring through this narrow neck.

We formed up into Companies as the men came in, and having reformed, reported to Brett. "B" Company was ordered to go back to the original map reference (O.22 central) given in the "Corunna" message, and Field led the Company back to an old German line running between Rocquigny and Barastre.

On our way back, we passed through Vimiera Camp, where we had rested on the morning of the 22nd. I noticed a man dart into a hut that had once been a cookhouse; presently he ran past me holding a small Union Jack, which he said the Germans could not have, though they were welcome to the Camp. When I last saw that man, the Union Jack was still protruding from his haversack!

We soon ran into the 19th Division on its way up to hold the ridge, which we had just evacuated. Having settled into the new position, we came under machine gun fire from Rocquigny on our right, and our own 4.5 howitzers mistook us for the enemy and started shelling us. Here the Company, about 40 strong, stayed until Field determined to go and join up with the 63rd Division, which was digging in on the next ridge behind Barastre, since there was no sign of the 52nd. Every moment we expected to see the remaining Companies appear. At midday there was still no sign of them. I went off to try and find out if any of the neighbouring troops had seen them, but all my enquiries proved fruitless. While I was in Barastre, looking for the Regiment, I saw the tanks go up into action to cover our troops' retreat. It was very interesting to watch. The Germans had several field guns in close support to their infantry, and as the tanks waddled over the crest of the ridge the German gunners knocked them out one after the other.

In Barastre, I gleaned the news that the 2nd Division was fighting a rearguard in conjunction with the 19th, between Haplincourt and Villers-au-Flos. I delivered my information to Field, who, thereupon, decided to go back to Beaulencourt and await the 52nd there.

We marched back to the Le Transloy-Peronne road, where we found the 1st 60th Rifles digging in. Field put the Company under the command of the Colonel, and we dug-in for the third time today, on a ridge commanding the Bapaume-Peronne road, which we had known so well during our rests in Divisional reserve during the past four months.

It was not until 5 p.m., when the enemy were in the outskirts of Le Transloy, that we met the 52nd again. It was a pitiful sight. A small column of men, led by Crosse and Brett, about 80 men all told, marched wearily up the slope. "D" Company had been cut off in Villers-au-Flos, and only 12 men under Eagle had managed to escape. David Barnes and Bailey were wounded and missing, and Vernon wounded. Ben Slocock had been killed.

Just before the 52nd came up with "B" Company, what remained of the tanks waddled through our line of posts. The enemy field guns, supporting the front-line troops, had done them considerable damage, and completely incapacitated not a few. I noticed one tank crew, through my glasses, coming towards us. They all looked very strange and I could not distinguish their faces from their uniform. As they approached I could see the cause of this. The officer's face was completely raw, all the skin off his forehead and face hung like an icicle from the tip of his nose, while the skin of his jaw and chin encircled his neck in a grey fold, like an Elizabethan ruff. His hands were raw too, and he gave me the impression of having been lathered in blood. Actually, he and his crew had been flayed in a burning tank, and he was the most badly burnt of all, as he was the last to leave. He asked for some water. I handed him my waterbottle, but he held up his hands and said he could not touch anything. So I poured as much as I could spare down his open mouth; then he went on back towards Albert. Wounded men came crawling up to our posts, too, beseeching us to carry them back to the main Albert road on our stretchers; these pitiful requests had to be refused, because our stretcher-bearers were already doing the work of four times their number.

One man with a shattered ankle, crawled up to me and asked me to get him taken back. When I told him that it was impossible, he started off dragging his ankle, and said he would get back to Albert as he was, rather than be taken prisoner. The pluck of the man!

At 5.45 p.m. the whole of the 5th Brigade moved back as a Brigade across the Somme battlefield from Beaulencourt, which was burning, to Ligny-Thilloy. The 52nd formed the rearguard for the Brigade, and "B" Company was detailed for the rear party and flank guards. My platoon formed the left flank guard. Away on our left marching in the same direction as ourselves at 2,000 or 3,000 yards interval was a German column. We took no more notice of them that they did of us!

The shell-hole country over which we had to march made our progress very fatiguing. Grass and weeds had, in the course of time, matted over the old shell-holes, preventing one from being able to see where the actual holes were. The troops were dog-tired after a hard day, and these last four miles, as dusk came on, were heart-breaking; stumbling first to the right, climbing out of one shell-hole only to step into another; up and down and round and never a solid step ahead, every minute of waning light making a path more difficult to find.

Eventually, at about 7 p.m., the 52nd halted at Ligny-Thilloy and we had an hour's rest by the side of the road, and never has a ditch seemed so soft. Every man was fast asleep as he threw himself down. At 10 p.m. ammunition was served out and the 52nd took up an outpost position between the 24th Royal Fusiliers and the 74th. The 6th Brigade continued the line on the right of the latter. The night was bitterly cold after the spring warmth of the day, and a frosty wind sprang up to make it chillier still.

Rations came up in the night, and we had lunch on tea mixed with tobacco and boiled in shell-hole water. The element of tobacco rather spoilt the tea, making it taste very bitter, but the shell-hole water was infinitely better than that which came up in petrol tins for our consumption, as it proved to be composed of about three parts of water to one part petrol, and was almost worse than nothing. The hot tea did us a world of good and made up for everything else. Thus ended the longest day of my life.

Diary. March 25th, 1918. At 2 a.m. orders came to move again, and the 5th Brigade marched, half asleep, through Le Barque on to the main Bapaume-Albert road. This was a silent march, as the enemy had been reported to be in our rear, in which case we were cut off. On reaching the main road, there was a halt of 30 minutes, to allow the 6th Brigade to catch us up.

There was a faint grey streak in the eastern sky as we passed the famous Butte de Warlencourt; the very road on which we were marching had been mended by the Regiment just a year ago, after the boche retreated early in 1917; and just as dawn was breaking, we wheeled off the road into the ruined village of Courcelette. The march along the road had been quite a pleasure compared to the Somme battlefield of yesterday, but it was galling to pass all the well-known landmarks and to realise that all this hardly won tract of country was slipping back once more into the enemy's hands.

At Courcelette, where the 52nd had held the line for three months in 1917, we had a really long rest of two hours, and moreover, a hot breakfast. Before falling out, the Commanding Officer formed the Regiment up in line and called it to attention. "A" and "B" Companies became No. 1 Company under George Field, and "C" and "D" No. 2 Company under Percy Bobby. Then he said, "When you fall out, I want to see every man get some wood and drum up at once."

No sooner had the men thrown off their equipment than wood was collected, and fires were going everywhere, in true Light Infantry style. By 7.15 a.m. the Regiment had had a hot meal, and the majority of men were already asleep.

Meanwhile, the poor old Brigadier was in a state of collapse. We had passed him on entering Courcelette, sitting on a blasted tree stump holding his head in his hands. Each Company had marched at attention, but he was far too weary to rise up and take the salute. Behind him, stood the Brigade Major, looking like death, and in this state, I saw the Brigade Staff for the first and last time, during these operations!

At 8.45 p.m. we took up a position, facing east, along the ridge overlooking Dyke Valley, and commanding Le Sars and the Bapaume-Albert road. This was a very fine position, indeed. The 6th Brigade continued the line to the left, and

behind us, we had one battery of 18-pounders. On the right
there was not a sign of a soul! In front, the 99th Brigade was
fighting a rearguard action, and was to retire through us to
another ridge behind.

Owing to the excellence of the position, and the fact that
the enemy had not been able to move his guns forward, we
could have held on for a long time. Our only difficulties were
scarcity of ammunition and our right flank; of the former we
only had the 120 rounds which each man carried, the latter
was completely in the air.

Here, however, was excellent scope for good and controlled
fire, and through field glasses I could see every movement of
the enemy. Though we only held here for half an hour, we had
some good fun bringing down the enemy as they advanced
across the open from Le Sars towards Courcelette. The Boches
were no fools; they were well trained and made excellent use
of ground and cover, and never exposed themselves unnecessarily. Their first consideration was, always, to manoeuvre the
light machine guns forward, to cover the advance of the rest.
Through my glasses, I picked up a man carrying one of these
guns, and directed my Lewis gun on to him; that man never
carried that or any other gun again! It was almost impossible
to miss the enemy from this commanding position, and our
Lewis guns were doing good execution and holding up the
enemy's advance, when we, once again, received orders to
retire, because the enemy, as was his cunning way, was crawling
round our flanks.

For the rest of the day we retired continuously across the
shell-scarred and desolate Somme Plateau, past the ruins of
Pys, where Eagle and I had spent an unpleasant evening in
February '17 pursuing the retreating Boche; back we trekked
from ridge to ridge with the enemy almost close on our heels,
and our flanks continuously exposed. The weather, too, had
changed and a bitter north wind was blowing.

At last, we halted on the left bank of the river Ancre, opposite Beaucourt-sur-Ancre. Here we had tea, the second meal of the day, at 6 p.m.

I never saw a Staff Officer after leaving Courcelette. There seemed to be nobody in command of the Brigade, and likewise, no one met us when we reached the river, to pass on orders! Brett had gone back, early in the afternoon, to report the situation to Divisional Headquarters if he could find them.

While we were having tea, some machine gunners on the heights of Beaucourt must have mistaken us for the enemy, for they opened fire on us. However, they were bad shots, and we were too tired to take any notice of them.

At dusk, we crossed the Ancre at the ford, and took up a position on the heights of Beaucourt on the right bank, with strong points pushed forward to guard the ford across the river.

So ended a fatiguing day, to be followed by a bitterly cold night and little or no sleep. The wind whistled over the river from Thiepval; the long-disused dugouts were damp and musty; the wind seemed to freeze one's clothes to one's body; and as bitter as the wind, was the fact that we were occupying the trenches held by the Regiment in November 1916, eighteen months ago.

Diary. March 26th, 1918. At "Stand-to," orders came to pack up and retire again. Accordingly, "B" Company descended the steep slope to the Beaumont-Hamel road. The morning was very cold and foggy, and I led my platoon through Beaumont Hamel, where I joined up with Bobby. Our orders were to retire on Auchonvillers, but, when we were half way there, Brett met us and told us that the retirement was cancelled. So we trekked back again to the position we had just left, the march being enlivened by 8-inch shells from our guns falling on the road at Beaucourt. So we left the road and took a short cut to our old position, as it is never wise to argue with an 8-inch shell.

The sun had just risen when we settled down to improve the position; and our aeroplanes were crowding the sky, which was a pleasant sight after four days without the sight of one. One of these 'planes, however, flew over us at 200 feet, and the observer, in a fit of misplaced efficiency, fired on us deliberately, which was a poor trick, because we could not retaliate. Luckily, he too was a rotten shot. We lit some flares and put them on the parados, to show him our position, and deter him from shooting us up. These seemed to tickle him so much that he turned and plugged at us again. At this moment, Brett came along the trench and cursed me into fits for giving our position away to the enemy by lighting flares. I told him the reason, and his answer was to the effect that — aeroplanes might shoot at us for a week and never hit us, but that I ought to know by now what the Boche gunners could do!!

No sooner had we made fire-steps in this old trench than the order came to retire, so we filed off and took up another position in the old British front line before the advance at Beaumont-Hamel in '16. It was not nearly such a good position: our field of fire was limited to 100 yards, and we could not see the ford across the Ancre: the trench was very narrow and shallow and digging in the chalk subsoil was very difficult.

No. 1 Company was on the right and No. 2 on the left; from the latter's position we could see the enemy's guns being brought into action, while, away on our right, across the river, we could see the enemy wandering about on the crest of the Thiepval ridge.

Ellam and I scrounged about and found an old dugout, which had partially collapsed at the bottom. It was damp and cold and musty at the bottom, and smelt of decay, rats, and putrescent vegetation and food. But, here I found a half-opened tin of bully beef, and picking out the biggest pieces of chalk with my penknife, ate the remainder of the contents. How the tin had got there, or how long it had been there, I never stopped to consider. We had been through strenuous days, marching far over shell-torn country on underfed stomachs, never knowing if or when we should see food again, and here, at least, was a form of food! But never shall I forget the taste in my mouth after it! For four days I had a dry stickiness in my mouth, incessant heartburn, and a feeling of overwhelming depression, which almost blotted out the instinct of life. Ellam would not touch it, and, therein he was wiser than I.

As a matter of fact the Regimental Transport had achieved a well-nigh impossible task by getting rations up to the Regiment all through the retreat, when roads were blocked for miles and miles with all manner of guns and transport. We never starved like some less fortunate regiments.

We had not occupied this trench for more than one and a half hours, before the enemy patrols entered the trench opposite. For the rest of the day No. 2 Company was kept busy sniping them.

At midday we heard the grim tidings of the Brigade Major's ride to find touch with the troops on our left. He had set off after we had left Courcelette, and had ridden for six miles and never seen a soldier. Divisions had seemed to disappear into thin air, and behind, there was not a single rifle to support us. Bar the 8-inch shells which had nearly blown the few remnants of the Regiment to bits in the early morning, not a single gun had barked at the enemy for 24 hours. Incidentally, Brett had told me that, when we had received orders to march on Auchonvillers in the morning, the village was already in enemy hands, and, luckily, he had met someone on the road who asked him where he was going, and on hearing his reply, had advised him to go elsewhere!

At 2 p.m. it started! Shells screamed over and crashed behind in the unoccupied support trench. We could watch the blighters serving the guns and were powerless to hinder them. For two hours it continued, but little damage was done as the trenches were so close together that a short one was likely to do the enemy more harm than us.

Then, at 4 p.m., the joyful tidings came round the line like wildfire that we were to be relieved at night, and that the Australian and New Zealand Corps were behind us. It seemed that the impossible and improbable was to happen, and I had visions of being allowed to sleep the clock round. The troops were hardly delighted; they probably didn't believe the tidings, and the majority were past caring what happened. Many rumours had floated round when we were trekking like hell yesterday. One was that we had made a counter–stroke and captured Lille and that the Belgians were advancing on Ostend! As usual, the yard had emanated from Refilling Point, that useful source of all lying rumours.

However, late in the afternoon, the tidings were confirmed in very truth, for we could see the Australians advancing in artillery formation along the sky line, away on our left. I don't think I have ever seen such a cheering sight.

A bitterly cold night drew on, and still no sign of the 12th Division, which was supposed to relieve us. Hope waned, flickered, and went out; and, then, suddenly at midnight, an order came for us to pack up once more and evacuate the line as the 12th Division was going to hold another position in rear.

From *The War Letters of a Light Infantryman* by Capt. J.E.H. Neville, MC. Privately printed by Sifton Praed & Co. 1930

A BETTER HOLE? 13TH JULY 1918

'There's a damned hedgehog down there'

The experience of 2nd Lieutenant W.H.H. Demuth, MC, of the 13th (Service) Bn. King's Royal Rifle Corps during a tour in the line near

Bucquoy from 7-20 July 1918 shows that bombs, bullets and bayonets were not the only occupational hazards faced in No Man's Land.

A curious incident happened during this tour. It appears that whilst patrolling 2nd Lieut. Demuth fell down a well sixty feet deep, within thirty yards of an enemy post; the remainder of the patrol had been unable to rescue the unfortunate officer, so returned and reported it. In broad daylight on July 15th 2nd Lieuts. Marshall and Carr went out with a covering party, erected a windlass over the well, and let down a rope. On shouting down the well Demuth, who had regained consciousness, answered. Fortunately there was just sufficient length of rope, and, having tied himself on to it, was very soon drawn to the top. It had been a painful business for the gallant officer, and he sat down to recover himself. The rescue party were much amused at his first remark after staring death in the face. He quietly said, "There's a damned hedghog down there." The officer was badly bruised and had a nasty cut on his chin, but was quite cheerful and stated that his steel helmet had saved his life. He was taken at once to the Aid Post, and then sent down the line. It was a wonderful escape from a very awkward situation.

2nd Lieuts. Marshall and Carr were congratulated by the Divisional Commander, and Rifleman Horrocks received the military medal.

From *The King's Royal Rifle Corps Chronicle 1918 (13th Battalion War Records)*. Winchester: Warren & Sons. 1919.

INTER-ALLIED CO-OPERATION: 23RD JULY 1918

'The battle was fought on a brilliant summer's day, and I saw a very handsome French youth lying dead in a field of clover'

Major Hervey de Montmorency, RFA, describes an attack in which he acted as liaison officer to a tank battalion detailed to support the 3rd French Division, which included French African soldiers. The piece reflects the grimness of battle at the same time as elevating its hilarious moments. Finally, at the end of a day of hand-to-hand combat, two captured German officers appear to be as proud when complimented on their conduct by a French general, their captor, as if they were being invested by the Kaiser himself.

On the 23rd July, 1918, the 3rd French Division, under Général Nayral de Bourgon, supported by a brigade of British tanks, opened the attack which led to the fall of Moreuil. One of the great problems before the battle was how to conceal the presence of the tanks from the enemy; so, while they were being assembled at Thory, several noisy aeroplanes were directed to fly to and fro above the German lines in order that the sound of their engines might drown the noise made by those of the tanks. The ruts or tracks made by their pedrails across the fields, too, were carefully raked over and obliterated, so that they might not be revealed in the enemy's aerial photographs taken of our zone. On my suggestion, French helmets were issued to all the personnel of the tanks. This led to a deal of fun and good-natured chaff; our fellows strutting about in their Gallic head-dresses, shrugging their shoulders extravagantly, exclaiming '*Mon Dieu*' and '*Sapristi*' and practising the somewhat ungainly French salute which reminds one of that insolent gesture often exchanged between school-urchins and which is known as cocking a snook!

Our attack was eminently successful all along the front, and by nightfall our lines had stabilised themselves beyond Sauvillers, with our right flank resting on the Bois du Harpon.

The French were loud in their praise of the tanks, which had saved them many casualties, but ours were heavy indeed, twelve cars being put out of action, and, if I remember rightly, the Tank Corps had ninety-five killed and wounded. I went into the firing line for a short time in one of these huge armoured cars, and found it most disagreeably hot; but I felt a sense of delightful security when I heard the bullets rattling against the steel walls; just as one often experiences a glow of pleasure seated by a comfortable fireside on a winter's night and listens to the rain and sleet pattering against the windows of one's home.

The Germans put up a tough resistance, their machine-gunners, as usual, displaying great heroism.

A French African battalion on our left advanced magnifi-cently. I have always held Ethiopians in affection, regarding them as brave, cheery, simple folk, and I was thrilled with their courage that day; a black corporal leading his platoon captured a German machine-gun at the point of the bayonet. In the rush at the gun more than half his men had been bowled over by the machine-gunners, who held up their hands and begged for quarter when the stalwart Ethiopians were about twenty yards away. The negro, the light of battle in his eyes, was about to fling himself on the German detachment and finish them off, when he was stopped by a French sergeant.

The negro corporal, maddened at being balked of his prey, plucked the safety-pin out of a hand-grenade and made a dash at an English Tank officer, mistaking his strange uniform for that of an enemy; but, somewhat puzzled by the French helmet the Englishman was wearing, he stayed his hand just sufficiently for the officer to rush up, catch hold of one of the buttons of the Ethiopian's tunic, and at the same time seize and wring his hand – the left hand, which was free – and, in halting, Britannic French, pour out compliments on the negro's courage. The negro dared not let go his bomb while the officer was clinging to him like a leech for fear that he might not be able to break away before the grenade exploded;

the officer, knowing this, gripped the black corporal like grim death. The situation was a critical one for some seconds, then everyone burst into roars of laughter, the negro himself joining in and hurling his grenade at the Germans, who, ducking down like ninepins, managed to escape the effects of the explosion.

On the battlefield I noticed two gigantic Ethiopians lying stiff and stark, surrounded by five dead Germans whom the negroes had evidently slain in hand-to-hand combat before they fell themselves.

The battle was fought on a brilliant summer's day, and I saw a very handsome French youth lying dead in a field of clover; two beautiful swallow-tail butterflies were playing around his head, which was pillowed on his arm.

During the heat of the battle, I was watching through my glasses a daring German who was peering at us from behind a tree barely two-hundred yards away. On a sudden I saw the flash of a shell, which burst apparently right on his face; the decapitated body fell back and lay motionless like a log, while the head, still in its heavy steel helmet, bounced away.

At eight o'clock at night I was standing alongside Général de Bourgon while our prisoners of war filed past us: the usual melancholy column of limping, dusty, depressed looking creatures with that wild staring expression in the eyes which men carry who have just escaped out of the Valley of the Shadow of Death. The general detained two officers, one a very tall, the other a very short man. In excellent German he put certain questions to them, and then asked if he could do anything for them: they requested a drink of water.

'Certainly,' answered de Bourgon; 'we never refuse water to our prisoners of war. I compliment you,' he added, 'on the splendid fight you put up. You conducted yourself like fine soldiers!'

The two German officers drew themselves up as stiff as pokers, saluted, and a glow of pride shone in their faces.

From *Sword & Stirrup: Memories of an Adventurous Life*, by Hervey de Montmorency. Bell & Sons. 1936.

ADVANCE VICTORIOUS: 20TH–23RD AUGUST 1918

'at mid-night, began the absolute worst night of my life'

2nd Lieut. H.H. Taylor, commanding a platoon in No. 1 Company, 13th (S) Bn. Royal Fusiliers records his part in an attack during the Second Battle of the Somme, on 23 August 1918. From 8 August 1918 onwards the Final Advance was officially on; this piece gives a feeling of the speed of the advance and the scale of an army on the move, with all the attendant arms and material then involved – tanks, cavalry, machine-gunners, supplies, as the old 1916 Somme battleground was completely and finally wrested from the Germans. But while victorious, the latter half of 1918 was still a bloody affair. Determined German soldiers defended every step of the way.

Arrived our trench, near Fonquevillers, at 3 a.m. Aug. 20th. Dugout at last. 4 beds (i.e. stretchers on a frame). Rather damp but happy. Breakfast 9.30 a.m. No stand-to. Road from F. Villers to Bucquoy, where up to 19th hardly a water cart dare go, filled with lorries, G.S. waggons, limbers, tanks and motor cars. Military Police at Pigeon Wood cross-roads! Rifle and foot inspection at 10 a.m. Meals quite decent, in a decent (big) elephant. Warned for stunt at 2.30. Sworn at by skipper, with Jones and Bally, re route for working parties. Bottle of scotch and one of lime juice in mess. Filled up w. bottles and marched off at 8.45 p.m. to Rettemoy Farm. Road packed. Picked up

wire, picquets &c. at Farm. On to Wasp Trench. Jerry bumping badly. Heavy gas shell bombardment, just round proposed
dump. Two men fell out, gassed. Dumped stuff just before
dump, to avoid big pocket of gas. Eyes in a devil of a state.
Whole party coughing and spitting! Back to R. Farm. Took
two gas cases to Yank doctor in the farm. O.K. 2nd load,
bombs and S.A.A. Got as far as P.H.Q. in Wasp Trench. Saw
C.O. and Capt. Walforde. Reported progress. Sent 12 men and
Sgt. Wing back to C.H.Q. as escort for German prisoners.

Aug. 21st. Carried on thro' the gas again with Lewis Gunners.
Carried box of S.A.A. myself. Damned hard work! Finished
finally at 2.30 a.m. Returned to Wasp Trench. Moved up at 5
a.m., when very heavy barrage opened & 63rd (Naval) Divsn.
passed thro' us. Casualties fairly heavy on leaving Wasp Trench.
Very misty. Only see about 10 yards ahead. Met returning
wounded first near old Platoon Hqrs. Devons, Cornwalls,
Drakes and Hawkes. Passed one man walking back with
empty left sleeve! Jerry shelled cross-roads by Platoon Hqrs.
very heavily. Pte. Lowe hit outside Platoon Hqrs. Huge piece
of shell tore half his throat away. Even then he managed to
get his field dressing out & crawl about a dozen yards. Very
hard luck, as Lowe had 3 wounded stripes up, and had seen
service in Mespot and Egypt. Put Platoon in position & then,
with Corpl. Massey, put myself on "point duty" at cross roads.
About half the division had lost all sense of direction owing
to the fog. Some wandering towards Bucquoy, others towards
Pusieux. Artillery and m-gun officers likewise lost. Owing to
previous knowledge of position, was able to send them all on
in right direction. About 400 prisoners passed down the path
to Wasp Trench during the morning. Formed them up in
batches of 8 for stretcher work. Got photo and shoulder straps.
Capt. Walforde hit through muscles of both legs, above knee.
Went down with Hun s-bearers & my wrist watch. Rum up at
9 a.m. Collier, my servant, drunk to the wide by 9.45. Put him

outside the dugout to dry! Jones rather shaky. He also had to resort to the same consolation. Neither he nor Bally came up much. C.O. came round about 10.30. Quite pleased. Tanks and cavalry passed on through Bucquoy between 5 and 7. Three tanks stranded. One by Bucquoy; one to right of B.; third on far ridge overlooking Achiet-le-Grand. Second had a direct hit on it. "Lunch" 1 p.m. Handed over posts to Middx. officer. Buried Pte. Lowe opp. Platoon Hqrs., near 3 German graves. Middle German grave had a large "humorous" wind vane on the top of the cross. Moved off at 1.45, down Bucquoy Avenue. One long line of transport on this road. Artillery firing by road. Jerry's heavies dropping all over the place. Turned off some 400 yards before reaching Pigeon Wood-Essarts Rd. Along Lees Avenue to trench. No bivvies or dugouts, so we annexed adjoining trench, with big Coy. Hqrs. & dugouts for men. Very hot. Gunners and other behind line people stripped to waist. Most of our men did the same when in position. 8 tanks drawn up just behind Coy. Hqrs. About 4 miles of cavalry, tanks, A.S.C., ambulances, ammn. waggons, motor lorries &c. in view from Coy. Hqrs, along Essarts road & Bucquoy Avenue. Had decent wash and decent dinner about 8 p.m. Then getting cooler. Rations up at 7 p.m. Managed to get 800 Woodbines for boys. Decent sleep on "chicken runs." Letters up with rations. Quite happy. Not much water about. Black bottle up with rations. First good sleep since leaving Souastre on the 9th Aug. Jerry sending up S.O.S. lights all night. We sent some up, when Jerry counter-attacked at Ablaineville & Logeast Wood. He was unlucky.

Aug. 22nd. Up 8 a.m. Beaucoup wind up. Other Coys. had been standing-to since 4 a.m., ready to move. Bosche counter-attacked heavily, but was again unlucky. We had breakfast and then held rifle and foot inspections. Couldn't get much water. Had to fill water bottles as best we could. Had a meal at 3 p.m. Managed to get 13 packets of Gold Flake from YMCA on Essarts Rd. Jolly fine. Dished them out to the boys. Moved up line again at 5.30 p.m., behind tanks, & rest of transport. Through Bucquoy again. Jerry sent over about half a dozen heavies "with their slippers off." Couldn't hear them coming. They landed on the road and upset a mule or two. Jerry smashing up what was left of Bucquoy. Place smelt very strongly of dead Bosches & dead horses. Many still unburied. Coy. Hqrs. heavily laden & lagged on the march. I helped with packs &c. On down sunken road to Achiet-le-Grand. Then came in sight of several dumps on fire. Also villages. Fired by Fritz on his retreat. Arrived near derelict huts about 11.15 p.m. Jones, then acting as Coy. Cdr., by this time was as drunk as a lord. He started off with a water bottle full of neat rum! We now came under German machine-gun fire. Couldn't get straight into trenches, as they were already occupied. The battn. we relieved didn't move out until we went over the top in the morning. Then, at mid-night, began the absolute worst night of my life.

Aug. 23rd 1918. Position of things then. Out in the open with Coy., 3 officers in charge. One drunk, other incapable, & babbling all kinds of impossible things, & myself, really inexperienced. Acting Coy. Cdr. became volubly drunk and started shouting out, within hearing of Fritz. Had to threaten to shoot him and then sent him into dugout before he would close down. Our No. 4 Coy. also without a home. At last found Coy. Cdr. of Bedfords, the people already in the trench. He didn't know where we could go; he already had a lost coy. of the Drakes attached to him. Also many machine-gunners for the barrage later in the day. Whilst looking over trench held by latter people, Jerry sent over dozens of gas shells. Eyes got in a rotten state, and breathing became rather painful. Managed to get men spread out along trench, but had difficulty in getting them to dig in. Most had fallen asleep, & seemed quite indifferent as to whether they got blown up or not. In some places they were lying shoulder to shoulder on both sides of the trenches. In one place they had stirred up some old gassed earth, & couldn't use that particular piece of trench. Got them to dig in at last.

Drakes coy. moved out at 2 a.m. Took over some of their trench. Jerry very busy with machine-guns and Very Lights. Another big gas shell attack at 3 a.m. Caught another dose. Jones still talking dippy in the dugout. Reported by Bedfords. Note from Bn. Hqrs. placing Bally in charge of Coy. vice Jones. This woke him up a bit. As soon as dawn broke five Jerry aeroplanes came over and started machine-gunning us. Only one of our combat aeroplanes in sight & he very wisely went home to breakfast then! Had a pot at Jerries with a rifle; a few Lewis Guns also potting. No luck. Could see the airmen quite plainly, as they were only about 400 feet up. Men, however, were fairly well dug-in by then, & there were no casualties in our Coy. Bread & bacon at 7 a.m. Took no notice of Jones. Two of Bedfords lit a fire to cook breakfast. Jerry saw the smoke. He had exact range of trenches & consequently the third shell dropped dead in the trench junction & blew their heads off. Killed instantly. Rather rotten for troops remaining in the trench. Received orders from Bn. Hqrs. at 10 a.m., after Jerry's aeroplanes had paid us several more visits. Zero to be at 11 a.m. Division on left had already taken Gomiecourt, so we need not expect much opposition. We also were living in hopes, as earlier in the morning we saw armoured cars & tanks chasing up and down the road along the ridge in front of us. Bedfords also were optimistic. Lined up Platoons at 10.45. 1 & 4 Platoons should have been in front, as 2 & 3 did last stunt. However, 1 & 2 went in front & reached barrage line at 11 a.m. Although was on at 11 for 8 minutes, front coys. had gone on, so we had to follow. Then the fun began! Our own barrage was very heavy; it was impossible to hear shouting. Then, when we reached the ridge between the road & the railway, we came into Jerry's barrage as well. Oh my! He mayn't have been holding the line on our left very strongly, but I am quite sure he was in full strength in front of us. We walked into a regular Fritz Christmas tree, 5.9's, pines, r-grenades, machine-guns & rifles, all "let rip" along that ridge. Machine-guns, fired low; kicked up earth and dust all round me, so that I could hardly see next man. Air became smoky from dozens of "Woolly Bears" & "Pip Squeaks." Had to grin at one wee boy, who was hit in the ankle directly we got out of the trench. He knelt down and started yelling "Sir, Sir, I am hit, I'm Hit. Over here!" Evidently had a notion that I should have stopped the war at once. Casualties getting heavy. I then did a silly thing. Walked right into a machine-gun traverse. Men on my right & left hit, but Smith, my servant, who was with me, remained untouched. I then sat in a shell hole while Smith put a field dressing on. Clung on to my tin hat like a shrimp. Tried to find out how far remnant of my platoon had gone, but couldn't see far for smoke. Gave it up & started for dressing station with Smith. Blood all over my head, tunic, breeches & equipment. Some knut! Met Jones & his platoon just coming up. Told them to give Jerry an extra one for me. Looks of surprise on faces of m-gunners, for I had only passed them a few minutes before, on the way over the top. Then had that curious feeling of uncertainty as to whether I should stop another packet before reaching the dressing station. Jerry's machine-guns were still very busy knocking spots off our parapet. Greatly bucked when Bennet, our stretcher-bearer, assured me that I was a sure "Blighty." Got machine-gunned when crossing roads to rear of trench. Reached field dressing station near derelict huts. Yank doctor & one of our own. Bosche and our own wounded all round the shanty. Under heavy shell fire. Dumped my webbing equipment & gas mask. Also revolver holster. Saw Lewis, one of my L.G. team, hit in wrist. Sun scorching down. Took tunic off & walk down the line at 11.30 a.m.

Diary and papers of 2/Lieut. H.H.Taylor formerly in the compiler's collection.

FIRST BITE AT THE HINDENBURG LINE: 18TH–24TH SEPTEMBER 1918

'Spotting a M.G. post about 40 yards away on the other side of the wire, Sgt. Ford calmly got up and rushed forward, hoping to find a gap through which to rush the enemy post. He fell riddled with bullets.'

One of the greatest feats of arms of the final advance was the capture of the Hindenburg Line by the 46th (North Midland) Division on 29 September 1918. This line was the German army's 'make-or-break' defensive position. It was a mass of mutually supporting trenches, machine-gun posts and barbed wire on rising ground to the east side of the St Quentin Canal, which was itself a formidable obstacle. The following account is of a preliminary attack (and the days preceding it) for the purpose of gaining possession of Pontruet, one of the outlying defences of the Hindenburg Line on the west side of the canal and obtaining observation over the Line before the general attack was launched. The narrator, Captain C.N. Littleboy, commanded 'C' Company of the 1/5th Sherwood Foresters and his devotion to his command is evident, especially when, towards the end, he takes pains to describe the sense of loss he felt by the death of several trusted and beloved non-commissioned officers and men of the 'Half-moon Company.' It is interesting to note that at the commencement of this action all four platoon commanders in 'C' Company were NCOs, and they were all experienced commanders. There seems to have been one other officer, presumably the second-in-command, whereas the establishment actually called for six company officers and earlier in the war it would have been highly unlikely to find platoons commanded by sergeants for any length of time.

September 18th. We went on parade as usual this morning, but at 11 a.m. a runner arrived and gave a pink form to the Adjutant. Those who saw the action, guessed it spelt *m-o-v-e*, and they were right. When the Battalion had been assembled, we marched back to Lahoussoye with instructions to be ready to move at 5 p.m. by lorry.

By five o'clock all was ready, and we sat outside our billets and waited, the monotony being only once relieved by a captured German car dashing along the main road to Albert. At 8 p.m. our waiting came to an end. We fell in and marched about two miles to a by-road, on which were drawn up a seemingly unending series of lorries that were to take the Brigade on its long midnight run.

At 10 p.m. a light flashed, a whistle blew, and the convoy started on its moonlight trip. 10.30 p.m. saw us going through the deserted streets of Corbei, and thence out into that bleak, devastated area east of Amiens. Ahead of us stretched the long, straight road to St. Quentin, shining like a ribbon in the moonlight. Passing the old aerodrome on the right, Warfusée was reached and left behind as on and on we went, with clouds of thick, white dust swirling about us. At Foucaucourt a short halt was made, and then on again once more, passing the old dressing station on the left, through Estrées, or where Estrées was, and across the old No Man's Land to Villers Carbonnel. Then slightly downhill to the marshy Somme, across a very rickety and narrow bridge to Brie, and up again to Mons-en-Chaussée. Here and there we saw a derelict Tank, a dead horse, a rifle stuck upright in the ground, and other relics of the battlefield, all looking weird and eerie in the moonlight. The whole countryside looked absolutely deserted and stricken. Men laugh at the idea of ghosts, but there were few who would have cared to walk alone in the ghostly stillness that lay brooding over this track of death.

And now, far away in the distance, we saw Verey lights shooting upwards, bursting into light, then slowly falling to earth again, and fading as they fell, and we began to think we were nearing our journey's end at last. We passed Estrées-en-Chaussée, and then, a long way ahead, we saw the road lit up by flashlight. The leading lorry had stopped. One by one, the lorries drew up (4 a.m.) and discharged their sleepy, and in some cases blasphemous, loads. The companies were got together, and then we struck off to the right, across country, to Larris Woods. There we lay on ground-sheets till dawn, listening to a distant barrage that told us somebody was going over somewhere. How different all this from March and April!

As soon as it was light we looked around to get our bearings. Pœuilly was about 400 yards to the north-east, and from the top of the hill behind we could see Vrainges and Fléchin to the north, and to the east the hollow in which Vermand lay – familiar country to some of us.

After eating our "haverbag" rations, we set about building ourselves leafy bowers in which to live in true alfresco style. Then, by the side of blazing fires, we slept the day and then the night away.

September 20th. Towards dawn in September, leafy bowers, even in the pleasant land of France, are a doubtful proposition, and we were thankful when the sun rose and warmed us. One hour's P.T. helped to pass the morning away, and then about 2 p.m. the Company Commanders were summoned to the Colonel's rustic dwelling. Briefly we were told the general situation, and then that we were going into the line that night, and, in all probability, would shortly take part in an attack.

When the meeting was over, I found Mr. W-Smith, D.F.C., 2/5th Sherwood Foresters, and now of the Kite Balloon Section, waiting for me. He pointed to his balloon up above and promised that he would look after us when we were in the line at Berthancourt. He told me afterwards that, whenever he saw the copse "getting it in the neck," he used to turn some "heavies" on to the Boche gunners.

After a Platoon Commanders' meeting, at which I explained the dispositions of the companies – B Coy. right front, A Coy. left front, C Coy. support, and D Coy. reserve near Bn. H.Q. – at 6 p.m. we moved off up the line. First at company intervals and then, after Vermand, at platoon intervals. Vermand was "stinking" with big guns, and, as we passed through, they started their "evening hate." We were very glad that we were at this end and not at the other. Villécholles was reached in about twenty minutes, and so on to Maissemy, outside which we halted for a quarter of an hour, while the cross-roads ahead of us were being shelled. Then on we went to these cross-roads, where we found the guides of the outgoing battalion, eager to be away from such a "hot corner," but their eagerness was apparently not shared by the C.O., who calmly sat on a wall, dangling his legs in great enjoyment.

It was now quite dusk, and not so very far away we could see "star shells" rising and falling, and hear the whine of gas shells and their "pop" as they burst in the valley in front of us. Quickly the word was passed: "Have your respirators ready." Half-way up the slope ahead of us we found our L.G.s and drums that had been dumped there by the limbers, and, picking them up, we went on past the trench on our left, where Bn. H.Q. was, and past the Cemetery on the right, which was to be the battalion dump, to Berthaucourt.

Here, by the Crucifix – as we discovered afterwards, the most "unhealthy" spot of all – we waited while the guide tried to find his own company, which we were to relieve. This done, and there being only two platoons to relieve, C Coy. was temporarily put in a field on the west side of the village, while O.C. C Coy., C.S.M. Lamb, D.C.M., and Pte. Mays took a walk round the copse to find other accommodation, but discovered none; so No. 9 (Sgt. Ford) "clicked" and took over the roughly dug shelters vacated by the two outgoing platoons; No. 10 (Sgt. Parnham, M.M.) and No. 11 (Sgt. Holmes) were given areas in the copse on the west side, and No. 12 (Sgt. Loomes) went into the dyke on the north side. Each platoon had begun work on "bivvie" construction.

It was a lovely, starry night, and Boche bombers were going over in an almost continual stream. Vermand and Massemy seemed to be getting the benefit of a good many cargoes, and bombs bursting along the ridge by the Tumulus made quite effective fireworks.

We had been at work about three hours when the Hun sent over a salvo at the copse, which unluckily burst among No. 11 and decided Sgt. Holmes to shift his men to the dyke in which Sgt. Loomes was already established.

September 21st. It was beastly in that copse: at dawn, at 10 a.m., at noon, at 3 p.m., at 5 p.m., and at dusk we were "strafed" with H.E. and gas, but we suffered fewer casualties than might have been expected, taking the "bivvies" into consideration, for their roofs were nothing but wood and branches. (Even a ground-sheet gives one a wonderful sense of safety.) Probably what security these shelters afforded was due to the fact that they were nearly all converted shell-holes.

Thinking that the unavoidable movement around C.H.Q. was perhaps partly the cause of our being shelled so heavily, I decided to move C.H.Q. to the dyke, a more secluded place. While Ptes. Cavanagh and Titley and Dmr. Johnson were making the necessary accommodation in the dyke, a gas shell landed right amongst them, killing Pte. Titley and wounding the other two. Pte. Middleton, stretcher bearer, rushed up and, being unable to tend properly to their wounds with his respirator on, fearlessly tore it off without any thought for himself.

It was so "unhealthy" in the copse that I begged Colonel Hacking to let us go into the front line for a rest, and this he did later, but not in the way I meant.

It will be remembered that B and A Coys. were in the front line, if such it could be called, for there was not much of a line. B Coy., on the right, occupied for the most part a sunken road running south from Berthaucourt, and also about a 100 yards of Gallichet Alley, ending in a bombing block, with the Boche somewhere round the corner. A Coy., on the left, had posts among the ruins of the village and just north of it, and also one at a bombing block up Beux Trench, which ran into Gallichet Alley a few hundred yards east of Berthaucourt.

We were not surprised to hear, therefore, on the night of 21st-22nd, that B and A Companies were to make a small attack to improve matters if possible. Their objective was the junction of Gallichet Alley and Leduc Trench. At 1 a.m. each company sent a party of one officer and sixteen men: "B" to work down Gallichet Alley, and "A" down Beux Trench. Both parties were heavily bombed, and "B", on the right, found unexpected opposition from machine gun fire at close range. It became obvious that no advance could be made with such small forces, and eventually Capt. Smith, M.C., O.C. A Coy., ordered a withdrawal to the original positions.

September 22nd. At dusk – we were still in the copse – a ter-rific "strafe" was put over by the Boche all around Berthaucourt, and drizzling rain and darkness did not improve matters. Our view was entirely blotted out by a veil of swirling smoke as the storm of shell-fire smothered the front line and the ruins of the village – everywhere was the sickening smell of H.E. and gas. It was while Cpl. Cook was fearlessly running round warning the men to put on their box-respirators that he was killed.

Through this inferno we could now faintly hear the sounds of bombing and rifle fire; so Mr. Banks, with a runner, went up to B Coy. to see what was happening, and to find out whether they wanted any help. All wires had gone "dis" as soon as the bombardment started, so we could not get any news that way.

The first news I received from B Coy. was brought by Dmr. Marshall, who told me that the Boche had captured Gallichet Alley, but B Coy. still held the sunken road. As we were about to move forward to counter-attack, L/c Crispin spied B Coy.'s red lamp winking merrily away towards Bn. H.Q., and read, "A and B Coys. O.K."

But meanwhile Mr. Banks and his runner had been making their way to B Coy. H.Q. As soon as he got into the sunken road he smelt Boche and said to his runner, "The Boche have been here anyway." A little further on they came upon a dead Boche lying at the end of Gallichet Alley, amid a heap of "tater-mashers" and one or two Hun rifles. On arrival at B Coy. H.Q., Capt. Jacques, M.C., told him what had happened. Under cover of a barrage, a party of about 40 Boche had forced in the post up Gallichet Alley and reached the junction of the C.T. and the sunken road, where Lewis guns held them up. Only one Boche had reached the road, and he was to have six feet of it for himself next morning. All B Coy.'s rifle and L.G. fire had then been directed on Gallichet Alley, and the Hun, finding he could make no headway, had begun to bomb the sunken road. Meanwhile a message had been sent to Mr. Barrows, who was on the extreme left of B Coy., to counter attack with his platoon, and, as soon as they approached, the Boche turned and bolted, throwing away rifles, bombs and equipment in their hurried flight.

September 23rd. After the midday hate, Pte. Colledge, M.M., came up to C.H.Q. with a message that I was wanted at Bn. H.Q. On arrival there, I was told that Sir D. Haig wanted some Boche land and some Boches with it; so the "Half-moon Company," with the aid of Mr. Crellin's Platoon of A Coy., were to attack on the morrow. First we were to occupy Leduc and Beux trenches, and then go on down the slope and capture the trench line in front of Pontruet. Troops would be attacking on our right and left; those on the left, the Lincoln and Leicester Brigade, would sweep down on Pontruet from the north-west (so that the Boche would be caught between two fires) and then join up with the Division on our right, and we, C Coy., would then be squeezed out and become "support." Armed with these instructions, I returned to the copse.

At dusk the four Platoon Commanders met in the dyke. The general idea was given them in outline, and also the various dispositions of the platoons: No. 12 Platoon would be on C Coy.'s right, with No. 10 in support in the sunken road. Next to No. 12 came No. 11 Platoon, and on the left again No. 9. Nos. 11 and 12 Platoons were to capture Leduc and Beux trenches respectively, and then push on to Pontruet, while No. 9 would make straight for Pontruet. On the left of No. 9 came Mr. Crellin's Platoon; they were to work up the dyke, and subsequently they did really valiant work. While these dispositions were being planned and noted, C.S.M. Lamb was seeing to the drawing of bombs, S.A.A., &c., from the Cemetery dump.

While the platoons were getting ready for the attack, O.C. C Coy., Mr. Banks and two runners walked round the A & B Coys.' front line, as their line of posts was to be our kicking-off place, and then we showed each Platoon Commander where he was to go. The latter returned to their platoons, loaded them up with bombs and S.A.A., and all set off to their own positions.

September 24th. Two hours later, at 2 a.m., the four Platoon Commanders met in A Coy. H.Q. cellar, when final instructions were given, zero hour told, also the time of the advance, zero + 17. The Platoon Commanders then returned to their platoons and we waited as patiently as we could.

At zero, 5 a.m., out barrage opened (a very feeble affair) and the T.M.s in the sunken road by B Coy. H.Q. began to fire at the Boche in Gallichet Alley.

At zero + 17 to the second, our advance began, but we met with a devastating fire from the Boche posts that had scarcely been touched by the barrage. At 5.40 a.m. Pte. Knight arrived with a message from Mr. Banks saying that No. 11 could not get on at all, and a similar report came from Sgt. Loomes (No. 12). So Pte. Mays and I hurried to the sunken road, arranged for another T.M. strafe and asked Capt. Jacques to send another platoon forward. While going back I suddenly heard a motor engine and thought, "What on earth is a lorry doing up here?" and then, "If only it was a tank!"

Bouyed [sic] up with this new hope, I hurried on and found "Milady" clanking through the ruins. As I went up to her I was covered by her guns, but luckily one of the crew recognised the British uniform and yelled to me to go round to the side. An officer appeared from the belly of the monster and asked where he was and whether he could be of any use. The situation was quickly explained and "Milady" trundled off towards the Boche post that was holding us up. The garrison of that post "did not like the look of things a bit," and surrendered, but not before they had received a drum of armour-piercing ammunition. I heard afterwards that some men of No. 11 Platoon under Cpl. Gale rushed the post at the same time.

Meanwhile, what was happening on the left? There was no word from No. 9 or Mr. Crellin. No. 11 Platoon at first was held up, but by dint of creeping forward bit by bit, accurate bomb-throwing, and the fine example set by Sgt. Loomes, Cpl. Roper and L/c W. Saville, Beux trench was captured at last, and then we saw the Lincolns and Leicesters streaming towards us from Pontruet. We were told that they had been through the northern part of Pontruet, but when we tried to advance down the slope, we found that the village had not been properly "mopped up" and the Boche was once more at his M.G. posts. This of course prevented the Lincolns and Leicesters from getting back, so they lined the dyke just to the north-west of Pontruet.

It was now 8 a.m., and in broad daylight it was not possible to attack Pontruet again, so we consolidated on the high ground where we were.

Still no word from No. 9 Platoon. We got our first news of them at dusk, when Cpl. Cliff and one man crawled back from in front of Pontruet and told the tale of Sgt. Ford and gallant No. 9. No. 9 Platoon, we learnt, had started off at zero + 17, heading straight for Pontruet. Very soon they met with M.G. fire, but Sgt. Ford, seeing that the attack on his right was held up, thought the reason was that No. 9 was not far enough forward, and pressed on. So, by means of rushes of a few men at a time, they found themselves at last up against the Boche wire. Spotting a M.G. post about 40 yards away on the other side of the wire, Sgt. Ford calmly got up and rushed forward, hoping to find a gap through which to rush the enemy post. He fell riddled with bullets.

So died Sgt. R.H. Ford, D.C.M., M.M. – the bravest little fellow we ever knew. When Capt. Smith was told of his death, he said, "I noticed Ford particularly when you were talking to your Sergeants in the cellar this morning. He looked so bright and smiling and intelligent. He might have been going on leave instead of 'over the top.'" I can picture him now as I last saw him, three or four minutes before the attack began – smiling, cheerful, perfectly confident, spotlessly clean, with a khaki muffler wrapped loosely round his neck. Sgt. Ford and I were together the whole time we were in France, and I had never known him fail. Memories of Ford crowd in on me as I write – how at Ypres he went on firing his L.G. during the Boche counter-attack, long after he was hit – how at Mount Kemmel he covered the withdrawal of his company with his platoon, on three occasions, amidst very heavy shelling, and how he used to go out on patrols by himself, "just to find out what the Boche was doing." Everybody liked him and everybody mourned his loss. I think that Sgt. Ford fulfilled all the conditions in Rudyard Kipling's "If," and was indeed a "Man" after the poet's own heart.

But to return to the happenings of this day, the 24th September. When Cpl. Cliff had finished his story, C.S.M. Lamb immediately went out with him, Sgt. Ford was brought in and his remaining men withdrawn. Meanwhile, under cover of darkness, we began to organise our position on the hill top overlooking Pontruet, so that everything should be ready to hand over to the 1/8th Bn. when they came to relieve us. While we were thus employed, the Boche began to put a few rounds into Pontruet, thinking evidently that we now held it. The Boche infantry, to warn their gunners of their presence in the village, sent up red Verey lights. The effect of these from our point of view, looking down as we did, on Pontruet, was most wonderful. The trenches and ruins of the village were lit up again and again by a brilliant red glow, and then faded into darkness. Red lights were not the only ones; green, yellow, blue each had its turn, and we might have been looking at a scene lit up by coloured limelights.

At 4 a.m. the 1/8th Bn. arrived, and the relief was completed just before dawn. Our tired platoons made their way through Berthaucourt and Pontru to Cooker's Quarry, where C.Q.M.S. Lane housed them in some old but comfortable "bivvies."

September 25th. At 12 noon we awoke, and the senior surviving N.C.O. in each platoon was summoned. We then took
the full toll of our losses. Within the compass of this small
book it would be impossible even to mention the name of
every man who, on September 24th, laid down his life for his
country. Reference has already been made to Sgt. Ford, but
we must refer to three more, Sgts. Loomes and Holmes and
Pte. Mays.

Sgt. C. Loomes, D.C.M., was hit very badly early on in
the attack, and subsequently died in hospital. Big, burly Sgt.
Loomes – never frightened, never worried, always cheerful
– an ideal N.C.O. The news that he was badly wounded was
brought to me by a man who came into A Coy. H.Q. and said,
with a break in his voice, "I have got Sgt. Loomes outside, Sir,
he is in a terrible mess. He and I have been pals together for
years, so may I take him back?" I told him to do so, and his
old pal, even bigger and broader than Loomes himself, went
out and bore his dying friend away.

Sgt. G.H. Holmes, M.M., was killed outright by a bullet
straight through the forehead, while leading his men in a
rush against the Boche post in Gallichet Alley. He was known
throughout the Battalion as a brave man – brave almost to
recklessness. He was never happy unless he was in No Man's
Land or "strafing" the Boche. Tall and thin, wearing four
wound stripes, we used to see him walking about over the
top, with his own peculiar gait, without the slightest regard
for whistling bullet or bursting shell.

And now just a word or two about Pte. "Flanny" Mays.
During the whole attack he had been indefatigable, running
hither and thither with messages. After the attack was over,
about 8 a.m., when about to enter A Coy. H.Q., he received
a direct hit from a "wing-bomb" and died almost instantaneously. Mays was a very fine soldier, always willing, always
cheerful, and the bravest of the brave. Many were the occa-

sions when his jokes and sallies cheered the drooping spirits of his mates. We missed him very much in the days to come.

From *'C' Coy. 1/5 Sherwood Foresters in the Battles of The Hundred Days* [by Capt. C.N. Littleboy]. Printed for private circulation. 1919.

A LAST BATTLE: 4TH NOVEMBER 1918

'two Germans came out of a dugout almost under my feet, I managed to kill them both'

In their last battle of the Great War the 13th (S) Bn, Rifle Brigade attacked successfully at Louvignies. But as Lt. R.N.R. Blaker, commanding 15 Platoon in 'D' Company, describes, many Germans were still putting up a stiff resistance, particularly machine-gunners when they got the chance. Blaker's Platoon came through this attack relatively lightly, largely due to his own initiative in undertaking a remarkable solo reconnaissance which earned him a Military Cross. Platoons on either side of him, both of which lost their officers in the advance, suffered heavily and the battalion's losses for the day were 157 killed, wounded or missing. But the method now in use was a long way away from the massed attacks of the earlier part of the war. Platoons were organised into three groups, mutually supporting each other as they moved through the German defences, and the defenders swiftly crumbled when they realised that they were being overrun.

The position the 13th R.B. had to attack was, first, a railway line (partly an embankment and partly a cutting); and secondly, orchards (both very strongly held – the orchards particularly so – according to our information). The 8th Lincolns were holding the line where we were to attack, and were (roughly) in possession of and just in front of the village of Ghissignies and about 100 yards from the railway.

We were in reserve at the village of Neuville, about four and a half miles from the front line.

We had orders to attack on the morning of the 4th Nov. 1918. Zero time was 5.30 a.m. There were, as usual, countless conferences, until everyone was quite conversant with their duties, etc.

We had some aeroplane photos which gave us a very fair idea what the country we were to attack was like – but the actual location of any machine-guns in the orchards had not been reported. I was told however that the position I was to be in was directly in front of the orchards and I should probably have a difficult job and must get on to the orchards as soon as possible, leaving the supports to clear up in the railway.

I may say here that as we came through the country before reaching Neuville I always, when I got the chance, went and had a look at the positions which the Germans had been driven out of and got a good idea where they were likely to put their machine-guns, etc.

We started off from Neuville at night, 12.15 a.m., to get to our positions, and after a tiring and muddy march over ploughed fields, and with a certain amount of shelling too, we were met about a mile outside Ghissignies by guides from the Lincolns and taken to spots near our starting points. The guides, however, took some of us wrong and 2nd-Lt. Macaulay, 16th Platoon, and I (15th Platoon) were taken quarter of a mile too far away, but after an hour we discovered this and had to get the men out of the cellar we had found for them and go through a pretty heavy shrapnel fire to a small stable right on the front line. We finally got settled about 3 a.m., but of course no one could smoke or speak, except in whispers, as we were only about 100 yards from the enemy and they kept putting down machine-gun fire and Whizz-bangs, and as there were no cellars and practically no cover we had to be careful. We were very lucky coming up as we didn't have a single casualty.

As soon as I had the men settled I went to find Capt. Davy, O.C. "D" Co., and report to him, and he told me to go with 2nd-Lt's. Park and Macaulay and take our Platoon Sergts. and arrange our positions to start off from. As this was in front of the Lincolns and out in No Man's Land, it wasn't pleasant, and as we came out of the cellar where Capt. Davy was, two Whizz-bangs pitched within 10 yards of us, right in our line, but beyond putting the "Wind up" and covering us with mud, fortunately we escaped. We then – after tripping over wires, tree-trunks, etc.–managed to get into our positions, but were very nearly fired on by the Lincolns, as no one had told them we were going out. I only just stopped them in time.

Park and I fixed up our positions roughly, we were greatly aided in getting them by a Very Light the enemy kindly put up, and it also enabled us to get a good view of the railway, but we had to stand very still while it was up. It's a very funny feeling standing there waiting and hoping they won't spot you, as you have the impression that you must look very prominent.

We then all went back and had a talk to the Section-Commanders and the men, and then, as time was getting on, got them out of the stable and by degrees to their positions. Shell fire was pretty heavy as the enemy were rather "windy" and seemed to suspect there was something up, but fortunately we escaped, although I thought my left section were "done in," as both machine-gun fire and Whizz-bangs for a minute or so seemed to be directed right on them, however, I went there and found they were all right, but it had been very close.

My Platoon was only 22 men and was divided into three sections – Riflemen and Rifle grenadiers on left and right and Lewis Gunners slightly behind in centre. We had to cover about 150 yards with the Platoon.

Nos. 13, 14 and 16 Platoons, "D" Co., only had 21 men each.
2nd-Lt. Ackroyd was in command of 13 and was in touch with
the K.R.R.'s on his right.

After a good deal of walking about, at last I managed to
get the section in position, and just before 5.30 a.m. the barrage started, it was supposed to land on the railway (but it
turned out that it was about 6 yards too far and went over
the railway). It was a grand sight. The whole front along the
railway seemed to be one vast sheet of flame, and earth, etc.,
was flying about, we immediately advanced so as to get up
close to the barrage, so that when it lifted we could be on
the enemy before he could resist, but unfortunately there was
a thick hedge with barbed wire between us and the cutting,
which was not touched by the barrage, and when I got there
it was difficult to see any opening, as it was still dark, but I
ran along the hedge and found a small gap near the ground
and scrambled through on hands and knees, my Sergt. (Packer)
was just ahead. As I went down the cutting (which was 15ft.)
two Germans came out of a dugout almost under my feet, I
managed to kill them both, then I went over the single line
and a German Officer came out of a dugout and fired at me
from 5 yards but missed, I then killed him and went up the
bank the other side and found my Sergt. there firing at some
Germans who were running away towards the orchards.

I could see the outlines of the orchards about 180 to 200
yards away across a turnip field, and as there was no cover I
at once made up my mind that if we went across the open
we would be wiped out (in my opinion) before getting there,
so I told Sergt. Packer to bring the men on and pointed
out the way and said I was going to try to have a go at the
machine-guns in orchard on our front, before they could get
at us. Sergt. Packer went back to the railway for the men and
I went on alone. To get to the orchards I had to walk through
our barrage, which was going at the rate of 100 yards per

4 minutes, but although I had some extremely narrow shaves and a very unpleasant time I managed to get there safely.

As I said earlier, I had studied the positions where the enemy were likely to put machine-guns and I now found this very useful. It was still fairly dark but beginning to get light. I immediately saw in a corner of an orchard a place where it was practically certain there would be a machine-gun and got there without being seen, and my surmise was right as I got right up to a machine gun dugout with two Germans on the look-out, but they had missed seeing me in the dark and also no doubt they didn't expect anyone so soon and were doing more sheltering that watching, on seeing me they immediately tried to put their hands down for their revolvers, but I killed them both before they could do so, as I was right close on them, thereupon yells came out of the dugout and I shouted "come out," and out came five pretty scared looking Germans with "hands up." I motioned them to go back through the barrage towards our lines, and after a slight hesitation, they had to do so. I then went to another likely place on my front and managed to do exactly the same as before to another machine-gun crew. I then looked about but could see no more machine-guns on my front.

It was then my intention to wait for my Platoon to come up with me after the barrage had lifted, but as it was getting lighter and I could see better, I saw all dotted about just round by the orchards and in the open grass fields beyond, enemy heads occasionally peeping out, so I thought it better to try to get them out of their holes, so I went on and did so, making them come out and drop their arms, they didn't like coming out into the barrage and why they didn't fire at me, goodness knows, I suppose it was funk a good deal as the hedges and ground were getting pretty well knocked about by the shell, and shrapnel was flying too, anyway I cleared out all I could see and sent them on their way to our lines. I could not hold them all in a bunch and so considered it would be best just to disarm them and send them back. I could see in the distance some of our men coming along and so I left them to escort the prisoners.

It was practically light now and the barrage was very hot, I had some extraordinary narrow escapes – being blown along about 5 yards by a shell which pitched very near indeed and half deafened me for a minute, but on the whole I considered that the method of getting onto the enemy whilst they were still sheltering seemed so successful that it was worthwhile going on a bit and risking it, especially as my men were coming along. So on I went disarming and sending back Germans here and there – but there were not so many beyond the orchards – until I came to the main road leading from Louvignies to Le Quesnoy, and on this road I came on a solitary house standing right on the road. I came from the back of it and went round to the front, where there was no door, and peeped inside a room which opened into the road and saw there a crowd of Germans, some sitting down and some standing. I don't know who was more surprised – they or I. Anyway I managed to pull myself together a bit quicker than they did and advanced just under the doorway holding a Mills bomb in my left hand and my revolver in my right, the only thing I could think of to say was "Kamerad," and so I said it, at the same time menacing them with my revolver, they didn't seem very willing to surrender, so I repeated "Kamerad," and to my surprise and delight they "Kameraded," 2 officers and 28 other ranks. My idea is that they were holding a sort of conference, as the barrage was not then reaching them in full force. Both officers and three of the other ranks had Iron Cross ribbons on!

My first idea was to hold them in the house, but they were a rather nasty looking lot and also I could see out of the corner of my eye as I stood in the doorway several heads beginning to peep out of dugouts, etc., along the road, so I made them drop their arms, i.e., those who had them, fortunately for me none of them had expected so early a visitor and so hadn't them actually ready for use, and then I made them file out of the house and pointing towards our lines I gave them to understand that they had to go that way, they didn't seem to like the idea, especially as the barrage was getting hot again, but I couldn't afford to stand any nonsense so off they went. I saw two blown up by a shell, but couldn't waste much time beyond seeing that the others were actually going the right way, as I was getting a bit anxious about the heads along the road which were peeping up, so I went along collecting them and succeeded without any trouble in getting the road quite clear and collaring two machine-guns and a trench mortar and the crews. I can only suppose their Officers and N.C.O.'s were among the lot in the house, or else I would have encountered more resistance, anyway, roughly 25 to 30 came in quietly including one pretty miserable looking young officer. I took them in front of the house, as it was some shelter from the barrage which was pretty nasty now. One of the prisoners, when we got to the house, wanted to know where the men were who were in it, and when I told him they had "Kameraded" he expressed great surprise to think they had done so to me alone. These prisoners seemed fairly harmless so I made up my mind to hold them, especially considering that I could see no more anywhere along the road and all our front for 200 yards at least was clear, so I lined them up along the front of the house and stood sentinel over them until my men came up later.

The barrage knocked things about a good deal and the Germans got a bit uneasy at times and wanted me to go down with them into a cellar under the house and road, but I was not taking any risks. I got a small bit of shrapnel in the face whilst guarding them and one of them wanted to dress it, but again I was not taking any risks, as my view of them would have been impeded.

Also, whilst guarding them, a shell hit a telegraph pole just above me and brought some of the wires down round my neck, but I soon got rid of them, and none of the Germans went for me. I was getting a bit anxious now as Germans kept coming back in twos and threes from the orchards, but none of our men appeared, I drove a few of these Germans back again and they never attacked me. At last to my relief I saw one of our men dodging along just by the road, and then another. I waved to them and think they saw me as they went back, and then the rest came along onto the road about 100 yards off with 2nd-Lt. Dion, "A" Co., and Sergt. Packer, together with about 14 men of my Platoon. I immediately marched the prisoners up to them and sent them off to the rear under escort and told 2nd-Lt. Dion that there were some revolvers and arms in the house and he went off with a few men and got them. I have in my possession now one of the German officers' revolvers from these.

I found my Lewis Gun and three of the team had been knocked out just before reaching the railway, but the rest of the Platoon had had very little opposition after getting over the railway, but the Platoons Nos. 14 and 16 on our right and left had practically been wiped out by machine-gun fire from the orchards, together with, I am sorry to say, Capt. Davy and 2nd-Lts. Park and Macaulay – all killed.

We were now only about 200 yards from our first objective, and after reforming, we went on – behind the barrage now – to the first objective and reached that without any serious opposition. "C" Co., on our left, were nowhere to be seen and it turned out that they were held up by machine-guns for some time. However, at the first objective, Lt. Gosney of "D" Co., who was with "A" Co. for the attack, came along with a few men and told me 2nd-Lt. Ackroyd had got through and was in touch with the K.R.R.'s on the right, and after a few minutes he turned up and we re-organised the men we had left of the Co. and decided to go ahead, as we knew the New Zealanders were on our left, although there was the gap between us and them where "C" Co. should be, but there seemed to be very little opposition now after we had got past the main road.

There is not much more to say except that we tried to start three times from our first objective to our final objective (which was about one and a half miles on), but on each occasion were forced to come back as some of our guns were firing very short right into us, but finally we got off and then kept in touch with the 10th Royal Fusiliers, who were going through the 13th K.R.R.'s, they being left to clear up the village of Louvignies. We finally got to our objective, just in front of Jolimetz, about 8.45 a.m., 10 minutes late according to programme, but our barrage, firing into us at first objective, was responsible for this.

We then had about 30 men between us, but men kept on coming in and we dug in quickly, and after rather an anxious time for half-an-hour or so, in case of a counter-attack, we got word the Essex Regiment had gone through on our left to follow up the enemy, and we had a bit of a breathing period, but shells came pretty freely from the enemy and we nearly all had very lucky escapes. However, beyond posting the men and getting the rest into the shelter of a barn with a cellar, we had not much to do, and my servant, Tubbs, who had come up at the first objective, managed to get me some tea to drink (without milk), but it still tasted excellent as I was very tired and thirsty.

We hung onto this barn and our line until 0.30 at night, when orders came for us to march back to Beaurain, about nine and a half miles. Poor old infantry, after all that, we had to march back, absolutely dead tired too, however we had to do it and we did.

I found next day I had 14 men left out of my 22 − 3 killed near railway and others wounded at various times.

I also found that some pieces of shrapnel had gone right through my leather jerkin at the back, just missing my spine, and also a hole was blown right through the top of my torch which was strapped on my belt.

The attack was completely successful and the enemy never stopped again till the armistice.

From *An Episode of the Great War, 1914-1918* by R.N.R. Blaker. Published anonymously for private circulation. 1919.

Biographical Notes

ANDREWS (Sir William Linton) had already embarked on a career as a journalist when he enlisted in the 1/4th Black Watch (T.F.) in 1914. He was born in Hull in 1886 and educated at Hull Grammar School and Christ's Hospital. His early experience was on provincial newspapers in Hull, Huddersfield, Sheffield, Dundee, Portsmouth, Paris and London. During the war he served for three years on the Western Front as a private, N.C.O., Orderley Room Clerk and Company Quartermaster-Sergeant. He received a commission in 1918 but did not see active service as an officer. He became sub-editor of the *Daily Mail*, 1919-23, editor of the *Leeds Mercury*, 1923-39 and of the *Yorkshire Post and Leeds Mercury* 1939-60. He was President of the Guild of British Newspaper Editors from 1952-53 and also held various honorary positions, directorships and so on. His knighthood was bestowed in 1954.

BLAKER (R.N.R.) served in the ranks of the Queen's Own (Royal West Kent Regt.) before he was commissioned in the Rifle Brigade (Special Reserve), 22 November 1916. He was awarded the Military Cross for the action described by him in this collection and it is interesting to compare the official citation printed in the *London Gazette* with his own version of events: *For most conspicuous courage and good work on 4th November, 1918, near Louvignies. While leading his platoon in the attack, he was temporarily cut off from it, and came single-handed on two enemy machine-guns in action. He dashed between the guns, capturing them both and their teams. Seeing his men a short distance ahead, and held up by machine-gun fire from a house on their flank, he again single-handed took them in the flank, clearing the house and capturing two officers and twenty-eight other ranks.* He graduated at Jesus College, Cambridge, in 1898, twenty years before he won his MC!

BOARDMAN (J.A.) served with the 6th Bn. The Cheshire Regiment (T.F.) during the whole four years of its active service, Nov. 1914 to Nov. 1918. Awarded the Military Medal and bar.

BOLWELL (F.A.) was a reservist of the Loyal North Lancashire Regiment recalled to the colours on mobilisation in 1914. He recalled: '...although a married man with two children, I was only too pleased to be able to leave a more or less monotonous existence for something more exciting and adventurous. Being an old soldier, war was of course more or less ingrained into my nature...' His active service lasted from 15 August 1914 to 11 October 1915, when he was wounded at Loos. Following some months of treatment he was discharged medically unfit.

CUDDEFORD (D.W.J.) came home from Nigeria early in 1915 and enlisted in the Scots Guards, with whom he trained at Caterham and did duty in London until commissioned in the Highland Light Infantry. He joined the 12th H.L.I., 15th (Scottish) Division on the Somme in August 1916; took part in the battles of the Somme, Ancre and Arras serving as a platoon commander, adjutant and company commander successively. In July 1917, before the Third Battle of Ypres, he was seconded to the King's African Rifles for service in German East Africa where he ended the war as adjutant of the 4/2nd K.A.R. By his own account he was twice recommended for a decoration during his service in France, but none materialised.

EYRE (Giles E.M.) enlisted in the King's Royal Rifle Corps in 1914 when he was eighteen years old; served in France with the 7th Bn. in 1915 when he was wounded, and on his return to the front in the spring of 1916 was attached to the 2nd Bn. and captured during the Somme fighting, in the attack on the switch line near Pozières on 23 July. According to the dust-jacket of the first edition of his war memoirs, published in 1938, he was: 'One of the few survivors of the Messina earthquake of 1908, journalist, wanderer in the far corners of the Empire, sailor before the mast, soldier, nearly drowned in swimming across the Vistula in an attempt to escape a German prison, lecturer and propagandist, supporter of lost causes.'

FLOYD (Thomas Hope) enlisted in the Royal Fusiliers and served with them in France in 1916 before being selected for officer training. He had not, however, seen action in the ranks. As a newly commissioned subaltern he was posted to the 2/5th Lancashire Fusiliers in the Ypres Salient at the beginning of June 1917. His time with them lasted just two months as he was wounded on 31 July 1917 on the first day of the Third Battle of Ypres. In 1931 the Orpington Press published his *Intolerance: A Lecture*.

FOLEY (H.A.) was educated at Clifton College and enlisted with his brother, Geoff, in the Somerset Light Infantry at Taunton Barracks on 31 August 1914, being drafted the next day to the 6th (Service) Bn. He accompanied the battalion to France as a lance-sergeant in May 1915. In November he and his brother were sent to the GHQ Cadet School at Blendecques, near St Omer and emerged as second lieutenants after the one month course. Both brothers were gazetted to the 7th (Service) Bn. S.L.I. Geoff was wounded and died of wounds in May 1917; H.A. Foley, now a captain, was captured during the German spring offensive in 1918.

GAUNT (F.) lived in Chelsea, London, enlisted in the Royal Fusiliers in February, 1912. He accompanied the 4th Bn. to France in 1914 and remained with them until wounded on 11 November 1914 during the First Battle of Ypres. On discharge from hospital in 1915 he was transferred to the 3rd Norfolk Regiment and eventually discharged from the Army in September 1916 in consequence of his wounds.

GREGORY (H.) enlisted in the Loyal North Lancashire Regiment in 1916, subsequently transferring to the Machine Gun Corps and serving in France with the 119th Company (40th Division). By his own account 'served eighteen months in the trenches, was awarded the Military Medal, wounded and captured by a German officer at Soissons, and afterwards worked as a Prisoner of War in a German salt mine.' He was demobilized in March 1919, and as well as his war memoirs, published in 1934, he wrote a play, *Prisoners of War*, published in the same year.

HOWSE (Harold Edward) was born in 1894 in Port Elizabeth, South Africa, where his father was a businessman. A great-grandfather was one of the settlers of 1820. In 1906, aged 12, he went to Rondebosch High School, near Cape Town, then in 1909 to the Grey Institute and in 1911 matriculated at the University of the Cape of Good Hope, going up to Rhodes University College, Grahamstown. He took a full part in university life: Debating Society, joint-editor of the Magazine, on the Students' Representative Council, Rugby football &c., narrowly missing a 1st Class Honours when he graduated in History in 1913. With reluctance he entered a business house in Port Elizabeth but was freed from this uncongenial employment on the calling out of the Defence Force in 1914, being posted to Cape Town with Prince Alfred's Guards, from where he managed to obtain several teaching posts. At the end of 1915 he took a passage to England to join up and received a commission in the Royal Berkshire Regiment in August 1916. He was killed in action during the third battle of Ypres on 16 August 1917. He was posthumously mentioned in despatches.

KAY-SHUTTLEWORTH (The Hon. Edward James) was the second son of Lord Shuttleworth. He was educated at Eton and Balliol College, Oxford, graduating in 1911 and being called to the Bar. He was commissioned in the 7th (Service) Bn., Rifle Brigade, immediately on the outbreak of war and served with them in France from May 1915 until invalided home in March 1916. In England he underwent a staff training course, but was killed in a motor-cycle accident on 10 July 1917 on the eve of his return to France. He was married in December 1914 and left an infant son and daughter.

KELLY (D.V., MC) was born in Adelaide, Australia in 1891 of Irish stock, educated at St. Paul's School and Magdalen College, Oxford. Resident in Stockholm in 1914 ('enjoying... my last year of comparative idleness') he came home and enlisted in the University and Public Schools Brigade, subsequently receiving a commission in the 6th (S) Bn. Leicestershire Regiment. During the whole of his active service in France, 1915-1918, he served on the staff of the 110th Infantry Brigade, selected by the brigade commander because he was the only Oxford man in his battalion. His long and distinguished post-war career in the diplomatic service included Ambassador to Moscow, 1949-1951. Knighted, GCMG. Memoirs, *The Ruling Few*, published 1952.

LITTLEBOY (Captain C.N., MC) was the son of a shipbuilder from Saltburn-by-the-Sea. Educated at Rugby and Trinity College, Cambridge, graduating in 1913, he received a commission in the 5th (Territorial) Bn. Durham Light Infantry in October 1914. He was quickly advanced to acting captain, but did not serve overseas with the D.L.I. Instead he was posted to the 2/5th Sherwood Foresters in Ireland in June 1916 as a captain and second in command of 'C' Company, which he subsequently commanded almost throughout its active service. The battalion went to France in February 1917 and he was awarded the Military Cross for gallantry at Passchendaele in September. In August 1918 the 2/5th Bn. was broken up and absorbed by the 1/5th Sherwood Foresters. Littleboy was given command of 'C' Company, retaining several of his old NCOs and men. He was severely wounded by a bullet in the stomach on 3 October 1918 during the Hindenburg Line battles, and awarded a bar to his MC for this battle. A younger brother was killed in action with the Royal Warwickshire Regiment near Ypres in October 1917. He wrote two books about his war experiences and was a major contributor to the history of the 2/5th Sherwood Foresters.

LUCY (John F.) an Irish Catholic from Cork enlisted with his brother in the Royal Irish Rifles – a Protestant regiment from Ulster – in 1912. They had worked together in a newspaper office but were 'tired of small wages, of lodgings, and of having to cook our own food... tired of fathers, of advice from relations, of bottled coffee essence, of school, and of newspaper offices... we were full of life and the spirit of adventure, and wanted to spread our wings.' Clearly gifted, both brothers were soon NCOs. Denis Lucy was killed on the Aisne but John survived the war although several times wounded. He became a sergeant and in 1917 was commissioned in the Royal Irish Rifles. He was wounded severely at Cambrai and came home for good, retiring after the war with the rank of captain.

LYNCH (Francis William [Frank]) came from a substantial Dublin family and was educated at the Oratory School. Commissioned in the Connaught Rangers Special Reserve 15 August 1914 and served with the 1st Bn. (composite 1st and 2nd Bns.) in France from 11 March 1915 until his death in action during the Second Battle of Ypres on 26 April. He is buried in La Brique Cemetery, Ypres.

NEVILLE (J.E.H.) was educated at Eton and Sandhurst and gazetted to the Oxfordshire & Buckinghamshire Light Infantry in 1916, joining the 2nd Bn. (52nd L.I.) in France in December. He was awarded the Military Cross in January 1918 and wounded in August. He joined the 1st Bn. (43rd L.I.) in 1919 and served with it in North Russia, where he was again wounded. A career soldier, he retired as a lieutenant colonel.

PARR (George Roworth) was gazetted to the Somerset Light Infantry, in which his father and brother both served, in 1912. He served with the 1st Bn. in France including Le Cateau, The Marne and the Aisne, some of the time as acting Intelligence Officer of the 11th Infantry Brigade. He was killed in action in an attack in Ploegsteert Wood on 19 December 1914.

PENNEFATHER (Lt. Charles Lewis) was educated at Marlborough College and gazetted second lieutenant in the Rifle Brigade, 15 August 1914. Went to France with the 2nd Bn. in November, surviving Neuve Chapelle in March 1915 but being wounded on 9 May at Aubers Ridge when all the company officers of the 2nd Rifle Brigade were casualties. He rejoined the battalion in November 1915 and was killed in action as a captain, commanding 'C' Coy., on 14 June 1916.

RIDDELL (Brig.-Gen. Sir Edward Pius Arthur, CMG, DSO) was a professional soldier who had seen active service with the Northumberland Fusiliers in the Boer War and transferred to the Rifle Brigade in 1908. He commanded the Cambridgeshire Regiment in France from June 1916 to September 1917 when he was given command of a brigade. He was awarded the DSO in 1916, a bar in 1917 and second bar in 1918; the CMG in

1919. Brigadier commanding Northumberland inf. brigade 1920-24, retired in 1925. He was honorary colonel, Northumberland Fusiliers from 1939 until his death in 1957, chairman of Hexham Conservative Association and knighted in 1945.

SHARPE (Pte. William A.) A married man with a young son, living at Hinckley, was called-up under the Derby Scheme, graded C1 and posted to the Northern Cyclist Battalion for Home Service. However, during the '3rd Ypres' manpower shortage he was peremptorily regraded A1 and posted overseas. He served with the 2/8th Lancashire Fusiliers in France and Belgium and was captured in March 1918. A very sad postscript to Sharpe's experiences were nightmares: 'Which wake me up in a cold sweat. Have seen dead men and skeletons get up under heavy shell fire and run in all directions.'

SMITH (Captain H.Raymond) enlisted in the 8th Bn. Worcestershire Regiment, a territorial unit, on 8 August 1914; went to France with the battalion in the spring of 1915 by which time he was a member of the machine-gun section. Early in 1916, following the formation of the Machine Gun Corps he was briefly transferred to it then posted home in August 1916 to train for a commission. He was sent to the MGC headquarters at Grantham and forgotten about, finally being sent to an officer cadet battalion at Bristol towards the end of the year. He was commissioned in the Rifle Brigade in March 1917 and joined the 11th (Service) Bn. in France on 26 April, serving with them as a platoon and company commander during the battles of Third Ypres and Cambrai until early 1918 when invalided out, returning to the front just before the armistice.

SYMONS (Noel Victor Housman, CIE, MC) was a nephew of Laurence Housman. He was educated at King Edward VI School, Bath, of which his father was the headmaster. In 1914 he was working in a bank in Bath and promptly joined the Worcestershire Regiment, later receiving a commission in the 2/8th Battalion and served with them in France being wounded three times and awarded the Military Cross on the Somme in 1916. He took to soldiering and would have liked to have stayed in the army with a regular commission, but this plan was finished when he lost an arm in 1917. After the war he entered the Indian Civil Service and served in a variety of appointments including Commissioner of the Presidency Division of Bengal, and Director-General, Civil Defence and Additional Secretary, Defence Dept., India, 1943. Appointed Companion of the Order of the Indian Empire in 1941, he retired from the ICS in 1946 and devoted much time to the magistracy in Hampshire in his retirement.

TAYLOR (2/Lieut. Harold Howes) Left Borden Grammar School in Kent in 1914, aged 16, becoming a bank clerk. Enlisted 1917 in the Royal West Kent Regiment. Commissioned in the Royal Fusiliers Feb. 1918. His brief active service was with the 13th (S) Bn. from 31 July to 23 August 1918, when he was wounded in the head at Achiet-le-Grand (as is related in this work). He was in action several times during his service in France. All that is known subsequently is that he was advised not to return to office work on account of his head wound and applied to study at an agricultural college.

THOMAS (Cecil) enlisted in the London Regiment in September 1914 but did not serve overseas until May 1916, when shortly after his arrival he was captured at Vimy Ridge and spent the remainder of the war in German prison camps, most of the time as 'forced labour' in a German coal mine at Dortmund.

VENNING (Captain Edwin Gerald) was an actor, educated at the Clergy Orphan School, who became a soldier in 1914, being commissioned first in the Royal Sussex Regiment then transferring to the Suffolk Regiment with whose 1st Battalion he served in France. He was killed in action on 6 August 1915, shot in the neck while observing from a point immediately in rear of a British trench. The Suffolks' regimental history records that 'All ranks of the battalion deplored the loss of a valuable, gallant, and popular officer.'

A Western Front Chronology

1914

BEF mobilises	5 August
BEF begins to land in France	12 August
Battle of Mons (encounter battle)	23 August
Retreat from Mons	24 August-5 September
(Battle of Le Cateau [British holding action]	26 August)
Battle of the Marne (Allied attack)	6-9 September
Battles of the Aisne (Allied advance)	13-15 September
Battle of Messines	12 October-2 November
Battle of Armentières	13 October-2 November
First Battle of Ypres (German offensive)	19 October-22 November

1915

Battle of Neuve Chapelle (British offensive)	10-13 March
Second Battle of Ypres (German offensive)	22 April-25 May
Battles of Aubers Ridge (British offensive)	9 May
Battle of Festubert (British offensive)	15-27 May
Battle of Loos (British offensive)	25 September-13 October

1916

Battle of the Somme (British offensive)	1 July-11 November
Battle of the Ancre (British offensive)	13th-19th November

1917

German strategic withdrawal to the Hindenburg Line	25 February-5 April
Battle of Arras (British offensive)	9 April-24 May
Battle of Messines (British offensive)	7-14 June
Third Battle of Ypres (British offensive)	31 July-10 November
Battle of Cambrai (British offensive)	20 November-7 December
German counter-attack at Cambrai	30 November-4 December

1918

Spring Offensive (German)	21 March-5 April
Lys Offensive (German)	9-30 April
Battle of Amiens (British offensive)	8 August 1918
Final Advance (British offensives)	Thereafter

Glossary

Archie – Slang for anti-aircraft fire.

Barrage – Concentration of artillery fire on a position to be assaulted, or laid down to cover a movement of troops. A creeping barrage was one that lifted forward by a set number of yards at set intervals, so that it could provide cover as infantry advanced close behind it. A box barrage was a barrage surrounding an area on four sides in order to isolate it from supports, often used during raids. Advances in artillery techniques and accuracy were crucial to the eventual breakthrough of the Western Front stalemate.

Battle bowler – Officers' slang for steel helmet.

Battle order – Reduced scale of equipment worn by infantrymen in an attack: packs and personal equipment left behind for collection later, countered somewhat by additional ammunition, wire-cutters, bombs etc. carried forward into the attack.

Battle police – Military Police personnel stationed directly behind attacking troops to apprehend any unwounded stragglers unwilling to remain in the fighting area.

B.H.Q. – Battalion Headquarters.

Billet – Civilian building in which troops were accommodated. In France, mostly barns, cottages and stables. A billeting officer would proceed ahead of his unit to its destination and make a tour selecting billets and chalking the number of occupants, together with their sub-unit, on the door.

Officers, senior NCOs and experienced old hands would secure the most appealing billets.

Blighty – Slang for England, or for a wound that would ensure one's return there, as in 'Copping a Blighty.' Derived from Hindi word for Home and 'imported' to Europe by old sweats who had served in India.

Bomb – hand-held explosive device such as Mills bomb or Stick bomb, in more modern parlance known as a hand grenade.

Canteen – As well as a place of refreshment a canteen was the tin eating receptacle carried by every soldier, into which his rations were placed when served. When providing for himself it would also act as a cooking vessel. Also known as a Mess Tin.

Chatting – removing lice from clothing, usually by running a burning cigarette down the seams where the vermin dwelt, or crushing them between finger and thumb nails.

Cold feet – Cowardice (but not fear: see Wind up).

Consolidate – Make secure and fortify a newly won position.

Counter-battery fire – Artillery fire directed upon known or believed positions of opposing artillery, to close them down or put them out of action.

Crump – A heavy shell or its explosion.

C.T. – Communication Trench, i.e. one running back at right angles from the front-line trench system and providing protected access to it.

Dixie – Large metal receptacle for cooking in, which could then be carried to where it was required if its recipients were in trenches. When at Rest the men would come to it to fill their Canteens (q.v.).

Draft – Body of men selected as reinforcements from the UK to a unit in the fighting line. Usually commanded by an officer also going to the front.

Duck Boards – Slatted wooden flooring of ladder-like appearance laid along the trench floor (or across difficult ground) to render walking/gripping easier. Generally in lengths of about six feet.

Dud – Shell which fails to explode, or an inefficient soldier.

Dugout − Properly constructed protection from shelling for front-line troops, these were dug underground with steps down, shored up with anything from old doors to miles of cut and imported British oak. The term covered any excavation of this type from small chambers holding just a handful of officers and men to extensive undertakings as deep as 100 feet below ground which could house hundreds of men, HQs, telegraphists, aid posts and so on.

Elephant shelter − Hut constructed of semi-circular sheets of corrugated iron − called Elephant Iron − which married neatly to each other. With a beam of around eight feet at the base the hut could be as long as available sheets of iron allowed, and afforded a certain amount of protection from blast and shell splinters, etc.

Emergency rations − or Iron Rations. Bully beef and biscuits carried at all times but not supposed to be touched except in emergency.

Enfilade − Fire from the beam, brought to bear on an exposed flank, along the length of the trenches rather than straight towards them.

Estaminet − Establishment found in smaller towns and villages behind the lines which provided a range of provisions: beer, wine, coffee, omelettes, chips, etc. Usually furnished with tables and benches, a fire, sometimes a piano. Not a pub as such, but a centre for recreation when out of the line, where troops would gather for food, warmth, a sing-song and civilian company.

Fatigue − Duty such as peeling potatoes, moving stores, cleaning billets. A group of soldiers detailed for such work was known as a Fatigue Party.

Field Punishment No. 1 − Punishment for crimes such as drunkenness and insubordination which consisted of the offender being tied to a wagon wheel in the crucifixion position for one hour each morning and evening when out of the line, up to a maximum of twenty-eight days, sometimes combined with pack drill and bread and water rations.

Fire-Bays − Sections of the front-line trench manned during Stand To (*q.v.*) or during enemy attacks, divided by Traverses (*q.v.*)

Firestep − Raised platform along the side of the trench nearest the enemy upon which a man standing upright could comfortably look over the top and use his rifle.

Flying Pig − Long, fat trench mortar bomb.

Footslogger — Infantryman.

Funk Hole — Protective cover scraped out of the side of a front line, support or communication trench (C.T.) (*q.v.*), usually accommodating one or two men and nothing like the properly constructed and shored dugout (*q.v.*). One problem with funk holes was that if the side of the trench was undermined too far it could fall in, lessening the protective cover of the trench and requiring labour to rebuild.

H.E. — High Explosive, as in shells.

Major — Field officer rank held by a battalion second-in-command, but also the name by which the regimental sergeant major was known to those in his battalion.

M.G.C. — Machine Gun Corps

Minenwerfer — Feared German trench-mortar projectile (also Minnie, or Moaning Minnie)

M.O. — Medical Officer

Mopping Up — Dealing with overlooked enemy soldiers and positions after an attack had taken place. As the attack progressed, special parties detailed as Moppers Up would follow behind to winkle out the occupants of dugouts, hidden snipers, etc.

No Man's Land — The strip of land, varying in width from just a few yards to perhaps a quarter of a mile, which divided the opposing trenches. Riddled with obstacles such as barbed wire, shell holes, etc.

O.P. — Observation Post

Parados — The side of a front line or support trench farthest from the enemy, spoil from the trench digging being thrown up along the rear side to provide a little further protection.

Parapet — The side of a front line or support trench nearest to the enemy, built up with spoil, sandbags, iron loopholes and so on.

Patrol — Party sent out into No Man's Land (*q.v.*), most often at night time, to obtain information on enemy positions, observe their works and movements, etc.

Pill Box − Concrete fortification containing machine gun(s). The 'Concrete Zone' from Passchendaele down to Arras was so called because the Germans built a system of mutually supporting pill boxes along this line during 1917.

Plum Pudding − Trench mortar bomb.

Raid − Offensive operation to enter the enemy trenches and cause casualties, obtain the identity of opposing regiments, etc. Raiding parties varied from a handful of men to a complete battalion, usually supported by artillery fire.

Red Lamp − Officially sanctioned brothel for the use of other ranks. There were a number in the larger base towns. Officers were privileged to have their own version, the Blue Lamp.

Runner − Soldier employed to carry messages during operations. Runners were attached to each platoon and company headquarters (Platoon and Company Runners) and battalion headquarters (Battalion Runners).

S.A.A. − Small Arms Ammunition, for rifles and machine-guns.

Sap − Small trench projecting forward into No Man's Land (*q.v.*) to allow attackers, raiding parties and so on to stay under cover until nearer their objectives.

S.I.W. − Self Inflicted Wound.

S.R.D. − Initials inscribed on rum jars sent up to front-line soldiers; stood for Service Rum Diluted but many soldiers knew it really meant Seldom Reaches Destination.

Stand To − The period at dawn or dusk when, in the half light, a German attack might be expected so all infantry in front-line trenches would be held in readiness to repel such an event.

Stick Bomb − German hand-held bomb with a wooden handle, detonated by pulling a string before the bomb was thrown.

Strafe − Particularly violent or heavy artillery attention on a given area. Also applied to a reprimand by a superior officer.

Sump Hole − Hole dug into the bottom or side of the trench to drain away excess rainwater and human waste. A most unpleasant excavation to stumble into on a dark night.

Toffee Apple − Trench mortar projectile with a spherical head (containing explosive) about the size of a football, with a haft about two feet long sticking out of it which was pushed into the barrel of the mortar prior to firing.

Traverses − Thick sandbag partitions built to confine the effects of shells landing in a trench, and to prevent enfilade (q.v.).

Trench Mortar − Portable weapon with a high trajectory which could be used from a trench (or specially dug emplacement in the front line) to fire missiles into the opposing trenches.

Valise − Officer's roll-up canvas kitbag in which he transported his kit and slept. The private soldier's equivalent was the Pack, worn on the back, which did not, however, double as a sleeping bag.

Verey Light − Flare cartridge fired from a Verey Pistol which illuminated the surroundings at night, so fired if enemy activity in No Man's Land (q.v.) was feared. Coloured Verey lights could also be used as coded signals, calling on artillery support for instance.

Whizz Bang − Light artillery shell. They seemed to arrive quickly and make a loud noise.

Wind up − Fear, almost universal, the sufferer being sympathised with rather than thought badly of.

Wire − Barbed, but far more viscious than the agricultural variety, deadly sharp, difficult to handle, awkward to get caught-up in. Both sides erected barbed wire in front of their trenches in order to prevent raiding parties getting to them. They were wound around wooden posts at first, but hammering these in attracted enemy fire so screw pickets were introduced. These were made of iron with a corkscrew at one end which could be wound silently into the ground, with ringlets along the length through which the wire would be wound. Some troops hung old tin cans on their wire which rattled on the wire being disturbed to alert them to prowling enemies.

Working Party − Group of soldiers selected for some duty usually associated with defensive works, such as setting up or improving barbed wire, digging trenches, etc.

Sources

Extracts from the following works are included in this compilation and grateful acknowledgement is hereby made to the respective authors and publishers.

Andrews (W.L.) Haunting Years: The Commentaries of a War Territorial. Hutchinson. nd (c.1932).

Aston (John) & Duggan (L.M.) *The History of the 12th (Bermondsey) Battalion East Surrey Regiment.* The Union Press. 1936.

[Blaker (R.N.R.)] *An Episode of the Great War 1914-1918.* Printed for private circulation. 1919.

Bolwell (F.A.) *With a Reservist in France: A Personal Account of all the Engagements in which the 1st Division 1st Corps took part, viz: Mons (including the retirement), the Marne, the Aisne, First Battle of Ypres, Neuve Chapelle, Festubert & Loos.* Routledge. nd (c.1919).

Cuddeford (D.W.J.) *And All for What? Some War Time Experiences.* Heath Cranton. 1933.

Eyre (Giles E.M.) *Somme Harvest: Memories of a P.B.I. in the Summer of 1916.* Jarrolds. 1938.

Floyd (Thomas Hope) *At Ypres with Best-Dunkley.* Bodley Head. 1920.

Foley (H.A.) *Three Years on Active Service & Eight Months a Prisoner of War.* Bridgwater, Somerset, Printed for Private Circulation. 1920.

Gaunt (F.) *The Immortal First: A Private Soldier's Diary with the original B.E.F.* Erskine Macdonald. 1917.

Grant (Capt. D.P., MC) *The 1/4th Hallamshire Battn., York and Lanacster Regiment, 1914-1919.* Printed for private circulation. [1931].

De Grave (Capt. L.W.) *The War History of the Fifth Battalion Sherwood Foresters Notts & Derby Regiment 1914-1918.* Bemrose & Sons, Derby. 1930.

Gregory (H.) *Never Again: A Diary of the Great War.* Stockwell. [1934].

Headlam (Cuthbert) *George Rowarth Parr, Prince Albert's Somerset Light Infantry, A Short Memoir.* Edinburgh. Privately printed. 1915.

Hills (Capt. J.D., MC) *The Fifth Leicestershire: A Record of the 1/5th Battalion the Leicestershire Regiment, T.F., during the War, 1914-1919.* Loughborough. The Echo Press. 1919.

Housman (Lawrence) Ed. *War Letters of Fallen Englishmen.* Gollancz. 1930.

Kay-Shuttleworth (Mrs Sibell) *Edward James Kay-Shuttleworth, Captain 7th Rifle Brigade, Staff Captain 218th Infantry Brigade 1890-1917.* Printed for private circulation. 1918.

Kelly (D.V., MC, formerly Captain, Leicestershire Regt.) *39 Months with the 'Tigers,' 1915-1918.* Ernest Benn Limited. 1930.

The King's Royal Rifle Corps Chronicle 1918. Winchester. Warren & Sons. 1919.

[Littleboy (Captain C.N., MC)] *'C' Coy. 1/5 Sherwood Foresters in the Battles of The Hundred Days.* Printed for private circulation. 1919.

Lucy (John F.) *There's a Devil in the Drum.* Faber & Faber. 1938.

Macmillan (Prof. W.M.) Ed. *A South African Student and Soldier: Harold Edward Howse 1894-1917.* Cape Town. T.Maskew Miller. nd (c.1918).

Montmorency (Major Hervey de) *Sword & Stirrup: Memories of an Adventurous Life.* Bell & Sons. 1936.

Neville (Capt. J.E.H., MC) *The War Letters of a Light Infantryman.* Printed privately by Sifton Praed & Co. 1930.

Riddell (Brig.-Gen. E., CMG, DSO) & Clayton (Col. M.C., DSO) *The Cambridgeshires 1914 to 1919.* Cambridge. For the Regiment. 1934.

Russell (Capt. R.O., M.C.) *The History of the 11th (Lewisham) Battalion The Queen's Own Royal West Kent Regiment.* Lewisham Newspaper Co. Ltd. 1934.

Smith (Charles) Comp. *War History of the 6th Bn. The Cheshire Regiment.* The Bn. O.C.A. 1932.

Smith (Capt. H.Raymond) *A Soldier's Diary: Sidelights on the Great War 1914-1918.* The 'Journal' Press. Evesham. 1940.

Thomas (Cecil) *They Also Served: The Experiences of a Private Soldier in German Camp & Coal Mine 1916-18.* Hurst & Blackett. 1939.

The War History of the 1st/4th Battalion The Loyal North Lancashire Regiment 1914-1918. Published by the Battalion History Committee. 1921.

Wylly (Col. H.C., CB) *The Green Howards in the Great War.* Published by the Regiment. 1926.

Illustration List

opposite side to the door. Such trees would be brought up during the night and would replace the remains of genuine trees, so that the landscape did not alter from the German perspective. Author's collection.

26. Derelict tank on the Ypres battlefield, 1917. This example was utilised as an Observation Post. Author's collection.

27. An old front-line trench at the Ypres Salient. Photograph taken in 1917 after the fighting had moved from this spot. Author's collection.

28. The Grand Palace, Ypres, 1917. Remains of the Cloth Hall with British Army hut and vehicles. Author's collection.

29. A mine crater in the Ypres Salient. Author's collection.

30. Overgrown sandbag dugout near Ypres, 1917. Author's collection.

31. Brothers in distress. Two destroyed Mark IV tanks on the Ypres battlefield, 1917. The one on the left still has its 'unditching beam' attached. This iron reinforced beam could be attached to the tracks by chains and used to haul a bogged-down tank out of a trench or other obstacle. Author's collection.

32. More abandoned tanks in the Ypres Salient, 1917, showing the waterlogged ground that so hampered the British offensive that summer and autumn. Author's collection.

33. 'Cheddar Villa', a large German pill box at St Julien. Once captured was used by the 1st Buckinghamshire Battalion (and no doubt other regiments) as a company headquarters, also housing a platoon and the Regimental Aid Post, despite the rather large entrance which, of course, faced the Germans. Author's collection.

34. Aerial photograph taken on 1 May 1917 of the Dammstrasse (the road running diagonally NE from left to right on the picture). The moated emplacement north of the road is Eikhof Farm. Author's collection.

35. Gas was first used by releasing it towards the enemy lines when the wind conditions were deemed to be favourable. Later, with greater effect, it was mainly released via gas shells. Here a team of signallers are able to continue to operate their equipment during a gas bombardment by wearing gasmasks. Author's collection.

36. The trench mortar bomb (or German Minenwerfer) was a lethal trench weapon. Fired from a transportable projector, with its high trajectory it could all too easily come whistling down on unprepared infantrymen. Author's collection.

37. Gunners' War: everyone in the front line lived with the constant fear and attendant stress of artillery bombardment, especially, as seen here in September 1917, in the ever turbulent Ypres salient. Author's collection.

38. Men of "D" Company, 7th (Service) Bn. Royal Sussex Regiment waiting for orders during the Battle of Arras, April 1917. Author's collection.

39. Tea and tobacco evidently cheer up these inhabitants of a front-line post at Croisilles in January 1918, despite the snow on the sandbags. Author's collection.

40. The German soldier was a rightly respected foe. His stormtroopers were brave and well-trained in minor tactics and use of ground. Here German soldiers are seen advancing to the attack. Author's collection.

41. German attack develops with stick grenades as they encounter barbed wire in No Man's Land. Author's collection.

42. The Western Front. Author's collection.

43. The Ypres Salient. Author's collection.

44. The Somme region. Author's collection.

45. Liquid Fire attack at Hooge. Author's collection.

Front cover illustration: British troops going over the top at the Somme. Author's collection.

Back cover illustration: Machine Gun Corps troops manning heavy machine guns just behind the front line. Author's collection.

Index

TEMPUS – REVEALING HISTORY

Private 12768 Memoir of a Tommy
JOHN JACKSON

'Unique... a beautifully written, strikingly honest account of a young man's experience of combat' *Saul David*

'At last we have John Jackson's intensely personal and heartfelt little book to remind us there was a view of the Great War other than Wilfred Owen's' *The Daily Mail*

£9.99   0 7524 3531 0

The German Offensives of 1918
MARTIN KITCHEN

'A lucid, powerfully driven narrative' *Malcolm Brown*

'Comprehensive and authoritative... first class' *Holger H. Herwig*

£13.99   0 7524 3527 2

Verdun 1916
MALCOLM BROWN

'A haunting book which gets closer than any other to that wasteland marked by death' *Richard Holmes*

£9.99   0 7524 2599 4

The Forgotten Front
The East African Campaign 1914–1918
ROSS ANDERSON

'Excellent... fills a yawning gap in the historical record' *The Times Literary Supplement*

'Compelling and authoritative' *Hew Strachan*

£25   0 7524 2344 4

Agincourt
A New History
ANNE CURRY

'A highly distinguished and convincing account' *Christopher Hibbert*

'A *tour de force*' *Alison Weir*

'*The* book on the battle' *Richard Holmes*

A *BBC History Magazine* Book of the Year 2005

£25   0 7524 2828 4

The Welsh Wars of Independence
DAVID MOORE

'Beautifully written, subtle and remarkably perceptive' *John Davies*

£25   0 7524 3321 0

Bosworth 1485 Psychology of a Battle
MICHAEL K. JONES

'Most exciting... a remarkable tale' *The Guardian*

'Insightful and rich study of the Battle of Bosworth... no longer need Richard play the villain' *The Times Literary Supplement*

£12.99   0 7524 2594 3

The Battle of Hastings 1066
M.K. LAWSON

'Blows away many fundamental assumptions about the battle of Hastings... an exciting and indispensable read' *David Bates*

A *BBC History Magazine* Book of the Year 2003

£25   0 7524 2689 3

TEMPUS – REVEALING HISTORY

The Wars of the Roses
The Soldiers' Experience
ANTHONY GOODMAN
'Sheds light on the lot of the common soldier as never before' **Alison Weir**
'A meticulous work'
The Times Literary Supplement

£12.99   0 7524 3731 3

D-Day
The First 72 Hours
WILLIAM F. BUCKINGHAM
'A compelling narrative' **The Observer**
A **BBC History Magazine** Book of the Year 2004

£9.99   0 7524 2842 2

English Battlefields
500 Battlefields that Shaped English History
MICHAEL RAYNER
'A painstaking survey of English battlefields... a first-rate book' **Richard Holmes**
'A fascinating and, for all its factual tone, an atmospheric volume' **The Sunday Telegraph**

£25   0 7524 2978 7

Trafalgar Captain Durham of the Defiance: The Man who refused to Miss Trafalgar
HILARY RUBINSTEIN
'A sparkling biography of Nelson's luckiest captain' **Andrew Lambert**

£17.99   0 7524 3435 7

Battle of the Atlantic
MARC MILNER
'The most comprehensive short survey of the U-boat battles' **Sir John Keegan**
'Some events are fortunate in their historian, none more so than the Battle of the Atlantic. Marc Milner is *the* historian of the Atlantic Campaign... a compelling narrative'
Andrew Lambert

£12.99   0 7524 3332 6

Okinawa 1945 The Stalingrad of the Pacific
GEORGE FEIFER
'A great book... Feifer's account of the three sides and their experiences far surpasses most books about war' **Stephen Ambrose**

£17.99   0 7524 3324 5

Gallipoli 1915
TIM TRAVERS
'The most important new history of Gallipoli for forty years... groundbreaking' **Hew Strachan**
'A book of the highest importance to all who would seek to understand the tragedy of the Gallipoli campaign' **The Journal of Military History**

£13.99   0 7524 2972 8

Tommy Goes To War
MALCOLM BROWN
'A remarkably vivid and frank account of the British soldier in the trenches' **Max Arthur**
'The fury, fear, mud, blood, boredom and bravery that made up life on the Western Front are vividly presented and illustrated' **The Sunday Telegraph**

£12.99   0 7524 2980 9

If you are interested in purchasing other books published by Tempus, or in case you have difficulty finding any Tempus books in your local bookshop, you can also place orders directly through our website
www.tempus-publishing.com

TEMPUS – REVEALING HISTORY

R.J.Mitchell
Schooldays to Spitfire
GORDON MITCHELL
'[A] readable and poignant story'
The Sunday Telegraph

£12.99   0 7524 3727 5

Forgotten Soldiers of the First World War
Lost Voices from the Middle Eastern Front
DAVID WOODWARD
'A brilliant new book of hitherto unheard
voices from a haunting theatre of the First
World War' *Malcolm Brown*

£20   0 7524 3854 9

1690 Battle of the Boyne
PÁDRAIG LENIHAN
'An almost impeccably impartial account of
the most controversial military engagement in
British history' *The Daily Mail*

£12.99   0 7524 3304 0

Hell at the Front
Combat Voices from the First World War
TOM DONOVAN
'Fifty powerful personal accounts, each vividly
portraying the brutalising reality of the Great
War... a remarkable book' *Max Arthur*

£12.99   0 7524 3940 5

Amiens 1918
JAMES MCWILLIAMS & R. JAMES STEEL
'A masterly portrayal of this pivotal battle'
Soldier: The Magazine of the British Army

£25   0 7524 2860 8

Before Stalingrad
Hitler's Invasion of Russia 1941
DAVID GLANTZ
'Another fine addition to Hew Strachan's
excellent *Battles and Campaigns* series'
BBC History Magazine

£9.99   0 7524 2692 3

The SS
A History 1919-45
ROBERT LEWIS KOEHL
'Reveals the role of the SS in the mass murder
of the Jews, homosexuals and gypsies and its
organisation of death squads throughout occupied
Europe' *The Sunday Telegraph*

£9.99   0 7524 2559 5

Arnhem 1944
WILLIAM BUCKINGHAM
'Reveals the real reason why the daring attack
failed' *The Daily Express*

£10.99   0 7524 3187 0

If you are interested in purchasing other books published by Tempus, or in case you have difficulty finding any
Tempus books in your local bookshop, you can also place orders directly through our website

www.tempus-publishing.com

TEMPUS – REVEALING HISTORY

The Defence and Fall of Singapore
1940-42

BRIAN FARRELL

'A multi-pronged attack on those who made the defence of Malaya and Singapore their duty... [an] exhaustive account of the clash between Japanese and British Empire forces' *BBC History Magazine*

'An original and provocative new history of the battle' *Hew Strachan*

£13.99   0 7524 3768 2

Zulu!
The Battle for Rorke's Drift 1879

EDMUND YORKE

'A clear, detailed exposition... a very good read' *Journal of the Royal United Service Institute for Defence Studies*

£12.99   0 7524 3502 7

Paras
The Birth of British Airborne Forces from Churchill's Raiders to 1st Parachute Brigade

WILLIAM F. BUCKINGHAM

£17.99   0 7524 3530 2

Voices from the Trenches
Life & Death on the Western Front

ANDY SIMPSON AND TOM DONOVAN

'A vivid picture of life on the Western Front... compelling reading' *The Daily Telegraph*

'Offers the reader a wealth of fine writing by soldiers of the Great War whose slim volumes were published so long ago or under such obscure imprints that they have all but disappeared from sight like paintings lost under the grime of ages' *Malcolm Brown*

£12.99   0 7524 3905 7

Loos 1915

NICK LLOYD

'A revealing new account based on meticulous documentary research... I warmly commend this book to all who are interested in history and the Great War' *Corelli Barnett*

'Should finally consign Alan Clarke's farrago, *The Donkeys*, to the waste paper basket' *Hew Strachan*

£25   0 7524 3937 5

The Last Nazis
SS Werewolf Guerilla Resistance in Europe 1944-47

PERRY BIDDISCOMBE

'Detailed, meticulously researched and highly readable... a must for all interested in the end of the Second World War' *Military Illustrated*

£12.99   0 7524 2342 8

Omaha Beach A Flawed Victory

ADRIAN LEWIS

'A damning book' *BBC History Magazine*

£12.99   0 7524 2975 2

The English Civil War
A Historical Companion

MARTYN BENNETT

'Martyn Bennett knows more about the nuts and bolts of the English Civil War than anybody else alive' *Ronald Hutton*

'A most useful and entertaining book – giving us all precise detail about the events, the places, the people and the things that we half-know about the civil war and many more things that we did not know at all' *John Morrill*

£25   0 7524 3186 2